Murder Most Foul!

STANLEY J. MARKS

Murder Most Foul!

The Conspiracy That Murdered President Kennedy

Edited with an Introduction
by Rob Couteau

DOMINANTSTAR

Dominantstar LLC, New York.

ISBN 978-1-7360049-4-4

1 2 3 4 5 6 7 8 9 10 04

(Library of Congress Catalog Card Number for the original, 1967 edition: 67-29387.)

An abridged version of "An Introduction to the Life and Work of Stanley J. Marks" previously appeared under the title "Stanley Marks and *Murder Most Foul!*–A Sequel to 'The Kennedy / Dylan Sensation'" at the Kennedys and King web site on June 6, 2020.

Special thanks to James DiEugenio, Jim Lampos, Bobbie Marks, Al Rossi, and Yongzhen Zhang for their help and encouragement.

Cover: Photo of President Kennedy in Fort Worth, Texas, parking lot rally on November 22, 1963, by White House photographer Cecil Stoughton (Office of the Military Aide to the President).

robcouteau.com

dominantstarpublications.com

CONTENTS

Editor's Preface

The Rube Goldberg Chain of Events Leading to
Stanley J. Marks and *Murder Most Foul!*

In 2013, I was involved in a long-distance relationship with a woman named Molly, who lived in Portland. After Molly learned of my interest in the JFK assassination, she called one day from Powell's Bookstore when she heard that they were handling an estate sale of some rare JFK books. Would I like to speak with the person in charge?

Molly passed the phone to a clerk who described the collection: mostly, first editions of early classics, such as Ray Marcus's *Bastard Bullet*. But one of the titles I'd never heard of before: *Murder Most Foul! The Conspiracy That Murdered President Kennedy*, by Stanley J. Marks. And what really garnered my interest was the subtitle: *975 Questions & Answers*.

Once the books arrived, I quickly thumbed through each one. At first glance *Murder Most Foul!* seemed to be focused on a subject I'd already reached a conclusion about–the hoax known as the Warren Commission–so I slipped it into my bookcase and soon forgot about it.

Five years later, after some spring cleaning, I placed the book for sale on eBay. In the past, there might have been one or two available online, but by now I appeared to possess the only copy. Yet there it sat for the next year and a half, without any buyers. But on March 26, 2020, a Dylan blogger named Scott purchased it. What I wasn't aware of was that, on this same day, *Variety* magazine had posted a story titled: "Bob Dylan Releases 17-Minute Song About JFK Assassination." And Dylan's song, also titled "Murder Most Foul," became his first release to go to "number one" on any Billboard chart. (As of this date–five months later–it's been downloaded 4,305,032 times.) The day the book was sold, when I went online I noticed that my photo of the cover of *Murder Most Foul!* appeared not only on Scott's Dylan blog but on dozens of other websites.

The following afternoon I uploaded this same photo to my Facebook page and wrote: "The title of Dylan's new song about

JFK is lifted from one of the early books about the assassination, *Murder Most Foul!* by Stanley J. Marks."

My colleague Jim DiEugenio spotted the message and wrote back: "I hate to admit this, but I've never heard of that book. Has anyone read it, or does anyone have it?" When I replied that I did, he asked me to summarize its contents. By now the book was packaged in a sealed envelope and ready to be shipped; but fortunately, thanks to my own laziness, I hadn't yet bothered to go to the post office.

The next evening I wrote to Jim: "The main text of the book is comprised of 975 questions and answers, reminiscent of a prosecuting attorney making his case before a courtroom. Many of these Q&A's are pointed attacks on the Warren Commission and illustrate why it was a sham. This comprises the first 137 pages. The final fourteen pages feature three short chapters: 'The Rape of the American Conscience,' 'The Conspiracy That Murdered President Kennedy,' and a postscript titled 'Jim Garrison, "St. George" Versus the Dragon.' These summarize the author's conclusions and, unlike the Q&A's, take the form of a narrative discourse. No doubt, you'll find some gems there. At first, I didn't feel compelled to read *Murder Most Foul!* because so much has emerged on the Warren Commission since 1967, but looking through it now I see that it was well ahead of its time. For example, the postscript contains well-reasoned critiques against the media whitewash conducted by NBC, ABC, and CBS. And it adds: 'That the CIA controls many of the news columns in both the press and magazines is now known. What is not known, and what will never be known, is how many agents of the CIA now work for various organs in the mass communication media.' There certainly weren't many people thinking about this in 1967. The back cover notes that Marks previously published a book on US-Soviet relations, *The Bear That Walks Like a Man.*"

After compiling this brief summary, I decided to look more carefully at *Murder Most Foul!* before shipping it to Scott. And that's when I discovered that, indeed, there was a *lot* more to it. So I scanned the entire book and sent Jim a complete copy. After he studied the material, he wrote back and confirmed my suspicion: "Thanks again for that. This guy was way ahead of his time. And if Dylan was referencing this book, it really speaks well for him."

Always a fast worker, on March 31, Jim published an article at Kennedys and King titled "Dylan / Kennedy Sensation." I was both pleased and excited to see that his essay included a pithy summary of the contribution of Stanley J. Marks. After discussing the Shakespearian connection to the phrase "Murder Most Foul," Jim goes on to say:

> But Kennedys and King contributor Rob Couteau has alerted us that the title may go even further than that. For there is a little-known book with that same Shakespearean title in the Kennedy canon. In 1967, writer Stanley J. Marks wrote a short volume on the case. He entitled it *Murder Most Foul!* From its appearance–Couteau actually has a copy of the book–it did not appear to be printer typeset. The volume looks like it might be self-published and, therefore, did not get much distribution. If so, that is understandable. The contents of the book and its political views on the assassination, especially those at the end, are far ahead of the intellectual arguments in classic texts like *Accessories After the Fact* and *Six Seconds in Dallas*, both published in 1967.
>
> The approach to the case taken by Stanley Marks is that of a magisterial judge out of the British system. During the course of the book, this judge (Marks) relentlessly asks question after question of the prosecution. By the book's finish, the question count tallies to 975. Quite accurately, through his questioning, Marks concludes that the Commission suppressed important evidence and neglected to question certain important witnesses. His penultimate chapter is called "The Rape of the American Conscience." There, one of his first conclusions is that the Warren Commission, contrary to what it wrote, discovered a conspiracy. Marks is utterly disdainful of both the efforts of the Commission and its aides. In that penultimate chapter, he accuses them of abusing legal procedure and the rights of witnesses. He calls the performance by the Commission both "negligent and slothful." He says that the report deserves all the criticism it has gotten, for it could not even withstand exposure by the noonday sun.

Marks then sounds a note that no other critic of that time voiced, but which is appropriate to Dylan. He says that because of the disbelief in the Warren Report, a cynicism has gathered in the public and this bodes ill for the future of the nation. "For a nation whose moral fiber has been torn and shattered cannot long live."

Marks expounds on this idea by writing on page 139 that the Constitution contains the American Creed in the preamble. The Warren Report violated that creed. Because the United States "was not born on the idea that its president could be shot like a dog on the street and his murderers be shielded" from that day on "because it would be 'against the national interests.'" He concludes his penultimate chapter with what could be called an ode: "How long, O how long, Americans, will we permit our silence to perpetuate the evil in the Warren Report?" This condemnation is a far cry from, say, Josiah Thompson who, at the end of his book, said he was not really sure that the evidence he adduced justified a conspiracy. (*Six Seconds in Dallas*, p. 246.)

In his final chapter, Marks again does something that neither Meagher nor Thompson did–quite the contrary. He praises and appreciates the efforts of New Orleans DA Jim Garrison. He compares Garrison's ordeal against the media to St. George galloping forth to duel with the dragon. He also says something quite prescient for the time: he accuses some of Garrison's attackers of being in bed with the CIA. Which, we now know, is an accurate assessment. Again, if Bob Dylan knew about this obscure book, even more praise to him.

Besides generating a tremendous response in the research community, Jim's article was posted on Facebook's "Dylanology," a group with 36,000 members, and on the largest Dylan fan site, Karl Andersen's "Expecting Rain," which generates up to 25,000 unique daily visitors. Soon the essay was attracting over 5,000 hits per day: the largest response ever received by an article at Kennedys and King web site. I mention this because it also represents the first time since the early 1940s that Stanley Marks has received any widespread public attention. And, as we shall see, this was just the beginning.

Jim encouraged me to dig deeper and to cobble together an article about Stanley J. Marks, so I began by searching through databases at Ancestry and Newspapers.com. The forgotten story of who this man really was gradually began to emerge: piecemeal and bit by bit. Eventually, I discovered references to Stanley's daughter, Bobbie Marks; and, after befriending her, the story of her hard-working father continued to flesh itself out.

Bobbie was particularly amused to learn about the series of events that led me to her father and his work, beginning with Molly's phone call from a bookshop in Portland. We dubbed this the "Rube Goldberg Chain of Events": for if Molly hadn't visited Powell's that day and asked the $64 question, none of this would have occurred. As a Frenchwoman once remarked to me, the expression *Cherchez la femme* really means: "If you look long and hard enough, at the base of anything interesting in life you'll eventually find a woman–going all the way back to Eve!"

There were many more links in this unusual chain; but, rather than spoil the surprise, I invite you to read on.

An Introduction to the Life and Work
of Stanley J. Marks, by Rob Couteau

"We seek not the worldwide victory of one nation or system but a worldwide victory of man. The modern globe is too small, its weapons are too destructive, and its disorders are too contagious to permit any other kind of victory.... We steer our ship with hope, as Thomas Jefferson said, "leaving Fear astern.""–John F. Kennedy, State of the Union Address, January 14, 1963.

"If you became a successful political leader and you spoke out effectively against the war in Vietnam, they'd kill you, too."–Former District Attorney Jim Garrison, speaking about the relationship between the assassinations of Martin Luther King and the Kennedy brothers, June 1968.

"The arms race became a strongly cooperative effort between the military establishments of the two countries, each doing what brought revenues, influence, and power to the other."–John Kenneth Galbraith, "The United States and the Soviet Union: Change and the Vested Interest in Tension," circa 1987-89.

Part I: A Murder Most Foul

In September 1967 Stanley Marks attempted to position himself at the forefront of a soon-to-be cresting wave of JFK assassination publications when he released *Murder Most Foul! The Conspiracy That Murdered President Kennedy: 975 Questions & Answers*. This self-published paperback represents a full-frontal attack against the official story promulgated by the Warren Commission (WC) and its lackeys in the corporate media, but it's also much more than that.

Giving it a quick first glance, a contemporary researcher might easily pass over the book. After almost sixty years of research and the release of millions of pages of government documents related to the assassination, a reexamination of the WC hardly seems necessary, especially one from 1967. In addition, it appears to be a privately printed Photostat copy of a typewritten manuscript, replete with minor typos and over-struck characters; and it's only faintly reproduced in a small font, making for a challenging read. Yet, a more careful examination reveals that, in many ways, Stanley J. Marks was far ahead of his time.

For example, *Murder Most Foul!* contains some well-reasoned critiques of the media whitewash conducted by NBC, ABC, and CBS, and concludes: "That the CIA controls many of the news columns in both the press and magazines is now known. What is not known, and what will never be known, is how many agents of the CIA now work for various organs in the mass communication media." There certainly weren't many people thinking about this in 1967. And Marks was correct: the tradition of "sheep-dipped" agents is as American as apple pie. But when Agency "journalists" and their prefabricated "stories" weren't directly inserted, the CIA relied on another grand tradition: turning established journalists into "assets."

Of course, President Kennedy had a markedly different view concerning the true function of the press. In an address before the American Newspaper Publishers Association on April 27, 1961, the president reminded his audience that the press was "protected by the First Amendment ... not primarily to amuse and entertain, not to emphasize the trivial and the sentimental, not to simply 'give the public what it wants'–but to inform, to arouse, to reflect, to state our dangers and our opportunities, to indicate our crises and our choices, to lead, mold, educate and sometimes even anger public opinion."

While most of the Q&A's comprising the first 136 pages of *Murder Most Foul!* serve to puncture holes in the Warren Commission Report and thus illustrate why it was a sham, there are also passages that go well beyond the usual framework of early WC critiques. For example, consider, Q&A #46:

> What is meant by "against the national interest"?
> The Warren Commission has never defined this undefinable phrase. However, after the publication of the Warren "Report," many commentators and historians interpret that phrase to

mean that whenever a future president is murdered his killers can escape capture and punishment if a future investigating committee decides their capture would be "against the national interest."

Marks' wry irony flourishes throughout the chronicle, and this is just one of many instances of the author's tell-tale, trademark style of humor mixed with outrage, born from insight. We should add that Stanley's reference to the "national interest" has been largely replaced by a term that we've seen with ever-increasing frequency over the last few decades: "National security," with its concomitant erosion of civil rights; violation of human rights; and censoring of information that rightly belongs in the hands of citizens.

Like other reputable texts on the assassination, *Murder Most Foul!* did not arise *sui generis*, as if from a vacuum. It's likely that Marks was inspired to borrow a "juridical" approach from Mark Lane, whose first essay on the assassination took the form of a "legal brief" in defense of Lee Harvey Oswald, which was published in December 1963, only a month after Kennedy's death.

Marks also cites several important titles and articles then available, including Joachim Joesten's *Oswald: Assassin or Fall Guy?* (1964), Harold Weisberg's *Whitewash I* and *Whitewash II* (1965, 1966), Gaeton Fonzi's groundbreaking reporting in the *Greater Philadelphia Magazine* (1966), Mark Lane's *Rush to Judgment* (1966), Richard Popkin's *The Second Oswald* (1966), and Edward Epstein's *Inquest* (1966). Like many other researchers who bucked the tide, Joesten experienced a great deal of difficulty in finding a publisher in the United States. His work was finally published by Merlin Press in England before being picked up by Carl Marzani in the U.S., in July 1964. (But Epstein, who continually steered his research staff away from the subject of CIA involvement, didn't seem to have these problems.) In such a political climate, Stanley's decision to establish his own publishing imprint makes sense.

Another seminal work appeared in the fall of 1967: Sylvia Meagher's *Accessories After the Fact*. Like other early critics such as Vincent Salandria, Mark Lane, Ray Marcus, and Maggie Field, Meagher's approach was to use the government's own officially sanctioned studies to prove that things didn't add up. Besides making a laughing stock of the Warren Commission Report (WCR), she accomplished this by engaging in a careful analysis of an FBI report on the assassination (first uncovered by Vincent Salandria) as well as by combing through documents that had been quietly shuttled over to the National Archives (many of which were excluded from the WCR). Such data portrayed a contradictory tale about what actually occurred, and it stood in direct opposition to the Commission's own conclusion.[1]

Before Meagher entered into the fray, the WCR and its accompanying text–the twenty-six volume Warren Commission Hearings and Exhibits–remained largely unindexed. Meagher said that an attempt to analyze its contents would have been "tantamount to a search for information in the Encyclopedia Britannica if the contents were untitled, unalphabetized, and in random sequence."[2] After a great deal of tedious labor, she published her *Subject Index to the Warren Report and Hearings and Exhibits* in 1966. (Even FBI Director J. Edgar Hoover ordered two copies for the Bureau.)[3] This would prove to be an essential tool for cracking the code of the Commission. Therefore, a year before the appearance of *Accessories*, the first generation of authors relied on Meagher's research. As we shall see, Marks was working out of this same tradition, but he attempts to push the case even further. He also reiterates this position in his last assassination-related book, *Yes, Americans, A Conspiracy Murdered JFK!* (1992), in which he writes: "As a defense attorney, my best witness would be the Warren Commission's "Report" and the 26 volumes issued by the Commission."[4]

Marks was also a stylistic innovator. Instead of a straight narrative that dissects events in the manner of a typical researcher, he shaped his investigation into a "question-and-answer book" composed of 975 queries and replies, most of them taking the form of quick, rapid fire, staccato bursts of ammunition that hit their target with a no-nonsense precision. In a blunt statement of intention, in the Preface he says: "The contents of this book have been arranged in the manner of an attorney representing a client in a criminal court and in the manner that a district attorney would present his case against the alleged criminal." (Just like that other great voice of dissent, Mark Lane,[5] Marks was also trained as an attorney.) He boldly concludes: "It is the proposal of this book to reveal the attempts of the Warren Commission to befuddle, delude, and deceive the American people who sincerely desire the answer to the question, 'Who murdered President John F. Kennedy?'"

Regarding the factual minutia of the case, although the work of early researchers has been largely absorbed and superseded by that of subsequent authors, Marks still remains ahead of the curve when it comes to the larger picture that he paints at the conclusion of his book, which enters into a broader philosophical speculation regarding what will happen to the collective psyche of America as a result of the magic trick that was performed in Dealey Plaza in 1963–a prestidigitation that even includes an officially approved "magic bullet." But first, Stanley picks his way through the evidence and attempts to shock the reader into a new awareness–step by step, prosecutorial question by question– relieved only by a series of black comedic asides that remind one of the rants of a Mort Sahl or a Lenny Bruce; or that mimic the goofy stage whispers of a Groucho Marx. Perhaps he felt this was the only thing appropriate enough to level against an equally goofy "logic" that was exhibited by those seven wise men who formed the Commission. Therefore, Marks breathes fresh life into the manner in which we reassess the case. This is also reflected in the biting humor of some of his chapter headings. For example, chapter three: "Rifles, Rifles, Everywhere," which refers to the various firearms that were first located in the Texas School Book Depository (TSBD), one of which would have served as a far more reliable weapon than the rusty, old, dilapidated Mannlicher-Carcano rifle supposedly owned by Oswald but which had undoubtedly been planted there. A gun, one should add, that even when preserved in pristine condition–brand new and fresh out of the box–was known for its poor performance when used against long-range targets. (In referring to the Mannlicher-Carcano's bad reputation, Marks cites an article from the October 1964 *Mechanix Illustrated* magazine, which I later acquired. In a piece titled "Big Bargains in Rifles" by Ken Warner, a review of the 6.5mm and 7.35mm Mannlicher-Carcano appears under a heading: "Not Worth Considering." Warner states flatly that the Mannlicher-Carcano is "Unhandy, crude, unreliable on repeat shots, has safety design fault." Of all the rifles reviewed in the piece, the Mannlicher-Carcano is also the cheapest: selling for about $8 as compared to $45 for the Mauser 98s and Springfields.)[6] As Marks also notes, photos of two distinctly different Carcano rifles appeared in initial press reports; and a far more accurate and deadly weapon, a 7.65 Mauser, was discovered by the Dallas police inside the Texas School Book Depository. Several of the officers identified the assassin's rifle as a 7.65 Mauser, as did Dallas Police Captain Will Fritz.[7] Thus, Marks opens the chapter with Q&A #79:

> Why was a "dead" Oswald better than a "live" Oswald?
> The Dallas police, if Oswald had lived to be tried, would have had to explain to a jury composed of rational men: (1) a 7.65 German Mauser, (2) a 6.5 Italian Mannlicher-Carcano rifle!

Marks hilariously comments on the fact that no one in the FBI could reproduce Oswald's supposed ability to fire three shots from this shoddy rifle in 5.6 seconds:

> 237. Were tests actually conducted by the Commission?
> Yes, on November 27, 1963.
>
> 238. What did the tests prove?
> That Lee H. Oswald was the world's greatest marksman. […]
>
> 240. […] That the Commission was living in a dream world. *None of the experts* fired three shots in the *maximum time limit* of 5.6 seconds.

As the author chronicles here, after an initial test failed to deliver a desired result, the Commission requested that the FBI conduct a second test. In addition, the Commission selected "Three riflemen who held the rank of Master Rifleman from the National Rifle Association. The *final* authority regarding marksmanship."

> 252. What would a Law Court say about this final test?
> That the test[s] were as phony as plastic boloney!

The author bases this Grouchoesque remark on the fact that the riflemen were positioned on a thirty-foot platform, whereas the sixth-floor window of the Book Depository was actually sixty-feet high. "Thus, the *angle* of fire was wrong, by fifty percent." In addition, "Each rifleman shot at a *stationary* target." Despite all this, they were unable to "hit the target area of the back, neck and head!"

Several pages later, Marks asks:

> 286. What did the Marine Corps think of Oswald's marksmanship?
> The Corps flatly stated he was a "poor shot."

Simple, and to the point. These are just a few of the ways in which Marks excoriates the findings of the Commission by using their own words against them.

In *Coup d'État! Three Murders That Changed the Course of History. President Kennedy, Reverend King, Senator R. F. Kennedy*, a book Marks published in February 1970, he titles his second chapter: "The Fraudulent Autopsy, Or How to Lie in a Military Manner." His dry humor is also displayed in chapter four of *Coup d'État!*, which bears the heading: "The Non-existing Paper Bag, Or How to Manufacture Evidence." This refers to a false claim that Oswald had slipped a rifle into a paper bag (even though the bag wasn't large enough to contain it) and then snuck it into work on the day of the assassination. In an earlier chapter of *Murder Most Foul!* the author also comments upon the "planting" of a bag after the assassination:

> 175. Who planted it?
> One of the conspirators converted himself into a newspaper man. Just as Oswald appointed himself secretary of a nonexistent club.

The latter sentence refers to Oswald forming his own one-man chapter of the Fair Play for Cuba Committee (FPCC): an organization closely monitored by the FBI as well as deeply penetrated–if not outright created–by the CIA.[8] But it would take many more decades for researchers to learn that the CIA's anti-FPCC program was run by Agency operators David Phillips and James McCord. Or to discover that Richard Gibson, the co-founder of the FPCC, offered his assistance to the CIA as early as July 1962 and that Gibson was employed by the Agency as a spy from 1965 to 1977.[9] (There are also many indications that Gibson's Agency ties go further back in time: at least to the late Fifties, when he forged letters supposedly written by leftists and worked to successfully sow seeds of discord in the African American ex-pat community in Paris.)

Then we have Stanley's comedic description of Lieutenant Day, a figure who, according to Marks, worked arduously to frame Oswald and who claimed to find the paper bag in an area that had already been thoroughly searched. Marks refers to him as "A man who leaves no fingerprints," since neither Day's nor Oswald's prints were ever found on this bag. In Q&A 156, Marks concludes that, as a result, Lieutenant Day "should join Lee Harvey Oswald and Captain Fritz in the Smithsonian Institute! For new species of mankind!"

The author's piquant sense of humor regarding the lieutenant continues throughout his oeuvre. In his second assassination-related study, *Two Days of Infamy: November 22, 1963; September 28, 1964*, Marks says that Day "was a police officer who always kept 'finding' or 'losing' just that type of evidence needed by the Commission. He 'found' fingerprints; he 'lost' palm prints; he 'found' a three-foot paper bag; he 'lost' memos and he 'found' memos. You name it and Lt. Day either 'found' it or 'lost' it. He was worse than the girl in the song 'who lost it at the Astor'; at least she knew where she had 'lost it' and also what she had lost." The latter refers to a tongue-in-cheek popular classic, "She Had to Go and Lose It at the Astor," written by Don Raye and Hughie Prince in 1939 and later recorded by Pearl Bailey.[10] Through the witty use of double entendre, the lyrics lead us to believe that a young woman has lost her virginity at the Hotel Astor, but by the song's conclusion we realize that the only thing lost was her sable cape.

One of the most ironic statements to appear in the Warren Commission Report is the claim: "In fairness to the alleged assassin and his family, the Commission … requested Walter E. Craig, president of the American Bar Association, to participate in the investigation and to advise the Commission whether in his opinion the proceedings conformed to the *basic principles of American justice*." (My italics.) This incident was reported in *Esquire* magazine in 1965 and is reproduced in Edward Jay Epstein's *Inquest*, Mark Lane's *Rush to Judgment*, and Léo Sauvage's *The Oswald Affair*. In turn, Marks seizes upon the absurdity of the phrase and runs with it. In fact, an entire section of *MMF* is devoted to this topic; chapter ten is titled: "The Commission & Basic Principles of American Justice!" There, Marks asks: "Did the Commission adhere to those principles?" Answer:

> No. The Commission permitted outright hearsay; it permitted perjury; it permitted its aides to use threats to obtain "evidence" to convict Oswald; it accepted fraudulent photographs; it *suppressed* evidence that would have proved the Commission's theory wrong; and the Commission permitted their aides to act above and beyond established legal rules of procedure.

Stanley devotes the remainder of this chapter to citing specific incidents of such wrongdoing. With a dig against the Dallas Police Department and a jab at the Commission for supporting the chicanery of that most corrupt of Texan institutions,[11] in a final coup de grâce he rhetorically inquires:

> 842. Did the Commission believe the police were efficient?
> Efficient? The Commission could not find enough words in the English language to praise the Dallas Police Department.
> To achieve this praise, this paragon of police departments did the following:
> They: (1) found evidence; (2) lost evidence; (3) had *no* stenographer at Oswald's interrogation; (4) had *no* tape recorder either; (5) conducted illegal searches; (6) seized private property which was never returned; (7) threatened witnesses; (8) committed perjury; (9) switched evidence; (10) did not know the difference between a German "Mauser" and an Italian "Carcano" rifle; (11) found chicken bones; (12) lost chicken bones; (13) took pictures of a "bag" that was not there; (14) found fingerprints; (15) had three members of the force who left no fingerprints; (16) found a holster; (17) lost vital radio logs; (18) reconstructed a murder site but first changed the street scene; (19) lost a revolver; (20) found a revolver; (21) arrested and then released men charged with "suspicion of murder"; and so on and on and on!
> For the above, the Commission *profusely praised the police.*

He concludes:

> 843. How can the interpretation of the phrase: "Basic principles of American justice" be made in reference to the Commission?
> On both Moral and Legal plateaus the Commission was a disgrace to "Basic principles of American justice."

* * *

In a recent post on the Education Forum, Jim DiEugenio remarks: "It's one thing to attack the Warren Commission, as Sylvia Meagher and Harold Weisberg did effectively many years ago. It's another thing to try to explain what really happened." This leads us to ask: Did Stanley Marks go beyond a mere WC critique and enter into that more challenging arena of attempting to explain what *actually happened* (and *why*) on November 22? Bearing this in mind, I will highlight a few of the ways in which Marks does so in his unique manner. And, unlike Meagher or Weisberg–who were unjustifiably critical of what District Attorney Jim Garrison actually accomplished–Stanley not only appreciated Garrison's efforts; he was also prescient in his analysis of how the Power Elite would attempt to foil him.[12]

The author begins *Murder Most Foul!* with an ironically titled chapter: "To Dallas We Go":

> 3. Who comprised the anti-Kennedy forces in Texas?
> The power structure of Texas in the political, economic, social, and educational life was all anti-Kennedy.

A few pages later, Marks begins chapter two by asking: "Who was Lee Harvey Oswald?" He answers: "Evidence is now accumulating that he was a minor cog in the CIA." Thus, by page six, without equivocation, Marks identifies Oswald as a minor player in the intelligence community. He goes further:

> 45. Was Oswald any type of Agent for the CIA?
> The evidence is accumulating that the answer is "yes."

In chapter seven, he issues a warning that even researchers today would be wise to heed:

> 66. How many "Hearings," "Witnesses," and Affidavits were produced?
> The FBI inundated the Commission with 25,000 reports; in fact, the FBI gave the Commission so many reports of its "investigations" that the FBI created a "fog" over the work of the Commission. It now seems to have been deliberate for, in a period of nine months, no group of fourteen lawyers could have read, digested, and analyzed each report to see what [effect] each report would have on an overall picture of the conspiracy.

Let's put this "fog" into context by examining an interview published seven months after *Murder Most Foul!* first appeared, in the April 1968 edition of *NOLA Express*.

Citing a source associated with the CIA, Mark Lane says that a number of false leads or "clues" were purposely left "scattered around Dealey Plaza like leaves on an autumn day." The "clues" led to "false sponsors" of the assassination (e.g., "The Mob did it"). About a year later, in a May 1969 interview with a European publication, Jim Garrison spoke about the "distribution of an endless amount of irrelevant information to cause confusion in the minds of those who might attempt a serious inquiry." In his first book about the assassination, *A Heritage of Stone* (1974), Garrison goes further and seems to be referencing Lane directly: "False sponsors are created by prior planning and by the planting of leads trailing away from the intelligence organization.... At a more superficial level, an abundance of leads is planted by prior planning to provide a frame-up of the pre-selected scapegoat."[13] And, in the mid-1970s, shortly before Gaeton Fonzi began his work as a researcher for the House of Representatives Select Committee on Assassinations, he was warned by attorney Vincent Salandria (one of the first critics to use the Warren Commission's own documents to prove that the WC Report was fraudulent) that they would attempt to bury Fonzi with pointless minutia. As Fonzi recalls: "He ventured that I would get lured into a quagmire of inconsequential details." In Salandria's own words: "I'm afraid we were misled. All the critics, myself included, were misled very early. I see that now. We spent too much time and effort microanalyzing the details of the assassination when all the time it was obvious, it was blatantly obvious that it was a conspiracy."[14] Just like Jim Garrison (who relied on Salandria's assistance and advice), Salandria had arrived at a painful conclusion: "Our national security state killed President Kennedy in order to perpetuate the Cold War.[15] (Perhaps the earliest and most prescient critic to take a "bigger picture" view of the assassination, in 1967 Salandria also predicted the murder of RFK: "They'll get Bobby killed and they'll get us all killed … they'll turn this into a closed, totalitarian military society. The assassination was just the start.")[16]

From the phony baloney of the rifle, we go to the phony baloney of the "Oswald killed Tippit claim." This is how Marks dispenses with it in three brief Q&A's:

> 365. What time did Mrs. Markham swear she saw the murder of Tippit?
> 1:06 p.m.
>
> 366. Where was Oswald?
> According to the Commission running from the bus stop, at 1:04 p.m., at a world record speed for nine-tenths of a mile, to murder Officer Tippit!
>
> 367. What did this event make Oswald?
> On this day: (1) the greatest marksman; (2) the fastest runner!

In Q&A #750, Marks dismisses the ludicrous notion of a "tumbling," magic bullet. He also cites the early work of Gaeton Fonzi:

> (1) You can't fire a bullet that "tumbles"; and (2) the Commission's own test bullets did *not* match Bullet No. 399 in any shape, manner or form! This admission appeared in the August, 1966 issue of "Greater Philadelphia Magazine," by [Gaeton Fonzi].[17]

Under the chapter heading, "Pictures Can Be Made to Lie," Marks presents a summary of the shenanigans surrounding the Zapruder film and how its frames were presented out of order in publications such as *Life* magazine. He begins:

> 757. How did the Commission compel the "camera's eye" to lie?
> The Commission again *suppressed* an FBI report which stated that the camera used by Mr. Zapruder was set for 24 frames per second but the Commission had it set for only 18+ frames per second.

Thus the "change of speed … changed the time between the shots." After explaining why a court of law would accept neither the testimony nor the reconstruction of events based on a manipulated film, Marks then focuses his literary lens on another picture that was "made to lie." For, by 1967, he was already convinced that the "man in the doorway" photo–taken in front of the Texas School Book Depository while Kennedy was traveling on Elm Street–was actually Lee Oswald (who, according to the WC, should have been up on the sixth floor, firing at President Kennedy). Known as the "Altgens photo" (snapped by AP press photographer James Altgens), this image continues to provoke debate among researchers today.

> 774. Who was the "man in the door entrance"?
> The evidence clearly supports the fact that it was Oswald.
>
> 775. Why did the Commission have to dis-approve this fact?
> Oswald in the doorway could not be Oswald on the sixth floor.

Again: incisive, witty, and to the point. Although the Commission claimed that the man in the doorway was Book Depository employee Billy Lovelady, Marks introduces as evidence a quote from none other than J. Edgar Hoover:

> 777. What did the "man in the door entrance" wear?
> The same color shirt, in the same manner, as Oswald's!
>
> 778. Did Mr. J. Edgar Hoover write a letter concerning this?
> Yes. A suppressed letter to the Commission, dated 3/9/64 to Mr. J. Lee Rankin, General Counsel. Mr. Hoover stated that Mr. Lovelady informed his Agents that when he wore his shirt it was buttoned up *all the way to the neck* and had red stripes!

In chapter fourteen, "The Conspiracy That Murdered President Kennedy," Marks takes CIA Director Dulles to task. He begins by quoting from an article that appeared in *Look* magazine in July 1966, in which Dulles remarks: "If they found another assassin, let them name names and produce their evidence."

"This contemptuous statement directed at the American citizenry," says Marks, "revealed the attitude of the Commission.

The Commission did not praise the president; they gave him a funeral and used his shroud to conceal his murderers." Taking a further dig at the former CIA director, Marks rhetorically asks: "Mr. Dulles, how can other assassins be named if material is *not* in the National Archives? Was there a conspiracy, Mr. Dulles? Of course there was!" At this point, the author offers a blunt appraisal of not only how the plot was covered up, but of why and how it occurred.

> The inception of the Conspiracy that murdered President Kennedy can be, and will be eventually, traced back to the disastrous "Bay of Pigs." The president relied upon the CIA, headed by Allen Dulles, whose information was one hundred percent wrong in the CIA's assessment of Castro's Cuba. Heads rolled but the CIA had many heads and the heads that remained never forgave President Kennedy [...] Thus, in the wreckage of the "Bay of Pigs" were parts and persons of the CIA apparatus who had directed that operation. The hatred of this apparatus for President Kennedy was to cease only when these forces fired four bullets into his body.

Next, Marks introduces the subject of Kennedy's foreign policy–the most probable reason he was killed. He begins with a discussion of U.S.–USSR relations:

> With the relaxation of tensions between the U.S. and the USSR after President Kennedy's confrontation with the Soviets in the Cuban Missile Crisis, the Batista–Cuban exile organization, with many members on the CIA payroll, decided that Kennedy must go. However, the murder of President Kennedy was the "spark," a means to an end.
>
> The Kennedy conspiracy had a major and minor objective: (1) An invasion of Cuba; (2) an attempt to involve the Soviet Union with the invasion so that a war would ensue between the U.S. and USSR.
>
> By early 1963, members of the Conspiracy, who were both U.S. citizens and exiled Cubans of the Batista faction, had been selected.

Three years later, in *A Heritage of Stone*, Jim Garrison would extrapolate on this theme of JFK's attempt to end the Cold War and how it may have led to his undoing. But Garrison was already drawing this connection at least as early as 1969, as can be seen by certain interviews he conducted, which we shall explore in a moment.

Marks then returns to the probable role of Oswald:

> It was during this period that Oswald entered the Conspiracy. He thought he had a perfect "front." To the world (and FBI?) he was a defector and he was branded as a "Communist." A perfect "patsy"! Oswald, to himself, was a patriot, misguided, but still a patriot. Was not Hale a spy and a patriot? Did not many American newspapers and commentators call President Kennedy a traitor? Oswald was happy to assist [in] the removal of a "traitor."

Many reputable researchers would agree that Oswald was a patsy, and one who may have considered himself to be a patriot (however misguided so many "patriots" may be), but few today would argue conclusively that Oswald knew that JFK was going to be killed. So here, Marks adopts a point of view that was shared neither by Garrison nor by many others in the research community. But it *is* fair to say that Lee Oswald had to be aware of the extreme right-wing zealotry and hatred that fueled so many of the anti-Castro Cubans that he associated with; not to mention that of leading intel figures such as Guy Banister, who had given Oswald an office to operate out of in New Orleans. These were the sorts of psychopathic personalities with whom Oswald spent a great deal of time. But by the time Marks published *Yes, Americans, A Conspiracy Murdered JFK!* in 1992, his views had evolved: "Whether Oswald was a part of the Conspiracy cannot be ascertained.... There is evidence that Oswald was used as a 'patsy'; that he executed a part of the conspiracy but he had no knowledge of what was to occur."[18]

Relying on Richard Popkin's *The Second Oswald*, in *MMF* Marks also comments on the widely reported phenomenon of Oswald look-a-likes that occurred shortly before and after the assassination. (As Popkin says: "Real Oswald's role was to be the prime suspect chased by the police, while Second Oswald, one of the assassins, could vanish.")[19] Marks believes that

> Oswald's role was strictly that of being a decoy. He had no idea that he was also selected to be a victim. To assist him in this decoy was another man who resembled Oswald. That this is true can be found in the "Hearings" of reliable witnesses seeing "Oswald" in two or three places at the same time.

The next paragraph opens up an entirely new can of worms. Although Marks couldn't have known the full extent of the connection between the various assassination attempts on De Gaulle and the Kennedy assassination, his instinct–coupled with his in-depth knowledge of European history–was already leading him in this direction:

> As history has shown a conspiracy spreads rumors. The various assassination attempts upon President De Gaulle were always preceded by rumors and the French agencies took care to track them down. Yet, in spite of this, De Gaulle narrowly escaped death when the attempted killers received word one hour before the attempt.

In fact, a figure linked to the numerous attempts on De Gaulle's life was lurking in Fort Worth and Dallas at the same time that JFK visited those two cities during his final day on earth. As Henry Hurt explains in *Reasonable Doubt* (1987), a man claiming to be Jean Souètre, a French army deserter and member of the renegade Organisation Armée Secrète (a dissident right-wing paramilitary group linked to assassination attempts against De Gaulle), was apprehended by American officials in Dallas shortly after Kennedy's murder and immediately expelled from the country.

The capture and expulsion did not occur thanks to any brilliant American intel operation: it came as a result of a tip from their French intelligence counterparts, who were alarmed that Souètre might be on his way to Mexico, to assassinate De Gaulle upon the latter's scheduled arrival there. As Jim DiEugenio points out, this mercenary was no stranger to our homegrown American terrorists: "Souètre had developed contacts with radical right-wing elements in Dallas and New Orleans, and also with anti-Castro Cubans."[20]

* * *

After ascending a scaffolding composed of such contradictory, incongruous official "facts," we then encounter a broader perspective. The concluding chapters of *MMF* dispense with Q&A's and summarize what the author believes actually occurred on November 22. And here, Marks unleashes the full thrust of his impassioned polemic. In fact, *polemical* is the principal adjective that defines why this work still stands out today.[21] Why *polemic*? Because Marks is enraged, and he's reminding us that we, too, should be equally outraged. To help get us there, he attempts to shake us up with the truth–as brutal as it may be to confront it.

According to Merriam-Webster dictionary, *polemic* derives from the French, *polémique*, meaning *controversial*. (Yes, to this day the truth about the assassination remains *quite* controversial.) This, in turn, derives from the Greek *polemikos*, meaning: "warlike, hostile"; and from *polemos*, "war." Receding further into the past, the term has a possible link to the Greek *pelemizein*: "to shake." Therefore, polemic shakes us up, produces controversy, and can be utilized as an instrument of war, in the sense that a pen may be mightier than a sword. (Something the CIA's Directorate of Plans was certainly aware of.) Indeed, *Murder Most Foul!* partakes of all these definitions.

Chapter thirteen begins with four final Q&A's. The first two sum up the principal thrust of the book:

> 972. What did the Warren Commission prove?
> That a conspiracy murdered John F. Kennedy.

> 973. What did the Commission believe?
> They believed that those who could read would not read; that those who could see would not see; that those who could [talk]

would not [talk]; and those who would investigate would not investigate.[22]

Marks then dispenses with his Q&A mode and, for the next seventeen pages, shifts into straight narrative. The chapter titles offer the reader a no-hold-barred window into the author's apoplectic indignation. This one is fittingly dubbed "The Rape of the American Conscience."

> The most perplexing question to obtain any answer to is the fact that the Commission, at the very first moment of its investigation, had in his hands the FBI reports and the Secret Service reports. Just on the basis of those reports the Commission could not find Oswald guilty of being the "sole and exclusive killer" […]
> The members of the Commission did not achieve their status in the American social, economic, and political scale by being stupid; therefore one can only conclude that these seven had some understanding, whether spoken or implied, that this nation of 195,000,000 souls would be torn asunder if the Commission reported to them that a conspiracy had murdered President John F. Kennedy. Yet, these seven men place their honor upon a report that would wilt in the noonday sun.

Therefore, the Commissioners–who certainly weren't "stupid"– must have assumed that the American people were. Marks also condemns the Commissioner's aides, whom he derisively refers to as "legal beagles," since nonlawyers weren't allowed to serve in this role. In Q&A #58, Marks adds: "The aides became known as 'legal beagles,' for they were neither or 'legal' nor 'beagles,'" i.e., the last thing they sought was the truth.

> The facts are clear that no control was ever exerted over these aides, who, time and time again, violated the rights of witnesses. The facts are also clear that these aides did not seek to bring forth the truth but sought only to confuse, to mislead, and to deceive the Americans.

After quoting President Truman's famous dictum, "The buck stops here," Marks concludes that the final responsibility rests upon the Commissioners and not the aides. Therefore, "That the Commission was negligent and slothful in its responsibility has been proven beyond a reasonable doubt.... the American People wanted the truth, not a whitewash." Marks also raises a point that should be carefully considered, especially in light of what was to follow over the next half century:

> Criticism is derived from critics and they should not be immune in turn. When, however, the critics are attacked on the basis of personality instead of the measure of their facts, then it is a sign that the criticism has been correctly established.

As a declassified CIA memo would later reveal, it was the CIA itself that first floated the strategy of attacking WC critics as mere *conspiracy theorists*. Right after the Agency issued this strategy memo on January 4, 1967,[23] the use of the phrase spiked in mass media, then rooted itself as a more commonly used expression in our culture. A closer examination of the memo is revealing, for it boldly states: "The aim of this dispatch is to provide material for countering and discrediting the claims of the conspiracy theorists, so as to inhibit the circulation of such claims in other countries." The Agency writer then proposes: "(a) To discuss the publicity problem with liaison and friendly elite contacts (especially politicians and editors), pointing out that ... further speculative discussion only plays into the hands of the opposition. Point out also that parts of the conspiracy talk appear to be deliberately generated by Communist propagandists ..." Hence, the same old pattern of slander. But now, watch what follows this so-called antipropaganda stance. In a sterling example of a U.S.–USSR "mirroring" effect, the agent encourages his CIA colleagues "(b) To employ *propaganda* assets to answer and refute the attacks of the critics. Book reviews and feature articles are particularly appropriate for this purpose." (My italics.) For some reason, "our" propaganda was deemed as "holier than thou's." And speaking of researchers being attacked merely on the basis of personality, we now know that, in the 1970s, FBI Director Hoover issued a memo calling for the "preparation of sex dossiers on critics" of the Warren Commission "probe."[24]

Returning to *MMF*, the author then poses a chilling question: "Thus, to whom does the American public go to seek the truth?" And the answer is horrifying:

> It can now be said that the American people do not believe anything stated in the "Report." Due to this lack of belief a cynicism has now gathered among the Citizenry that bodes ill for the nation. A Nation whose moral fiber has been torn and shattered cannot long live; for when the Nation's spirit is destroyed, no Nation will live.
>
> The American Creed, which is expressed in the Preamble to the Constitution of the United States, has been violated and this violation has been condoned by the Warren Commission.

This might be a good place to reexamine the Preamble (a document that law courts often rely on when interpreting the Constitution). It reads: "We the People of the United States, in Order to form a more perfect Union, establish justice, insure domestic Tranquility, provide for the common defense, promote the general Welfare, and secure the Blessings of Liberty to ourselves and our Posterity, do ordain and establish this Constitution for the United States of America." Marks repeatedly emphasizes the fact that four principle elements enumerated in the Preamble–*justice, domestic tranquility, promoting the general welfare* (the "People" part of "We the People"), and *securing liberty* were blasphemously violated by the conspirators and the Commissioners (at least one of which–Allen Dulles–may have served in each of these roles). Therefore, the Commission's actual message to the American people is that justice, domestic tranquility, promoting the general welfare, and securing liberty will now no longer be taken for granted. The violation of justice also calls to mind J. Edgar Hoover's remark: "Justice is merely incidental to law and order." According to Marks (as discussed in one of his later books), Hoover issued this statement after RFK's murder. As the author highlights in his last assassination title: "There can be no 'liberty' where 'justice' does not reign."[25]

Marks sagely concludes:

> People, in all nations, must stand for an ideal. The United States of America was not born on the idea that its President could be shot like a dog in the street and his murderers be "shielded from this day on" because it would be "against the national interests."

Thus, with the murder of an idealistic president comes the death of our own youthful idealism. He continues:

> The Spirit has in this year of 1967 been replaced by cynicism of everything "American." There was a Spirit when John F. Kennedy was president of the United States. There was a feeling that the United States of America was moving toward a goal enunciated in the Preamble of the Constitution. The Youth … which a Nation must have to exist, had a feeling within them that the nation did not care for the future. There is no Spirit today.
> How can there be? A Congress that laughs at black children, brown children, white children being bitten by the rats of the slums? This is the Spirit of America? A Congress that passes a law which drafts only the poor, white or black?

How touching that Stanley capitalizes both Nation and Youth, as if to highlight their equivalence and remind us that these are potentially sacred forces, crucial to society's future well-being. Later on, he capitalizes another term normally rendered in lower-case: Citizen. (And for those too young to remember: the "draft" mentioned above is a reference to the military draft during the Vietnam War. It was unfairly structured, since economically deprived minorities were less likely to avoid military service by qualifying for exemptions as university students.) Marks also includes several remarks that appear to be aimed directly at Ronald Reagan, a future president of the United States who was then governor of California, where Marks currently resided:

> A governor that destroys an educational system? A governor who believes that only the youth who has parents with money should enter the universities and colleges of his state? A

governor that believes mental health can be cured with pills?
This is the United States of America?

Such challenges remain with us now: racial injustice, poverty, unequal educational opportunity, and mental illness problems that are addressed primarily with government approved pill popping.

One might easily gloss over this last point or regard the author as being somewhat "naive" when we consider the devastating street-drug problems that grip the nation today. But I view this as another forward-looking remark–and one linked to a hidden agenda behind much drug abuse in the 1960s (see below).

As Marks has clearly noted, the optimistic, progressive spirit embodied by President Kennedy was eclipsed and replaced by a widespread cynicism. President Johnson's seemingly endless Vietnam War was an additional reason that it morphed into an international cynicism about everything "American." Domestically, the American flag was burned in public, often by agents provocateurs (an action that turned many working-class Americans against the war protestors). The election of Richard Nixon in 1968–and, even more so, his re-election in 1972– snowballed into such an avalanche of cynicism and despair that many simply dropped out and gave up. For those who didn't live through this period in the early Seventies, the palpable sense of paranoia, mistrust in institutions, and loathing over the intelligence community's intrusion into the lives of ordinary citizens is difficult to imagine.

And while Nixon and his Secretary of State–a war criminal named Henry Kissinger–were aiding and abetting South American death squads as they rounded up thousands of protesters and forced them into stadiums where they were tortured, killed, and "disappeared" via Operation Condor, the youth in the U.S. were lured into similar stadiums that served as concert venues, where they were anesthetized by drugs and distracted by the kaleidoscopic hallucinations of LSD: a toxin manufactured via Agency contracts with Eli Lilly under the direction of the CIA's mind control operation, MK-ULTRA.[26] The Agency also relied on the services of drug dealers such

Ronald Stark (who played an important role in the Italian Gladio operation) to distribute the drug on the street level. Encouraging the use of such mind-altering substances was actually a form of psychic terrorism akin to those broader programs of violence and terror unleashed upon the left. And the brainless, apolitical, feel-good lyrics that dominated so much popular music (with few exceptions, such as Bob Dylan) added to this intentional distraction. Another (unwitting?) Agency asset, the LSD Pied Piper, Timothy Leary, encouraged young people to tune in, turn on, and drop out. And Leary pointedly instructed his acolytes to avoid politics. ("The choice is between being rebellious and being religious. Don't vote. Don't politic. Don't petition.")[27] For the Establishment, Woodstock was preferable to a half million political protestors showing up at the National Mall.

The result of all this was that "sex, drugs, and rock'n'roll" became the new opiate of the masses. While South American youth were tortured and killed, North Americans were "disappeared" on a purely psychological level, via drug abuse. Marks would later make a direct reference to this in his study on monotheism, *Jews, Judaism and the United States*, where he warns: "Both the U.S. and the USSR have been using 'mind-controlling' drugs since 1970! However, various states have also been using such drugs to control 'unruly' children (see S. J. Marks' *Through Distorted Mirrors*, 1976)."[28] Thus, as early as the mid-1970s (decades before the widespread public indignation over the use of Ritalin to control so-called unruly schoolchildren), Marks was already drawing a connection between drug abuse fostered by intelligence agencies and a broader pharmaceutical industry abuse. (We'll never know how much of the growing market for the latter came as a direct result of a youth culture that had been encouraged to destroy their own psychic equilibrium … as a true "Lost" Generation.)

In the last book that Marks published (at the age of eighty-two, just three years before his death), he once again took up this theme. *If This be Treason…!* (1996) is, in part, an exposé of the "Reagan-Bush administration's involvement (through the CIA-Contra movement) in the distribution and sale of hard drugs to Afro and Latin American youths." And in *Coup d'État!* he employs the term "LSD" as a metaphor to signify the illusions spun by the Warren Commission. Hence, *Coup*'s chapter five is titled: "LSD–Hallucinations and Charades." Returning now to *MMF*:

> Was the Commission, morally, an accessory after the fact, when it refused to question witnesses whose evidence was contrary to the theory created by the Commission? [...]
>
> The use of words to obscure the truth, the suppression of photographs, charts, film, X-Rays, the FBI report (yes, the 5-vol. FBI report *is not in the* [Warren Commission] *"Report" or the "Hearings"*), the Secret Service report, the destruction of material evidence, the theft of evidence, is the reason why the "Report" is considered untruthful.
>
> Was it planned this way?
>
> Many years ago, Walter Lippmann wrote:
>
> "The decay of decency in the modern age, the treatment of human beings as things, as mere instruments of power and ambition, is without doubt the consequence of the decay of the belief in man as something more than an animal animated by highly conditioned reflexes and chemical reactions.
>
> For, unless man is something more than that, he has no rights that anyone is bound to respect, and there are no limitations upon his conduct which he is bound to obey. This is the forgotten foundation of democracy in the only sense in which democracy is truly valid and of liberty in the only sense in which it can hope to endure. The liberties we talk about were established by men who took their conception of man from the great religious tradition of Western civilization, and the liberties we inherit almost certainly cannot survive the abandonment of that tradition."
>
> The Commission agreed and accepted the first paragraph only.

Lippmann's first paragraph represents an acute rendering of the mentality of many factions of the ruling class, which, if judged by their actions, must be regarded as psychopathic. A counterpoint philosophy–one reflecting man's potential to incarnate a noble, empathic spirit–was embodied by leaders such as JFK, MLK and RFK. This is precisely why Jim Garrison, in a

June 1968 interview, called Kennedy and his spiritual kin *humanists*: a word that, unfortunately, has fallen out of vogue.

Stanley Marks also belongs to this New Frontier "humanist" sensibility, and his text tells us precisely why. For he raises a sort of clarion call when he asks: "How long, O how long, America, will we commit our silence to perpetrate the evil in the Warren Report?" One could just as easily replace the term "Warren Commission" with a different phrase to describe the situation we find ourselves in today: "How long, O how long, America, will we commit our silence to perpetrate the evil in the *National Security State*?" (Which, as others have pointed out, has usurped a New Deal philosophy by positing the military as the most powerful influence determining a nation's direction, as well as its highest form of authority.)

Next, Marks explores a crucial pattern in the puzzle: the post-assassination plan. He asks: "What was the plan after the murder of the President?"

> There is now evidence that three persons, one who looked like Lee Oswald, attempted to rent a plane from the "Red Bird Airfield" for a long-distance flight. The operator of the flight was contacted on November 20 for a flight to take place in the afternoon of November 22, 1963. One of the persons asked the field owner if the plane could fly direct to Cuba.

The Red Bird Airfield event, which was already being commented on in the early days of research, was later explored in depth by Matthew Smith in *JFK: The Second Plot* (2002). Smith conducted extensive interviews with Wayne January, who ran a sales and charter business at Red Bird. January said that, shortly before the assassination, there were three individuals who approached him about renting a plane for a flight to Cuba. He immediately regarded their behavior as suspicious, and he later recalled that one of them resembled Oswald.

On the day of the assassination, a tower operator at the airfield made repeated attempts to contact the FBI when a plane scheduled for a long-distance flight lingered on the runway well past its scheduled time. The plane departed only after it was announced that a JFK murder suspect had been apprehended.

Marks continues:

> Oswald was a Communist, the FBI said so. A "defector" had fled to Cuba, that "Red" Godless Country, and had admitted it. Why did he fly down to Cuba if Cuba was not involved? That was the plot. The President's murder was only the spark. "Remember the Maine!" Remember Kennedy!

By citing the phrase "Remember the Maine!" Stanley is reminding us that what happened at Dealey Plaza was, in effect, a false-flag operation whose trademark mantra would be "Remember Kennedy!" That is, if this part of the post-assassination plan had not been scuttled by LBJ and the forces that stood behind him and pulled his puppet strings.[29]

Marks then engages in a discussion about how the assassination actually unfolded: "Three killers were involved and the gunfire was synchronized at 12:25 p.m. when the Dallas police flashed their first radio alarm. The President was hit in the classic 'cross fire,' from the back and the side." The author adds that the limousine's prior position at Elm and Houston Street would have provided a perfect opportunity for Oswald to fire from his supposed position in the Book Depository, yet he did not.

Then Marks reaches a conclusion that surely would have led the FBI to open a file on him (except for the likelihood that he had one already, as we shall see).

> Now, if Oswald was the assassin, he had a perfect target from the sixth floor. Mr. Hoover said Oswald did not shoot because trees blocked the view. It can only be said that Mr. Hoover should have his glasses repaired. There is not a tree on Houston Street! But no shots ring out. The car proceeds.
>
> As the car continues on Elm Street, the rifleman on the second floor of the Dal-Tex Building is waiting until his target approaches. He cannot fire at the President while the car is stopped at the corner of Houston and Elm Streets for the simple reason that the fire escape outside the window acts as a shield. Furthermore, he has a better shot when the car will proceed

down Elm Street. About 175 to 200 feet down Elm Street the trigger is pulled and the president is hit in the back. At the same instant, the two riflemen behind the fence on the grassy knoll pull their triggers, and the deed is done.

A fusillade of shots is released, all directed at the president in his automobile. Two types of rifles were used. It was all over in seconds. Within fifteen minutes the Dallas police had three suspects, two of them with rifles, but since none of them was Oswald, the police let them go.

The evidence is clear and uncontradicted that many witnesses heard five or more shots. It was in the newspapers and in the testimony given to the Commission. A bullet struck the curb and fragments of that curb hit a man [later identified as James Tague]. The bullet striking the curb did not come from Bullet Number 399; even the Commission admitted that fact. Parts of a bullet, some say the nose and base portion, were found on the front seat of the President's auto. No one has claimed, not even the "legal beagles," that those portions came from either Bullet Number 399 or the President's head. But what about the bullet that hit the windshield? So, Mr. Dulles, there was a conspiracy.

Even to this day, this remains a pretty accurate assessment of what probably occurred. Marks also speculates on how a "sniper's nest" was assembled by two men who later disappeared to the seventh floor of the TSBD (which had not yet been searched). Marks believes they later blended in with a crowd of reporters who entered the building, thus easily allowing for their escape, possibly with fake press credentials. (In the aftermath of the assassination, "security" at the TSBD was indeed porous, to say the least. As Joachim Joesten reported in 1964: "People who said they were reporters or showed their cameras were allowed to leave.")[30]

Marks concludes this chapter by directly addressing Allen Dulles and, with a lovely touch, issues his own verdict against both Dulles and the Commission (one very much in the spirit of Publilius Syrus, who once wrote, "The judge is condemned when the guilty is acquitted"):

No, Mr. Dulles, it was not the responsibility of the American citizen to find and name the assassins; that was your task. Your lack of responsibility to the task is the cause for your failure. You issued the "Report" under your name; you had at your disposal the entire operating machinery of the government of the United States. We citizens have only what you and your fellow Commissioners wrote. We read, we looked, we analyzed, we thought; and we, nearly seventy percent of us, now deliver a verdict on your work:

The Warren Commission was a failure.

The Postscript of *MMF* is graced by a telling title: "Jim Garrison, 'St. George' Versus the 'Dragon'!" Unlike other researchers who were snookered by the mainstream media's constant assault upon Garrison (one that we now know was orchestrated by the CIA), Marks realized that Garrison, as "St. George," was up against a State-sponsored dragon. He begins with the statement: "By the time this book appears in print the Kennedy Conspiracy may claim another victim: none other than Jim Garrison, the District Attorney of New Orleans whose 'lance of truth' has pierced vital organs of the conspiracy that murdered President John F. Kennedy."

Was Marks right about Garrison being turned into a victim? Yes, if we consider the phenomenon of "character assassination." As Gaeton Fonzi discusses in *The Last Investigation*, the Agency had long since perfected its craft of sullying and destroying the reputation of world leaders who refused to toe the line; such black arts were applied even in the early 1950s.[31] And "character assassination" would also prove to be a second, posthumous conspiracy launched against JFK himself: the lies, distortions, and propaganda that the media continue to twine into the Kennedy "story."[32]

After crediting Garrison's work ("There is no question that Mr. Garrison's investigation has created a firm base in the theory that President Kennedy was the victim of the Batista backed anti-Castro groups in the United States. These groups, in turn, have the full support of the CIA"), the author returns to the evidence of character assassination and the media's obsequious role. In four stunning little paragraphs, Marks illustrates just how prescient his views really were when, fifty-three years ago, he first composed this text.

> Various members of the mass communication media bribed witnesses, hid witnesses, issued fraudulent interviews, had "witnesses" file suit against Mr. Garrison, produced nationwide television programs which upheld the findings of the Warren Commission. How incredible! Why?
>
> The answer to "why" can be found in the fact that many of the inactive and active participants of the Conspiracy will be found in the ranks of the government and the economic strata of our nation.

What Marks is saying here about fraudulent "witnesses" was confirmed two years later by Jim Garrison. In his June 1968 interview, Garrison remarks: "Those people we felt from the beginning were sent in by the other side because they were so unconvincing and we never intended to use them as witnesses at all.... We had endless penetrations and endless appearance of different people and then they were not convincing after they gave us a statement, so we paid no more attention to them. So now, they suddenly appear and say we were witnesses for Garrison. That has no meaning." Garrison adds that, as a result, "Some of the press has made us look like monsters."

Also note that, by way of a reply to the question "why?" Marks introduces a crucial subject: the ruling economic elite, which exists one level above the CIA. This concept was rarely broached by assassination researchers until Fletcher Prouty (the Pentagon's liaison officer to the CIA) published *The Secret Team* in 1972. In a Preface to the second edition, Prouty says "intelligence gathering" is akin to a "cover story" for the Agency. For, although it does gather information, its real task is to serve as a "willing tool of a higher level Secret Team, or High Cabal, that usually includes representatives of the CIA and other instrumentalities of the government, certain cells of the business and professional world and, almost always, foreign participation."[33] This line of thought was further probed by author Donald Gibson, whose insights were assembled into articles such as "The Creation of the Warren Commission"

(1997) and then expanded in *Battling Wall Street* (1994) and *The Kennedy Assassination Cover-up* (2000). As Gibson reveals, the finger-pointing cannot stop at the level represented by the CIA or military intelligence, because above and beyond this there lurks a barely visible force that utilizes the Agency as its police: the economic "Power Elite," as it was dubbed by C. Wright Mills in a book with that same title published in 1956. But Gibson goes a step further, because he identifies specific individuals within this hierarchy.

Such concepts would certainly not have been alien to Stanley. In his 1971 attack on the Nixon administration, *Watch What We Do ... Not What We Say!* he includes a chapter titled "The Establishment" in which he sums it up nicely: "It can be said that not more than 8,000 persons (out of a population of 215,000,000) comprise the Establishment. They control every major decision, foreign and domestic, made in the nation. It is not a 'conspiracy' but a 'meeting of the minds.' They sincerely believe that 'what is good for them is good for the country.'"

He continues: "At the foreign policy level, the 'Establishment' works through the following four agencies: (1) the Council of Foreign Affairs; (2) the Committee for Economic Development; (3) The National Security Council; and (4) the CIA." Much of the rest of this chapter is comprised of lists of other organizations, foundations, and corporations funded by Establishment forces and tasked with "the movement of policy directed by the Establishment." (E.g., the Rand Corporation, the Brookings Institute, the Ford Foundation, and dozens of others.)[34]

All this has a direct bearing on Allen Dulles,[35] who also worked as a partner on the law firm of Sullivan and Cromwell (along with his brother, John Foster Dulles, President Eisenhower's Secretary of State). Sullivan and Cromwell represented leading multinational corporations and interests such as those of the oligarchic Rockefellers. As a principal law partner there, Dulles was positioned at the very apex of a visible pyramid of power. But above this first structure one can also imagine a second, inverted pyramid: one far less visible, and inhabited by those *éminence grises* who compose the real Power Elite.[36] The Dulles brothers served as interlocutors between these two structures, via institutions such as Sullivan and Cromwell.

Figures within the first pyramidal group were also linked to Operation Gladio, a worldwide clandestine network that targeted perceived "leftists" all around the globe. Gladio operatives were also tied to the 1978 assassination of Italy's Prime Minister Aldo Moro. And in the 1960s, plans were developed at the School of the Americas and the Conference of American Armies to coordinate such "security forces" in South America. The U.S. was directly involved in the overall planning, as well as in the training of torture techniques. Such Gladio-like operations in South America eventually took the form of Operation Condor (officially titled in 1975, but in operation since the Sixties), resulting in approximately 50,000 tortured and killed; 30,000 "disappeared"; and 400,000 "leftist sympathizers" imprisoned.[37]

The assassins connected to both Condor and Gladio behaved like mercenaries for hire who drifted in and out of various locations and operations. For example, speaking of agents involved in the assassination of Chile's Orlando Letelier in Washington, DC, Gaeton Fonzi writes: "The interconnections among these men are Byzantine, stretching over dozens of years and thousands of miles." The Condor operations are documented by declassified memos in the National Archives, which prove that these events occurred with the direct involvement of every presidential administration from Johnson to Reagan.

Therefore, by raising the issue of De Gaulle, Marks places Kennedy's death into a broader perspective: a worldwide war on the left, sanctioned and manipulated by an economic elite. We cannot obtain any real understanding of why Kennedy was killed without examining his assassination from this wider perspective. Otherwise, if we remain mere Warren Commission critics, we will fail to see the forest for the trees. One must also bear in mind that figures that were far less "threatening" to the Power Elite were also murdered by the Allen Dulles–Richard Helms CIA without a second thought. So, why not John Kennedy?

To jump ahead for a moment: although Marks was not familiar with the name "Operation Gladio" (which remained secret until 1990), he was well aware of Clay Shaw's involvement with organizations such as Centro Mondiale Commerciale and Permindex, which both appear to be linked to Gladio as funding mechanisms. In his 1970 publication, *Coup d'État!*, Marks discusses the connection between these mysterious entities and the assassination attempts on President Charles de Gaulle:

> After World War II, Mr. Shaw became associated with a mysterious "Centro Mondiale Commerciale" and a company known as "Permindex." Shaw was also associated with a highly classified CIA operation known as "Force III" and with this operation he was given the code name of "Dreyfus" (ironic, for both Oswald and Shaw were to become "patsies" as had Dreyfus).
>
> This "Centro Mondiale Commerciale" had within its organization such stalwart believers in democracy as the OAS, which attempted to murder De Gaulle five times, and also to overthrow the French Republic; various members and officials of Mussolini's Fascist Party; a few Nazi Hungarians; such as Mr. [Ferenc] Nagy, still wanted for war crimes in turning their own people over to the Nazis; and a man whose daughter-in-law was none other than the daughter of Hitler's financial wizard, Hjalmar Schact. Another associate of Mr. Shaw in this Italian corporation was none other than G. Mantello who was evicted from Switzerland, with the Nazi Nagy, for "criminal activity."
>
> Mr. Shaw was no mere employee–he was a member of the Board of Directors so he could not claim loss of memory as to the reputations and characters of his fellow members.
>
> A few persons who were involved with this Italian "Centro Mondiale Commerciale" company were to die violent deaths, and after their deaths their personal funds and property mysteriously disappeared. In fact, the rancid activity of this company, supplied with CIA funds, led to that company's expulsion from Italy. No other European nation was interested in permitting that company to settle on its soil, so the all-white nation of South Africa is now its spawning ground–with the "Four Horsemen" riding free as the wind.[38]

So let us pause for a moment to consider all this. Clay Shaw, an international businessman with links to the CIA, who was known to associate with Lee Oswald, is also a member of two organizations staffed with neo-Fascists, and these organizations are believed to be linked to assassination attempts against leftists and world leaders such as Charles de Gaulle. Espionage and murder are sometimes frowned upon; and, for this reason, Shaw's Permindex was given the bum's rush out of Europe. In addition, Shaw was associated with the maniacal anti-Castro activist, David Ferrie–Oswald's old flight instructor–whom Garrison was also investigating in the murder of JFK. Documentary proof would later emerge that "Shaw was an active covert operator for the CIA while Garrison was investigating him."[39]

In other words, Shaw was one of those rare birds who transit the orbs of an elite economic strata as well as the shadowy world of street operators such as Ferrie and Oswald. District Attorney Garrison was far ahead of his time in seeing this bigger picture– so far, that many remained blind to it and instead mocked him for seeking the truth along such pioneering trails. And so, Stanley Marks should be given credit for following in Garrison's footsteps in the unhesitating manner that he did and for encouraging others to do so as well.

Marks was also aware of the CIA's chicanery south of the border. Shortly after Chile's Salvador Allende became the first Marxist president in Latin America (assuming office on November 30, 1970), Stanley published his critical attack on the Nixon presidency: *Watch What We Do ... Not What We Say!* During a discussion on the dangers of the Agency ("It can, and does, murder both foreign and national leaders"), almost as an aside, he accurately predicts what will happen next in Chile. And he does so by comparing the fate of Chile to that of Vietnam:

> After the extermination of the Indo-Chinese nations as nations, the CIA will then proceed to "exterminate" another nation–Chile. The Establishment's propaganda is already being published with the same old trite and dreary slogans: "The Chileans pose a threat to our security." A nation that is more than 5,000 miles away from the territorial mainland of the United States, with no navy, army, or air force that cannot even drop leaflets on our mainland!

Thus, with the CIA "protecting" the people from "invasions" and the FBI maintaining its ever-vigilant status over the "dissenters," the people calmly lockstep their way into a prison of their own making.[40]

Just two years after this was published, on September 11, 1973, the CIA organized and staged the coup that would overthrow the democratically elected government of Allende and usher in a murderous right-wing dictator, General Pinochet, who dissolved all remnants of democracy and replaced them with a military junta that ruled by fear, torture, and the "disappearance" of those who had the courage to resist. Stanley saw it coming, because his in-depth historical research had trained him to recognize broader historical patterns. Although none dare call it "extermination," he was correct about that as well: The CIA conducted extermination.

*   *   *

In his second book about the assassination, *Two Days of Infamy: November 22, 1963; September 28, 1964* (published in March 1969), Marks would briefly expand on some of these same ideas. "The citizens of the United States," he says, are "living in a dream world concocted by the mass communications systems" that have convinced them that such a "secret could not be kept"– despite the fact that the public usually remains in the dark until the actual conspirators are apprehended. But although we may not be able to "name the assassins,"

A conspiracy has been proven beyond a reasonable doubt. But what was the purpose of the conspiracy?

History has shown that an invisible *coup d'état* occurred when President Kennedy was murdered. It is the belief of the author that more than the murder of a head of state was involved. This belief is based on two events that occurred during the three years President Kennedy occupied the White House; (1) The Bay of Pigs; and (2) the Cuban Missile Crisis. [...] The life of President Kennedy was only an incident to bring into operation the main purpose of the conspiracy. The conspiracy was a 4-pronged affair: (1) the murder of President

Kennedy; (2) the invasion and overthrow of the Castro regime in Cuba with the installation of a right-wing dictatorship under the direct control of the CIA, which is[,] in turn, controlled by the Fascist forces in the United States; (3) involvement with a war with the Soviet Union, but if that not be possible, a complete diplomatic break with the Soviet Union isolating that nation by the new government in the United States by exerting economic pressure upon NATO and nations receiving our foreign aid; and (4) a "Coup d'état."[41]

Twenty-five years after he published *MMF*, in his final book about the assassination, *Yes, Americans, A Conspiracy Murdered JFK!* (1992), Stanley Marks would tie the strands of economics and media together in a single statement:

Many persons cannot understand the reason why the powerful newspapers and the ABC, CBS, and NBC television and radio chains have kept a constant drumbeat against the critics of the Warren Commission. The reason is quite simple– when the president was murdered the power structure shifted both economically and politically.[42]

At the end of *MMF*, on the penultimate page of his Postscript, Marks condenses everything I've said about the public's manipulation by the media into one blockbuster sentence: "To whom does the mass communication system owe its loyalty? To the people who have fought, are fighting, and will continue to fight for the ideas of the 'freedom of the press,' or to its advertisers?" (As a veteran who served in World War II, Marks has earned the right to make such a statement.) Then he puts his money where his mouth is with a courageous challenge: "The NBC and CBS programs dealing with the Warren Commission in 1967 [are] nothing more than a distortion of the evidence and a deliberate misrepresentation of the truth. If this sentence is libelous then NBC and CBS have the right to sue this author for libel. Unfortunately, this will not occur, for it would be a means of obtaining a trial before a court of law where the 'basic principles of American justice' would be invoked."

Most authors with limited economic resources would not risk a lawsuit launched by a major corporation (with its handsomely paid legal team) for slander or defamation. As an attorney himself, Marks was well aware that "freedom of speech" does not automatically cover pointed attacks against businesses, even when such remarks may be justified. And if an author was proven "not guilty" in a court of law, he could still go broke while attempting to obtain such a verdict. We should keep in mind that, in the days before Internet or cable TV, the three main networks on American television were CBS, NBC, and ABC. Even a major city such as New York boasted a total of only seven television channels. (Besides the three media giants, there were three local stations and "Channel 13," a grant- and donation funded educational network, the latter now known as PBS.) Therefore, "news" was a lot easier to control (especially before the advent of an underground press). This was the sort of information barrier that so many independent researchers were attempting to breach.

On the final page of *MMF*, Marks makes a prediction that, sadly, comes to pass:

> The media may succeed; for as the day for the [Clay Shaw] trial approaches, the greater the use of the media for the perpetration of the lie increases. If the forces behind the Conspiracy cannot destroy Mr. Garrison's case, they may decide to destroy the man, either physically or by reputation.

Indeed, this proved to be the case: the powers-that-be went after Garrison's reputation and attempted to sully it.

> That the CIA controls many of the news columns in both the press and magazines is now known. What is not known, and what will never be known, is how many Agents of the CIA now work for various organs in the mass communication media.

As I mentioned earlier in regard to this quote, even now, many Americans remain unaware of this arrangement. Yet, this cozy relationship has only intensified, with major networks routinely hiring "former" intel operators who don't even bother to hide such "past" credentials.

> The facts speak for themselves, but if the public is never given the facts those facts are worthless.

This harkens back to Stanley's critique of Dulles, who claimed that critics merely need to step forward with their facts if they have any. Indeed, the critics did step forward–and with a whole array of evidence–but their case was effectively censored, their speakers effectively banned, from mainstream networks.

In conclusion, the author invokes a fellow lawyer and philosopher who served as the third American president and whose words Marks uses to plead his case.

> Thomas Jefferson once said that the most important factor in a democracy is a free press; he did not say a "privileged" press.
>
> The hideous activity of NBC, CBS, ABC, and other organs of the mass communication media can lead to a conclusion that certain members of that media know that President Kennedy was murdered by conspirators and the conspiracy must never be allowed to face the light of day.

Stanley ends on a note that continues to resonate, because what he calls the "light of day" has yet to emerge–for reasons we know all too well.

We are still facing the same challenge.

Part II: Footprints of the Bear

All this may lead a reader to wonder: but who was this guy Stanley Marks, and what were the circumstances that helped to shape him? As we shall see, Stanley's story is indeed a "story of our times."

As described in the Preface to this edition, I first stumbled upon the work of Stanley J. Marks in 2013, when I purchased a bunch of rare JFK assassination titles from an estate sale at Powell's, a bookshop in Portland. I conducted the purchase over the phone, without examining the text, so I had no idea what I was in for. Over the years, I rarely encountered any other copies of *Murder Most Foul!* for sale. After doing some spring cleaning, in August 2018 I listed it on eBay, where it attracted little attention for the next year and a half. Then, on March 26, a fellow named Scott purchased it. What I wasn't aware of was that, on this same day, *Variety* had published a story titled: "Bob Dylan Releases 17-Minute Song about JFK Assassination," and the tune featured the same title as Stanley's book (minus the author's trademark exclamation point). The similarities between the two Murder Most Fouls are indeed intriguing. For example, the ninth line in Dylan's song–"shot down like a dog in broad daylight"–echoes a phrase on page 139 of Marks' *MMF* when the author says that our president was "shot like a dog on the street." By the time Dylan's song was released, I had the only available copy of the book for sale. This is how Scott–an aficionado who runs a Dylan blog–first encountered Mr. Marks.

Once he posted my photo of Stanley's book cover, Dylan fans began to wonder about this unknown author and his treatise of 975 questions and answers. And I started to wonder as well. With only a handful of clues about Stanley, I began to search databases at Ancestry and Newspapers.com. One of the biggest–and only–leads was printed on the back cover of *MMF*: a note saying that Stanley had previously authored a book called *The Bear That Walks Like a Man. A Diplomatic and Military Analysis of Soviet Russia*. Once I ordered a copy, I discovered another clue on the acknowledgments page: a note to "my wife, Ethel, and my daughter, Roberta, for their encouragement and inspiration."

With this information in hand, I was able to locate a record of Stanley and Ethel in a 1940 Federal Census, where our biographical tale begins. Not long afterward I successfully tracked down Stanley's daughter, Roberta. Once she received my letter requesting help, she kindly provided enough information to fill in the gaps that, until then, had remained a mystery.

According to the census, Stanley Jacob Marks was born in Waukegan, Illinois on April 26, 1914, just three years before the birth of John F. Kennedy. When he was four years old, his parents died from the 1918 influenza pandemic, also known as the Spanish flu, which infected a third of the world's population. The names of Stanley's biological parents are not known. According to Stanley's daughter, after their death Stanley was placed in the care of foster parents: Sarah and Samuel Markowitz, from whom Stanley took his surname, later changing it to "Marks." ("When he was going into sales, my father had a mentor who said to him: "Stan, it's a rough world out there. 'Markowitz' really makes you very Jewish. Life will be easier if you simplify your name. 'Stan Marks'–there we go!") According to Roberta, in later years, there was a lingering suspicion that the Markowitzs' motivation for helping Stanley was primarily financial, rather than altruistic (foster parents were given a stipend by the state). "I think my father was a really brilliant man; and, if he had been brought up differently, he might have achieved greater things. What he didn't have was a family that nurtured or supported his intelligence. No one encouraged him." But she also recalls that Stanley bonded strongly with the Markowitzs' son Willy, who was a few years older than Stanley and who took him under his wing.

One of the few things Roberta knows about her father's upbringing is that Stanley often said "he never had enough food. When you see pictures of him as a youth, he was bone-thin and skinny. That is, until he married my mother, whose cooking he adored. Then he started to gain weight." One is tempted to surmise that Stanley's privations and experience with hunger on Chicago's hardscrabble streets may have helped to open his eyes to a certain political awareness–or at least helped to mold him into a lifelong FDR New Dealer.

On May 9, 1936, shortly after his twenty-second birthday, Stanley married Ethel M. Milgrom, a nineteen-year-old Chicago native. Ethel would later "co-author" several of his books, although primarily she served as his editor, helping to polish Stanley's sometimes awkward, strident prose.[43] After obtaining a history degree from the University of Illinois in 1934, in 1937 Stanley graduated from the affiliated John Marshall Law School, which is still Chicago's only public law school.

Thanks to a yearbook that someone posted on Ancestry, we have two professionally composed photos of Stanley. One is a traditional portrait that captures a smiling, bespectacled young man bearing a bright-eyed, notably intellectual look. The other features full-length figures of eight young men and two young women in the midst of a debate broadcast by Chicago radio station WJJD. Stanley, standing at 5'9" (according to his World War II draft card), appears as the third figure from the left. He's positioned before an old-fashioned stand-up mic, dressed in a smartly tailored suit and tie. A caption reads:

> THE DEBATORS' FORUM IS ON THE AIR. By the time this appears, these words will have been broadcast from Station WJJD, Chicago, one hundred twenty-four times. Every Saturday the Debaters' Forum brings you members of the John Marshall Law School faculty, Alumni Association, and Student Body who deliver talks on timely, interesting, and important topics of the day.

Stanley graduated during a precarious moment in history, and perhaps this explains why a law school graduate was soon working as a salesman. The Great Depression (1929-1939) was still in progress, and it would continue its devastation for another couple of years, until America's entry into WWII became inevitable, and the defense industry kicked into place. At the peak of the Depression in March 1933, fifteen and a half million were unemployed: over a quarter of the work force.

As a result of President Roosevelt enacting new labor laws, workers became more emboldened to make demands, leading to stronger unions, sprawling picket lines, and strikes that the government now had limited power to prevent (thanks to these new laws). It was also a time of raging debate about capitalism versus alternate political systems. As John Kenneth Galbraith later remarked in an unpublished paper on U.S.–Soviet relations, "The Great Depression, when it came, suggested an intractable weakness in capitalism."[44] Galbraith adds that fears of its collapse may have served to energize the more dictatorial, right-wing elements within the Establishment, who believed the only way to prop it up was to curtail civil rights. But in order to preserve the system, FDR decided to make accommodations to the left rather than take a sharp, dictatorial turn to the far right.[45] In the midst of this whirligig of change, Stanley's political allegiances were ultimately cast.

According to the 1940 census, Stanley and his wife were living in Chicago, sharing a household with Ethel's parents. Ethel's father, Joe Milgrom, had immigrated to the U.S. from Kazimer, Poland, in 1913. Ethel's mother, Eva Wolovoy (later Anglicized to Eva "Wool"), hailed from Russia and also arrived in 1913. Since Stanley would later publish a well-received tome about Russia's military prowess and significance, one cannot help but wonder how his views may have been enhanced and enriched by conversations with Ethel's headstrong mother, a native of Kiev.

During this post-Depression period when the economy was still shaky, Stanley was employed as a salesman by the Illinois Vending Company. Ethel was listed as a "Saleslady," working in a department store. Her father's occupation was "Laundryman": one who owned his own business. The census adds that Mr. Milgrom worked a total of seventy-three hours: more than ten hours a day if working seven days a week. His highest educational level was the sixth grade. Ethel's mother had completed the eighth grade, and her employment status was: "Unpaid family worker" in the "laundry." She worked forty-eight hours a week while simultaneously raising Ethel's teenage sister. The census also indicates that Ethel had completed all four years of high school. Therefore, we can conclude that our future researchers came from humble, hardworking backgrounds. Roberta recalls that her maternal grandparents also ran a grocery store in a predominantly African American neighborhood, where they regularly extended credit to customers and developed a reputation for being well liked and respected. And she clearly recalls her father giving her an early lesson in racial injustice: "He always used to make this comment, and it stuck with me. He'd say, even though we were Jewish, and, through the centuries, have seen very bad times, obviously, our skin was white. And we didn't suffer the way Black people do, because of their skin color."

What the census doesn't mention is that, by 1939, Stanley had begun research on what would eventually become a 340-page book about Soviet Russia. One of the remarkable things about this accomplishment is that he conducted his research and put the finishing touches on this tome while employed as a salesman and personnel manager for a wholesale company that manufactured billboards. This fact is noted in *The Billboard: The World's Foremost Amusement Weekly* (the well-known music industry magazine). Its March 13, 1943 edition features an enthusiastic piece on Stanley that contains some crucial biographical data:

Salesman Author Making Plans for Second Book Soon

Chicago, March 6.–Stanley J. Marks, sales representative of Gardner & Company here, is the author of a book that has received creditable mention by reviewers. The Gardner firm manufactures sales boards.

The title of the book is *The Bear That Walks Like a Man* and is published by Dorrance & Company, Philadelphia. Marks says he spent four years in research and study of the foreign policy of Soviet Russia as a preparation for writing the book, which deals with the strength of the Red Army, its organization, tactics, and strategy. Marks is also known as an aviator and commentator on foreign and national affairs.

Among those who have recently reviewed the book are Sterling North, of the *Chicago Daily News*, A. C. Spectorsky, of the *Chicago Sun*, and the book reviewers of the *New York Herald Tribune* and the *New York Times*.

The publishers report that present sales are encouraging.

Marks is working on a second book which deals with military science as practiced by the United States Army.[46]

The inside dust jacket of the *Bear* features a Marksian list of questions: "Will the United States defeat Japan without the assistance of the Soviet Union? … Has the airplane displaced land and sea power? … Why were the experts so wrong in their predictions about the Soviet Union when Hitler invaded Russia? These questions and many others are discussed and answered by Mr. Marks….The author lifts the curtain that has veiled the Soviet Union in mystery since 1917 and discusses the tragedies that have resulted from the policy of isolating Russia from normal intercourse with the rest of the world."

This latter remark represents an important point. Bringing the Russian "Bear" back into a normalized channel of communication–and no longer insisting upon its isolation–would prove to be one of the most important efforts made by President Kennedy, as well as being one of the most likely reasons he was killed. Soviet Premier Khrushchev even spelled it out for JFK in an urgent telegram delivered October 26, 1962 in the midst of the Cuban Missile Crisis, when Khrushchev bluntly stated: "Let us normalize relations."[47] (How that must have made Cold Warriors in the State Department cringe!)

Marks dedicates his book to "The leaders of the United Nations, upon whose shoulders rests the responsibility of leading their people in their struggle for survival against the barbarous monster of Fascism." And he ends the *Bear* with a prophetic warning against isolationism: "There has been a growing tendency among the Anglo-Saxon nations to treat the Soviet and Chinese people as poor relations."

In his brief Introduction, the author remarks: "Today, the American people, engaged in a life and death struggle, not for the preservation of their philosophy of government, but for the preservation of world liberty, want to know why and how their ally, Soviet Russia, has been able to stop the onrushing forces of fascism. That is why this book has been written." One could easily argue that, three decades later, Mr. Marks might amend this statement. For, after the murder of JFK, the American people were indeed engaged in a struggle for the "preservation of their philosophy of government." And, by then, the "onrushing forces of fascism" were embodied by a group of overzealous, unaccountable, out-of-control right-wing despots working for institutions such as the CIA and military intelligence, or positioned in various other shadowy enclaves of clandestine power.[48] In fact, these are some of the issues that Stanley Marks *would* explore in subsequent publications.

So, what led this intelligent, well-adapted member of society—a lawyer, to boot–to fall prey to the rabbit-hole allure of Kennedy assassination research? Was it the same unwavering belief in justice that compelled so many other self-sacrificing researchers to step into a void that should have been filled by an earnest, government sponsored, fact-finding mission? If we can judge anything from the idealism that drives the narrative of the *Bear*, a good guess might be: an unmitigated passion for truth, and a steadfast belief in the value of its importance. However, there may have been additional factors at play; for, as we shall see, Stanley was himself victimized by the government's encroachment on the civil rights of its citizens. And the event that triggered this was the publication of his first book.

A publishing contract for the *Bear* was signed on September 11, 1942 (perhaps a propitious date for a future "conspiracy researcher"), and it was copyrighted in 1943, a couple of months before Stanley's twenty-ninth birthday. Shortly afterward, copies were circulated among journalists in the mainstream press. One of the first reviews appeared in the February 28 edition of the *Democrat and Chronicle Sunday Magazine* (Rochester, NY), just four days after the book's official release date. It's a glowing and lengthy treatment, featured prominently between a review of an H. L. Menken memoir and a review of William Saroyan's latest novel. But Stanley receives more column space than either of these celebrated authors. Titled "A Forceful Espousal of Russia's Cause," it opens:

> With a partisan enthusiasm which first affronts and then convinces his reader, Stanley J. Marks uses his diplomatic and military analysis of Soviet Russia ... to show that had the Western democracies not isolated the USSR there needn't have

been a world alliance of heavily armed forces to chase Hitler and Tojo back to their lairs.

The reviewer adds that Marks "drips vitriol paragraph by paragraph when he mentions the isolationists of the United States, when he refers to Chamberlain, the Cliveden Set, Daladier, Laval, or their associates-in-theory. He has no verbal thrust too bitter when he says political leaders of England and France tried to use Russia as a sacrifice to Hitler's expansion dreams." (This uncompromising dripping of "vitriol" coupled with bitter verbal thrusts clearly anticipates the author's later writing.)

In a telling summation that foreshadows why Stanley would soon get into trouble, the reviewer adds: "In no less fulsome manner does Marks praise everything Russian, its strategy, its fighting qualities, its armed forces, its economic power, and above all its diplomacy, which at all times protected Russia against the 'inevitable' day when Hitler threw the might of his triumphing army against the Soviet's strength. And, with Russian soldiers now hurling the Nazi legions westward after one of the greatest defensive struggles in world history, who can say him nay?" The reviewer also touches on two major points in the book: Stanley's innovative analysis of the Blitzkrieg ("He credits the Soviet leaders with evolving much of its strategy and explains technical aspects of the Blitz"), and an in-depth discussion of Stalin's decision to forestall the conflict for as long as possible:

> Long before Munich, Soviet Premier Stalin was working for collective strategy against the Nazi menace which, according to the author, the Russian recognized alone among his democracy-ruling contemporaries. But, rebuffed time and again by the appeaser cliques, Stalin had no choice but the non-aggression pact with Hitlerite Germany … Marks doesn't dodge the question: Was there a double-cross of England and France by Stalin? He … answers with italics and implied desk thumping: NO! … the writer finds the double-cross was on the other side. Stalin needed his acquired years of peace to prepare for the war with the Nazis which he knew was coming and feared he would fight alone and unaided … Marks shows in

this chapter how the Soviet proffers of alliance were met by the appeasers' efforts aimed solely at finding out the military strength and disposition of the Soviet armed might.

Exactly one month later, on March 28th, 1943, the widely read *Chicago Tribune* featured a major piece titled "A Recital of Russia's List of Grievances." The reviewer was the highly accomplished Harvard graduate John Cudahy, a World War I veteran who served in the American Infantry against the Bolsheviks in Russian's Civil War. He later authored a book critical of U.S. involvement in Russia: *Archangel–the American war with Russia.* Cudahy's credentials were impressive; he served under FDR as ambassador to Poland and Belgium, and as minister to Luxembourg and the Irish Free State. By 1941, Cudahy had published five other books. That same year, *Life* magazine commissioned him to interview Hitler.

Although Cudahy's review is mainly a summary of Marks' work, early in the piece he remarks: "It is a detailed recitation of Soviet past grievances against the Democratic Powers–all the more painful for being irrefutably true." Cudahy also refers to his own past experience: "The Allied intervention in Archangel and Siberia twenty-five years ago in an undeclared war against the Russian government is not easy to justify." Gaining the attention of a reviewer of Cudahy's status in one of Chicago's major newspapers was no small accomplishment, and reading of this ambassador's approval must have been thrilling for both Stanley and his immigrant in-laws.

On April 4, 1945, another highly positive and lengthy appraisal appeared in Georgia's *Atlanta Constitution*. The reviewer praises the *Bear* as "remarkable," adding: "it could not appear at a more propitious time. For, regardless of the magnificent fight the Soviet Union has been waging against the Nazis and in spite of Russia's selfless contribution in blood and property for the common cause of the United Nations, there still exists, unfortunately, a great deal of prejudice and animosity against the country whose people have suffered most in stopping and destroying the heretofore invincible foe of mankind." After this encouraging opening gambit, he adds that Marks has "written a powerful book in which, without mincing words and without fear of stepping on any toes, he lifts the veil behind which the truth about the Soviet Union has been hidden all these many years." Directness and having the courage of one's convictions are also qualities that animate Stanley's later publications.

In a follow-up paragraph that would make many within the Establishment bristle with irritation, the reviewer concludes: "Ever since the formation of the USSR, the reactionary press in the United States has so perverted the truth about Soviet Russia that the average reader in America has received a distorted impression of the political, economic, and military strength of that country." Referring to the *Bear*'s fifteen chapters, he adds that each one contains "authentic and often dramatic information on Soviet Russia and her policy toward the rest of the world." "Mr. Marks' book should be read by all clear-thinking Americans in order to divest themselves of the unfortunate and harmful propaganda that may have poisoned their minds against the Soviet Union." As if to illustrate how quickly and pendulously opinions might swing during this period, in support of Marks' thesis, the reviewer ends with a quote from General MacArthur: "On the glorious banners of the Red Army rests the future of our civilization." In what would later prove to be an odd twist of fate, Stanley would serve in the Infantry under Douglas MacArthur in the Pacific theatre.

More ominously, on the same day the *Democrat and Chronicle* review appeared, the *Hartford Courant* published an essay titled "New Facts about Russia." The reviewer opens by stating: "Stanley J. Marks' leaning toward communistic philosophy is apparent" (a remark that, in itself, would have been enough to bring Stanley to the attention of the FBI), but then adds, "but this in no way detracts from the value of the book. His diplomatic and military analysis of Soviet Russia may not tell the whole truth, but then the whole truth is impossible at this stage of the game, and he does acquaint the reader with a great deal of fact with which the American public is unacquainted." A few paragraphs later, he continues: "Mr. Marks points out that the international policies of the past decade were not conditioned by love of France, Poland, Finland, or any other country, but by hate and fear of Russia. In this he does thinking Americans a favor; he intimates that future relations with the Soviets must be based on better understanding and mutual faith." Thus, even despite certain caveats, Stanley continued to be received favorably.

I was able to trace notices, brief reviews, or full-scale essays on the *Bear* in over thirty mainstream periodicals. Although Stanley is on record as saying that a few of the reviews were "stinkers," the only negative piece I could find appeared in the form of a one-line dismissal in the stodgy, predictably conservative *Foreign Affairs* journal (still being published today). A so-called Capsule Review, it merely states: "An only moderately successful summary of recent diplomatic history and an analysis of the Soviet's military strength." Yet, even there, the reviewer still felt compelled to include the adjective "successful."

A first-time author could not have asked for a better reception for his thankless labor. Even the professional journal of the U.S. Army, *The Command and General Staff School Military Review* (April 1943), notes that Stanley's book had been added to their library. It's also cited in several other publications, such as *Maxim Litvinoff* by Arthur Pope (a scholarly biography of the Soviet Union's Commissar of Foreign Affairs, reviewed favorably by the *New York Times*) and *The Russian Treason Trials 1936-37-38*, a 1946 thesis by Stanley Wilson deposited in the Stanford University library. In 1986, the *Bear* was listed in *Transformation in Russian and Soviet Military History*, a bibliography published by the Defense Technical Information Center and "prepared for use at the 12th Military History Symposium on 'Transformation in Russian and Soviet Military History' at the Air Force Academy." The report (partially redacted) indicates that the *Bear* was still circulating in the Air Force Academy library.[49]

What makes Stanley's accomplishment all the more noteworthy is that his publisher, Dorrance, was a vanity press. In the days before independent authors were blessed with self-publishing software and online distribution networks, vanity presses were notorious for charging high fees to naive, amateur writers, who dreamed of seeing their name in print. Once a trunk-load of books was paid for and delivered to the author, the publisher would usually vanish from the scene without offering that most crucial follow-up necessary for a text to survive: mainstream publicity. Yet Dorrance (which is still in business today) must have been more reputable than a typical vanity house. Stanley's hardcover is handsomely produced and features attractive cover art, a red cloth binding embossed with gilt lettering, and professional offset lithography. And either through their own efforts or the author's, the *Bear* not only thrived; it became a bestseller.

And–even more exceptional–Stanley's contract with Dorrance indicates that it was the publisher and not the writer that footed the printing bill: it's a standard book contract with a normal, ten percent royalty fee paid to the author. (Stanley's daughter recently found the original contract, stored in a box in her garage.) Stanley's only financial obligation was to pay for advertisement; and, being a natural-born salesman, he must have handled this exceptionally well. I also learned that the company was founded by Gordon Dorrance in 1920, after a book he was editing for Scribner's failed to reach the publication stage, and he decided to publish it under his own imprint. In 1954, on the *I Love Lucy Show*, Mr. Dorrance was portrayed by the actor Pierre Watkin in an episode called "Lucy Writes a Novel."

*   *   *

Perhaps as a result of such success, Stanley decided to pursue a teaching career at the Abraham Lincoln School for Social Science, which opened in Chicago in the spring of 1943. The venue was a perfect fit for a man of his beliefs. It was founded by William Patterson, an African American civil rights activist, who sought to establish a "nonpartisan school for workers, writers, and their sympathizers" that would assist African Americans who were migrating from the South, to work in Chicago's factories. It also welcomed Europeans fleeing "religious and economic persecution," with whom Patterson hoped to foster a "common interracial ground." According to Ian Rocksborough-Smith, author of *Black Public History in Chicago*, "given the repressions of Cold War America," the institution operated full-time for only three years. "The school was a collaboration between Patterson and various Chicago-based liberal educators and philanthropists ... and business people who supported New Deal liberalism."[50] Artists and writers such as Rockwell Kent, Howard Fast, and Paul Robeson also lent their support. Chicago-based literary authors such as Nelson Algren and Richard Wright (who was monitored by the FBI and later targeted by the CIA) were invited to lecture there. As we shall see, all this would lead to the kind of attention that was guaranteed to drive another nail into the author's vocational coffin.

Around this same time, Stanley was the editor of a periodical called *Book Marks, A Nation's Books on Review*. On April 24, he also became engaged in a brief career as a weekly book reviewer for the *Chicago Defender*, a widely celebrated African American newspaper. (One of the editors of the *Defender* also served on the board of directors for the left-wing Abraham Lincoln School.) For their International Workers' Day edition of May 1, 1943, the *Defender* printed an announcement introducing "War and Warfare: A New Column on Military Strategy and Tactics" by Stanley J. Marks.[51] In the issues that followed, Stanley was featured as both a reviewer and an essayist, publishing two separate pieces per edition. In his first column on warfare, he composed these powerful words:

> This writer believes that in a democracy, the leaders should be subject to criticism by the people. To do away with criticism is to do away with the theory and philosophy of democracy. The theory often expressed by military authorities, that only a soldier knows what war is about and therefore should control the destiny of a nation in time of war, is valid only if the citizens themselves know nothing of war. However, only in a Fascist dictatorship does the theory hold true that the army knows more than the citizenry.
>
> History ... has shown that whenever a democracy has given its army the right to control the life of the nation, dictators arise. To understand war, the conduct and methods, is one way to prevent dictatorships. Once war is understood the place of the army in a democracy is understood. The dividing line in the past may have been very thin between the army and the citizen;

but [in] today's war there is no dividing line, for this war is total.

To give the army complete control over the citizen life of this country is to establish a military dictatorship and this is not what the American people are fighting for. The cry that only a dictatorship can beat another dictatorship is an admission that our democracy is a failure. The writer of these articles is not willing to admit that American democracy is a failure.[52]

It remains difficult to read this without feeling as if we have been lured into the same trap that Stanley had warned his compatriots about seventy-seven years ago.

Politically speaking, the *Defender* was another perfect fit. The paper was founded in 1905 by a young African American named Robert Abbott, who designed it on his landlady's kitchen table and then printed 300 copies for its debut. Abbott had been trained in commercial printmaking, but when he was prevented from earning a living because of racial discrimination he decided to create his own paper. The *Defender* gradually rose in prominence to become one of the most important periodicals for African Americans in America, and it would play a vital role in the Civil Rights Movement. According to its web site, "The *Defender* did not use the words *Negro* or *Black* in its pages." Instead,

African Americans were referred to as "the Race" and Black men and women as "Race men and Race women" ... Agents distributed the paper surreptitiously to avoid persecution and prosecution. In many cities in the South, it was illegal to distribute or carry the *Defender*. In spite of efforts to keep the newspaper out of readers' hands, gradually achieving a circulation over 100,000, it soon became the nation's most influential Black newspaper. Single-handedly, Abbott and the *Defender* set in motion "The Great Migration." Abbott kicked-off his Great Northern Drive on May 15, 1917, much to the chagrin of Southern employers. By 1918 over 110,000 people had migrated to Chicago, nearly tripling the city's African-American population.

During the Second World War, the editors of the *Defender* and other Black press leaders promoted the "Double V Campaign": a proposed "Dual Victory" over both foreign *and* domestic "enemies" who remained opposed to racial equality and justice for all. The campaign grew out of a "letter to the editor" written by one James Thompson of Wichita, titled: "Should I Sacrifice to Live 'Half American?'" Published by the *Pittsburgh Courier* on January 31, 1942, Thompson's words had touched a nerve, and a Double V Campaign rapidly blossomed across Black America. Double V baseball games, "victory gardens," and dances were organized by African American communities; and Double V clubs staged protests, met with Congressmen, organized bon voyage parties for soldiers shipping off, and pressured businesses to halt discriminatory hiring practices. As a result, FBI Director Hoover–who considered such acts to be "treasonous"–almost convinced Roosevelt to allow him to arrest and prosecute Black press leaders under the Sedition Act.[53]

Only a wise, courageous intervention by the *Defender*'s editor in chief, John Sengstacke (who had taken over the paper in 1940, after the death of his uncle Robert) prevented all this from occurring. According to author Patrick S. Washburn, Sengstacke reached out to Mary McLeod Bethune, an African American who was FDR's special advisor on minority affairs, who contacted Attorney General Biddle to arrange a meeting of these two men.[54] In mid-June 1942, Sengstacke and Biddle finally sat down together and engaged in a frank exchange. As Sengstacke tells it, at first Biddle was none too pleased, claiming that such newspaper campaigns were damaging the war effort. But Sengstacke held his ground, even under the threat of being prosecuted for treason, and went on to explain the kinds of problems Blacks were experiencing in the country. And somehow, minus the poisonous presence of Director Hoover, the men achieved a compromise. Biddle would back off if the newspapers agreed not to intensify their campaign.

Sengstacke may not have been aware of the fact that, during the FDR administration, Biddle was almost single-handedly keeping the calls for suppression, censorship, and "Sedition" at bay. Such pressure originated not only at Hoover's FBI but also from military intelligence, postal examiners, the Office of Censorship, the Office of Facts and Figures (innocuously named to disguise that it was essentially a propaganda agency), the Office of War Information, and Biddle's own aides at the Justice Department. These forces were continually exerting pressure on the president to threaten or prosecute the Black press for treason and to arrest its editors. But Attorney General Biddle, a protégé of Oliver Wendell Holmes who "called the 'protection of the right to dissent' the 'ultimate safeguard' for democracy," held firm. As Patrick Washburn concludes in *A Question of Sedition*:

> Most historians have failed to recognize the government's strong antilibertarian feeling during World War II. [....] At the FBI, the domineering Hoover, who was a master at compiling damaging information on both individuals and groups, insisted that dissenting journalists and publications were subversive. The Office of Censorship and the army also endorsed censorship.
>
> These were powerful forces, and if unchallenged they might have imposed massive press suppressions, maybe rivaling or even surpassing those of World War I. In their path stood Biddle, a man later described as believing "in the Bill of Rights and in tolerance almost without stint or limit." He stubbornly held his ground, forcing a compromise from Roosevelt. His leadership also frustrated Hoover's attempt to go to court against the black press and ensured that the Post Office would not have Justice Department support if it chose to revoke the second-class permits of black publications. These were important victories for Biddle, who surely derived great satisfaction from them. But with almost the entire drama fought out behind the scenes, few knew of the breadth of his accomplishment. Almost single-handedly, with no apparent regard for the popularity of his actions, he had forced his interpretation of First Amendment press freedom on a reluctant and sometimes angry government.[55]

And historian Richard Steele remarked that "Biddle served as the administration's conscience, reminding Roosevelt of the purist view of civil liberties."[56] Biddle also "pushed for equal rights before the war," and "he threatened to resign as an honorary member of the Federal Bar Association if Blacks were excluded. His stand resulted in the policy being changed."[57]

However, the civil rights historian David Beito has expressed an alternate view in assessing Biddle's legacy. While crediting Biddle's sometimes heroic stance, Beito adds:

> In some ways, the outcome for the Black press was worse than had FDR actually tried to prosecute them or pull their mailing rights. As a result of the deal with Biddle, they had to increasingly pull their punches and, in some ways, became adjuncts of the administration for the rest of the war. This compliance was fortified in great part by frequent FBI visits and warnings to toe the line. There were good political reasons, of course, why neither Roosevelt nor Biddle would want to attack them legally, since they would drive away Black voters in droves had they tried. I also found evidence that Biddle was literally scraping the bottom of the barrel to prosecute seditionist newspapers during the war. Extreme measures were used to find someone to prosecute, because so few papers, compared to World War I, continued to oppose the war, at least in an outright manner. Biddle was instrumental in the pulling of the mailing rights of the *Boise Valley Herald* (a rather harmless pacifist paper) and the *Militant* (the Socialist Workers Party paper) on very, very dubious grounds. In many ways, the standard he used was just as permissive as the one used by the government in WWI. The main difference was that so few papers qualified.[58]

In any case, Biddle's meeting with Sengstacke occurred just a year before Stanley went to work for the *Defender*. Thus, he'd stepped right into a hornet's nest. Although Hoover was forced to end his plan to censor the Black press and imprison its leaders, this didn't stop him from continuing to spy–as the FBI files on the *Defender* attest to. In decades to come, Hoover's irrational animosity would find a new incarnation in the COINTELPRO machinations, which led to assassinations of Black Panther leaders.

* * *

Stanley's *Defender* articles (April 24–July 10, 1943) give us a direct glimpse into both the author's political philosophy as well as the larger issues that engulfed the nation in the 1940s. For example, in the April 24 edition of the *Defender*, Stanley reviews *One World*, a memoir by Wendell Willkie, a Republican nominee for president in 1940 who subsequently made two trips abroad as FDR's informal envoy.

A lifelong civil rights advocate, Willkie argues in favor of anticolonialism and racial equality. Stanley features a moving quote from the book: "America must choose one of three courses after this war[:] narrow nationalism, which inevitably means the ultimate sacrifice of our own liberty; international imperialism, which means the sacrifice of some other nation's liberty; or the creation of worlds in which there shall be equality, of opportunity for every race and every nation." (Unfortunately, our leaders chose the first two options; we are still awaiting the third.) Stanley concludes with another telling Willkie quote: "The best answer to Communism is a living, vibrant, fearless democracy–economic, social, and political."[59] This calls to mind JFK's later remarks about competing with the Soviet Union on an economic basis instead of a military one.

In a review published on May 8, 1943, Stanley begins with a fiery summation of two titles, *Germany's Master Plan* by Joseph Borkin and Charles Welsh; and *The Coming Showdown* by Carl Dreher: "A detailed picture of the methods by which various business and industrial interests in this country either sold out or were 'duped' by the Axis cartel system into slowing down U.S. war production is given in these two volumes." He also discusses hot topics such as "how American business was tied hand and foot to I. G. Farben," and how "DuPont has always flirted with the various reactionary organizations that spring up in this country under high-sounding names such as the 'Liberty League' or the 'Crusaders." He concludes: "It would be useless to defeat Germany and then allow the German industrialist, with the able assistance of the Anglo-Saxon businessman who recognizes no patriotism but his pocketbook, to rearm, under the kind guidance of the men who deal in death and destruction."[60]

With his banking ties to Nazi and Fascist business interests, Allen Dulles would not have been thrilled to read about this. Nor would Senator Prescott Bush care to be reminded of such embarrassing contretemps. (As the *Guardian* newspaper reported decades later, the father of President George H. W. Bush was a "director and shareholder of companies that profited from their involvement with the financial backers of Nazi Germany," and "his company's assets were seized in 1942 under the Trading with the Enemy Act.")[61] In a splendid example of the marriage of big business and the State, during the 1954 Guatemala coup that was manufactured by the CIA at the behest of United Fruit Company, Dulles was serving as CIA Director while United Fruit was represented by Sullivan and Cromwell: an all-powerful law firm that represented the interests of a corporate and economic elite, such as the Rockefellers. Both Allen and his brother, Secretary of State John Foster Dulles, were partners of this same law firm. As summarized by Hugo Turner in "Sullivan & Cromwell: The Dulles Brothers, Corporate Power and the Birth of the CIA," "Allen Dulles at least had the sense to pretend to be anti-Nazi while working closely with the Nazis' American backers, like the United Fruit Company and their German corporate backers, like IG Farben, before the war (and during)." Allen Dulles also "helped the Germans buy American Potash and Chemical, which controlled a valuable strategic mineral, bauxite. John Foster Dulles represented the IG Farben subsidiary General Aniline and Film. Many believe that if FDR had lived, the Dulles brothers might have been tried for treason along with other executives at a 'banker's trial.'"[62] In his groundbreaking Dulles biography, *The Devil's Chessboard*, David Talbot also discusses how "the Dulles brothers had helped launder Nazi funds during the war"–and how Allen's wartime position as Swiss Director of the OSS helped him to do so.[63]

Allen Dulles and the Nazis also shared another thing in common. As John Kenneth Galbraith writes: "Nothing was so central to Nazi doctrine as the eradication of [Soviet] communism."[64] And just like the Nazis, both Allen Dulles and J. Edgar Hoover believed that the ends justified the means.

* * *

On April 15, 1945, an intriguing notice appeared in the *Fort Worth Star-Telegram*, sourced from an AP dispatch. Under the heading "Army Writer at Camp Hood" we read: "Pvt. Stanley J. Marks, author of 'The Bear That Walks Like a Man' and a 750-page 'History of the U.S. Army and Military Science,' is in training at the Tank Destroyer Replacement Training Center." Stanley's research on this history text must have been commissioned by the Army, since the War Department had granted permission for the entire book to be published after the war.[65] Similar articles appeared on this same Sunday in several other Texan papers, such as the *Kilgore News Herald* ("Colonels Don't Tell This Private Much," the implication being that Stanley knows more about military-science history than his superiors); the *Victoria Advocate* ("Army Private is Army Authority"); and the *Taylor Daily Press* ("This Rookie 'Knows it All'"). Four days later, on April 19, the *Llano News* in Llano, Texas, featured an in-depth piece on Marks.[66] Besides mentioning his new 750-page tome, it adds that while Stanley was researching his book on Russia he received assistance from none other than Secretary of State Cordell Hull, who gave Stanley direct access to State Department files. Hull was the longest-serving Secretary of State in U.S. history, under FDR. (Seven months after this article appeared, Hull received a Nobel Prize for his central role in establishing the UN. President Roosevelt even called Hull "The Father of the United Nations.") The *Llano News* article also provides one of the best extant sources of data on Stanley's professional life:

Camp Hood Man Authority on Military Tactics

Camp Hood, Texas, April 17th: The Tank Destroyer Replacement Training Center is now training one new soldier who has a distinct advantage over fellow-trainees during classes in Army history, tactics, and administration.

He is Pvt. Stanley J. Marks, 31-year-old-Chicagoan and also author of the best-selling "The Bear That Walks Like a Man" and a 750-page "History of the U.S. Army and Military Science."

Marks spent three years putting together his "Bear," a book about the diplomatic and military career of Soviet Russia, gathering much of his material from the files of the State Department, opened to him by Secretary Hull, and the vast military library of the Command and General Staff School at Fort Leavenworth, Kansas. Reprints of the book are still selling three years after publication and a chapter on the Red Army was reprinted by a national digest.

His history of the Army has been published in part and the War Department has given permission to print it as a whole after the war. The book includes chapters on the military arms and tactics of other nations as well as the United States, and sections on sea power, logistics, and military administration. It took two years to write.

Marks attended the University of Chicago, was graduated from the University of Illinois, and also John Marshall Law School in Chicago.

His varied career has included service as personnel manager for a Chicago company employing 800 persons, teaching military science at the Abraham Lincoln School in Chicago, writing for the Chicago Sun and Daily News, and serving occasionally as a commentator for the Columbia Broadcasting System. His hobbies include piloting his own plane and reading from a library of 5,000 volumes, on mainly military and political subjects, that he has accumulated.

For a time he worked for an aircraft company, writing technical manuals illustrated with "explosion" drawings of famous warplanes and cargo aircraft. The manuals are used by the Army and Navy in the field. He thinks there will be great opportunity for writers in this field after the war. During the last three national political campaigns, Marks was on the Democratic National Committee, engaged in writing publicity.[67]

Roberta Marks later uncovered an article from an April 12, 1945 edition of *Camp Hood News*, which Stanley had pasted into an old scrapbook. Titled "So You Want to Write a Best Seller– It's All In the Contacts, Brother," the piece says that besides utilizing State Department files, Stanley also obtained documents from the Soviet Embassy and the British Consulate in Chicago. It adds that he was inducted into the Army on March 8 at Fort

Sheridan, Illinois; worked on the *Bear* "four or five hours a night, five nights a week … for three and a half years"; and that the profits enabled him to purchase "a nice home."

Then something rather strange occurs. After all this glowing media attention, the author seems to vanish from public view, from 1945 to 1966. I began to wonder if Stanley had been blacklisted; for this period overlaps with the witch hunts of the House Un-American Activities Committee (HUAC) in the Forties, as well as the subsequent plague known as McCarthyism in the Fifties (1950-54). When I shared these suspicions with my colleague Jim Lampos, a local historian who has conducted extensive research on post-WWII politics, he found the answer in less than a minute: "Stanley's name turns up in a House Un-American Activities Committee hearing in 1944, and it cites his book on Russia. Yalta was February 1945, and this hearing was in '44, so something was already afoot even while FDR was alive and we were allied with the USSR. It was a whiplash turn from 'Uncle Joe,' our ally, to the Cold War." Indeed, the oligarchs were already planning the infamous Cold War–and how to profit from it. "Poor Stanley," Lampos concluded, "clearly, he got into some deep borscht."[68]

Jim's search at Internet Archive had unearthed a diabolical document titled *Investigation of Un-American Propaganda Activities in the United States* (U.S. Government Printing Office, 1944) in which Stanley's name appears on three separate pages.[69] His thought crimes include working as an instructor at the progressive Abraham Lincoln School; composing "articles for labor papers"; and "having written favorably about the Soviet Union" (since the *Bear* highlights the positive role of our Soviet ally during World War II, including its sacrifice of millions of lives in the process). Stanley also made a grave error by including a discussion in his book about antilabor campaigns launched by reactionaries in the U.S. (E.g., "The new Congress is greatly reactionary due to the combination of Southern Democrats and Northern Republicans whose record of antilabor and antiprogressive laws needs no repetition here.")[70] The HUAC report even includes an entire chapter on the Abraham Lincoln

School for Social Science (pp. 292-309) and notes that it "makes a special effort to cater to members of trade unions." Heaven forbid!

HUAC's investigation of the school seems to have been neatly prepared by an obliging exposé published in the October 12, 1943 edition of the *Chicago Tribune*. Under a glaring banner, "Red Teachers on Faculty of Lincoln School," a reporter breathlessly intones that the school "represents one of the most ambitious attempts yet made by the internationalists allied with advocates of communism to train a large corps of expert propagandists to further their attacks against the American republic."[71] How ironic that the same paper that hosted John Cudahy's exuberant review of Stanley's book just seven months before now referred to Stanley as "the author of the radical book, 'The Bear That Walks Like a Man.'"

For readers unfamiliar with the rabid-dog mentality that infected America in the period leading up McCarthyism, one should perhaps cite as an example the crimes and misdemeanors committed by another faculty member of the Abraham Lincoln School, Vera Mirova, whose name is listed slightly below Stanley's on these same pages. Vera appears to have made an unforgivable error: "Studied the ballet in Russia." (President Lincoln would have shuddered in his grave!) As a result of such exaggerated reactionaryism, innocent people's lives were ruined, their careers destroyed, their ability to earn more than a subsistence "living" eliminated. "No one knows how many individuals, from ordinary workers to university professors, were driven from their jobs by false allegations."[72]

Yet, a full year after the publication of this devious report, Stanley is serving in a military tank corps unit in Texas. And he was then sent to the Pacific Rim, to serve in a special division under General McArthur. Marks would have been thirty-one and the father of a daughter, but by the end of the war even older men were being drafted. Or did he enlist to prove his patriotism? Perhaps, the service of this blacklisted soldier was merely one more example of how conflicting forces within the Establishment were playing themselves out during this time. While the military welcomed leftist veterans from the Abraham Lincoln Brigades (who had fought against Franco in Spain), J. Edgar Hoover remained deeply suspicious of them, and he demanded they not be promoted through the military ranks.

A subsequent search for material on the Lincoln Brigades yielded a 1948 publication prepared by the California State Legislature: the *Fourth Report of the Senate Fact-Finding Committee On Un-American Activities*, in which Stanley's name again appears, in a section titled "Part Two: Communist Front Organizations." Under the subsection "Abraham Lincoln School," we read: "This Communist institution was established in the early part of 1943 ... as a streamlined version of the Workers' School which was openly run by the Communist Party [...] Among those with Communist or Communist fellow-traveling records connected with the Abraham Lincoln School are the following ..." Stanley's name is listed along with thirty-three others (one of whom is actually named "William Blake," author of *An American Looks at Karl Marx*).[73] This same California HUAC report also features nine pages on author Dalton Trumbo's "Communist" record. (Trumbo, who was also a screenwriter, was one of the "Hollywood Ten" who refused to testify before HUAC.) During this period, Ronald Reagan, then president of the Screen Actors Guild, was secretly cooperating with the FBI as an informant (Reagan's code name was "T-10"), handing over names of fellow actors whom he deemed to be "Communist sympathizers." By then, HUAC's Hollywood hearings were in full swing and getting plenty of press coverage. As Marilyn Monroe's husband, the playwright Arthur Miller, later remarked, what better way to get front-page coverage than to talk about "Commie" movie-star celebrities?

Two years later, on September 2, 1950, an article linking Stanley's school to the Red Scare appeared in *Billboard,* the very magazine that had once given his *Bear* such a boost. In an article titled, "Subversive Groups–Duck 'Em,"[74] it features a list of Communist organizations, although it cautiously notes: "The Department of Justice did not name any schools as subversive organizations." (Perhaps, this was a carefully worded, cover-your-ass statement that still had the intended effect: to slander those mentioned.) "It stated, however, that the following organizations appeared to be adjuncts of the Communist Party." ("Appeared" to be? Again, a clever use of legalese?) At the very top of an alphabetized list, we read: "Abraham Lincoln School, Chicago." By this time, the Bureau had opened files on the school and its members. The National Security Agency also had an eye on the school. In a June 3, 1953 NSA memorandum, "Affiliation or Association with Organizations Having Interests in Conflict with Those of the United States," the Abraham Lincoln School is sandwiched between a listing of the Abraham Lincoln Brigade and the Action Committee to Free Spain Now.[75]

And–ironies of ironies–page one of this same *Billboard* (which showcases five lead stories that stoke fears of a Red Threat) features an article about how Brigadier General David Sarnoff had positioned himself at the head of a frontline attack against those dirty, filthy Commies: "U.S. Media Can Lick Red Lie."[76] How nimbly–and predictably–the actors assume their proper role on stage! In 1929 Sarnoff became president of RCA, which later became the "technological base of the National Security Agency (NSA)."[77] He also organized NBC, in 1926. Sarnoff was a good friend of Allen Dulles (as their cozy Cold Warrior correspondence demonstrates so well),[78] and he frequently served as a CIA tool.

David and his brother Robert (the latter was NBC's longest serving president) also stood at the forefront of numerous media attacks against Jim Garrison. (The Sarnoff's shameful roles are further explored in Jim DiEugenio's interview for Our Hidden History, "The JFK Assassination in the Press & the Public Eye"; in William Davy's "'Shoot Him Down': NBC, the CIA and Jim Garrison," and in Davy's masterful book about the media conspiracy against Garrison, *Let Justice Be Done*). The *Billboard* article on Sarnoff concludes with a chilling remark made in the context of battling the Red Threat:

> Sarnoff estimated that, by the end of 1950, there will be approximately 10,000,000 TV receivers in as many American homes. This means, according to Sarnoff, a potential daily audience of between 35,000,000 and 40,000,000 persons. "Through television they form a powerful nucleus for

concerted action in time of emergency, for television is one of our great media for the dissemination of information, instruction, and training.

"If we had international television today," he continued, "and I believe we shall have it within the next five years, the *Voice of America* would be the voice and vision of America. What a powerful weapon of propaganda that would give us!"

The same mass-media propaganda machine that the CIA's Deputy Director of Plans once dubbed a "Mighty Wurlitzer"[79] would launch its assault on Garrison via NBC TV, the network closely associated with both David and Robert. The brothers were also behind a hatchet job that NBC attempted to perform on the district attorney during a televised appearance on January 31, 1968. The interview was conducted by a talk-show host named Johnny Carson, who behaved in a particularly belligerent manner that evening; but it was carefully prepared and orchestrated by NBC's lawyers. The lawyers interviewed Garrison for several hours before the broadcast, more in the style of an interrogation than of a pre-show warm up. The results–dozens of trick questions–were condensed into cue cards that Carson obligingly read from, in the fashion of a Grand Inquisitor. But Garrison stood his ground and, by the end, even managed to get the audience on his side.

Apparently there were plenty of "spooks" who also tuned in. A CIA memo that I recently uncovered titled "Diary Notes" and dated July 19, 1967, reports: "Films: The other night NBC had a one-half-hour interview of Jim Garrison, District Attorney in New Orleans[,] and his charges of conspiracy in the assassination of President Kennedy. Mr. Helms asked that we obtain a copy of this film for agency showing."[80] Mr. Helms was CIA Director Richard Helms, who, during a recess in his testimony before the House of Representatives Select Committee on Assassinations (HSCA), "told reporters during a break that no one would ever know who or what Lee Harvey Oswald … represented."[81]

In any case, by the mid-Forties, the final footprints on the trail of Stanley Marks appear all the more ominous because, suddenly, he disappears from view. The political tide was changing, and the blacklistings of HUAC would eventually morph into McCarthyism. According to former Canadian diplomat Peter Dale Scott (author of *Deep Politics and the Death of JFK*), J. Edgar Hoover and his friend Louis Rosenstiel, "founder of the liquor company Schenley Industries," "had helped to invent McCarthy's anti-communist shtick, before even [Clint Murchison] got into the act. They did so by playing upon the internecine feuds splintering the postwar U.S. intelligence and political communities. McCarthy's famous list of Communists in government was originally prepared inside the FBI, then leaked to a member of military intelligence."[82] Toward the end of his career, during Joe McCarthy's waning days of power, when McCarthy begged Hoover to hand over the names, Hoover refused to return his calls. The "list" that McCarthy had so famously waved during many of his histrionic appearances before Congress was actually a blank sheet of paper.

Scott goes on to say that McCarthyism might be better termed "Hooverism"; but he later amends this proposal: "If what we mean by [McCarthyism] is the ruthless destruction of opponents and dissidents, without regard to legal or juridical restraint, then surely McCarthy was no more than a temporary foot soldier in a much more extended, far reaching, and vicious system. Even Hooverism is too superficial and externalized a label for a system which both antedates, and has outlived, the man who survived every attempt of Presidents, Congress, and the law to displace him." Scott finally reaches a bitter conclusion: the problem outlives any one individual. In fact, it's systemic. Therefore, "a better name for our system would be a system of accommodations … which is characterized by alliances or symbiosis with lawless forces."[83] But in any case, it was Hoover, McCarthy, and the home-wrecking wraiths seated at their august positions in the House Un-American Activities Committee who assumed the latest incarnation of this "vicious system" that meted out a "ruthless destruction" to figures such as Stanley.

Thus, Stanley's life mirrors in microcosm what was happening all across a broader political spectrum. He was caught in a vise between an old liberal FDR guard and an increasingly powerful right wing, the latter embodied by the likes of the Dulles brothers; Hoover and his puppet McCarthy; and the whole Eisenhower–Nixon clique; not to mention the burgeoning force of a clandestine intelligence community. Although Stanley was blacklisted by such overly zealous forces in 1944, he may have also been benefitting from his contacts within the Democratic Party throughout 1945. Thus, his status in the military may have seemed secure. After all, how many Army privates have contact with figures such as Secretary Hull? How many receive the sort of media attention that Stanley garnered–despite being slandered by HUAC? And, in a real smack in the face to the opposition (although it was probably unwitting), the *Fort-Worth Star Telegram* article–"Army Writer at Camp Hood"–even mentions that Marks taught at the Abraham Lincoln School: the very institution that the opposition considered to be a "Commie front," and which led to Stanley's public condemnation.

HUAC was originally founded in 1938. It continued its uniquely un-American existence until 1969, at which point it became known as the House Committee on Internal Security. The latter was abolished in 1975 by the House of Representatives. But by the early Sixties, the effects of the blacklist were beginning to wane. One incident that played a significant role in this sea change occurred in December 1960, when a newly elected President Kennedy crossed an American Legion picket line to view the film *Spartacus*. (The Legion was notorious for doing the bidding of J. Edgar Hoover, with whom it shared a special relationship.) The movie featured a screenplay by the blacklisted writer Dalton Trumbo, author of a 1939 bestselling antiwar novel, *Johnny Got His Gun*. And the film is based on an eponymously titled novel by Howard Fast, another blacklisted author. (As a result of being blacklisted, Fast was obliged to self-publish *Spartacus*, which underwent seven printings and sold 48,000 copies before being reissued by a major publisher, Dell.) According to social activist Danny Goldberg, author of *In Search of the Lost Chord: 1967 and the Hippie Idea*, by crossing the picket line "The new president effectively ended the blacklist that had excluded hundreds of left-wing writers, actors, and directors from working in Hollywood films and network television, thereby creating the space for a more rebellious and diverse mass audience."[84]

*　　*　　*

Tracing Stanley's footprints from 1943 to 1945 is a relatively easy task, thanks to the preservation of digital archives. But after Marks is given the honor of being called "un-American" in the government reports of 1944 and 1948, the trail grows thin and peters out. We know that he served under General MacArthur only because Stanley makes note of it on several of his book covers, which were published decades later. One says that he was stationed in the Armed Forces "SoWesPac T.O. under General MacArthur." In another blurb, he says he was a "veteran of World War II in the Pacific Theatre of Operations." In *Coup d'État!* he reproduces a challenging letter he wrote to author William Manchester, in which he says: "I, too, am a combat Infantry veteran, World War II, SoWesPac, T.O." *SoWesPac* refers to the South West Pacific theatre, a principal battleground after the December 1941 bombing of Pearl Harbor. "T.O." stands for the Territories of Papua and New Guinea. MacArthur was appointed Supreme Commander, South West Pacific Area, in 1942 (the Territories comprised one of the seven principal regions of SoWesPac). John Laffin, a distinguished military historian, calls the New Guinea campaign (January 1942–August 1945) "arguably the most arduous fought by any Allied troops during World War II."[85] Since the *Fort-Worth* article from April 1945 is very detailed and includes all sorts of biographical data but says nothing about Stanley serving under MacArthur, I concluded that he probably arrived in the South Pacific sometime after April. According to the back cover of *If This be Treason...!* Stanley was "honorably discharged in 1946."

Some of these questions were answered when I received a call on May 13, 2020 from Stanley's daughter, Roberta, in response two letters that I'd sent her about her father; and we finally had a chance to speak for the first time. Roberta said that her parents never told her about the blacklisting, or about Stanley's work at the *Defender* and the Abraham Lincoln School (or even that he'd been assisted by Secretary of State Hull, or reviewed by Ambassador Cudahy), and she was shocked to learn that her father's name had appeared in two separate HUAC reports. "I'm the world's greatest worrier," she added, "so maybe there were things they didn't want me to know. My father was very left, and very progressive, but I never heard anything about this."

Roberta did recall Stanley speaking about MacArthur; and she verified that, while he was in the army, Stanley had been stationed in the Philippines. "He brought me back a necklace composed of seashells from the Philippines that I kept for many years. I still have the shells. And he used to joke ... because I don't think he saw any actual warfare. Instead, they put him in the publicity office; he wrote and edited the staff newspaper. I think he came in after the activity there." MacArthur became commander in chief U.S. Army Forces Pacific in April 1945 and announced the liberation of the Philippines on July 5, 1945. He also maintained a base in Manila, through the summer of 1945.[86] So the dates would match Stanley's own biography, particularly if he shipped out of Camp Hood after April. The day after we spoke, Roberta forwarded an artist's sketch of Stanley that was originally composed in the Philippines, dated 1945. And she later uncovered a carbon copy of a letter of commendation written by Major Forrest E. Kimmerle, Commander of the U.S.S. Funston, praising Stanley's work as editor for the ship's daily newspaper. (An attack transport ship, the Funston was stationed in the Philippines from October to early December 1945.)

I also learned that, in 1963, shortly before her twenty-first birthday, Roberta moved to LA to seek her fortune in the art-and-design field, since there were few opportunities in Chicago. Her father visited during a business trip just a couple of weeks after the president's assassination. Roberta still recalls his reaction:

"He was very depressed. We were all depressed. It was such a traumatic time. There was an overall heaviness and gloom. Everyone was heartbroken; it was devastating. And anyone who was a *normal* person would be depressed! Like most people, I think my father felt the election of Kennedy was like a breath of fresh air. Someone younger, to move the country forward. My impression is that he was totally enchanted by JFK." It was also a challenging period because, in the midst of this catastrophe, Stanley was looking for work and attempting to gain a foothold in LA. "It was just not a good time," she said. "There was a lot of confusion going on."

We also spoke about how it was possible that Stanley's career in law may have been hindered by his being labeled a Communist sympathizer. I recalled that, in his memoir, Mark Lane discusses how "Passing the bar does not qualify you to become a lawyer in New York State. First you must appear before the official Committee on Character and Fitness and seek its approval." Lane adds that, in 1937 (the year Stanley graduated law school), the National Lawyers Guild had been formed to serve as a counterpoint to the medieval mindset of the American Bar Association, which "refused admission to Black lawyers and opposed the concept of social security and other legislation as left-wing plots." Lane adds: "At that time applicants for the bar were being rejected for their progressive beliefs." By the 1950s, the Guild was under attack by the U.S. attorney general, who unsuccessfully attempted to have it condemned as a subversive organization.[87] Membership in groups such as the Guild proved to be hazardous for young lawyers. Although one of Stanley's dust-jacket blurbs indicates that he was admitted to the Illinois Bar Association upon graduation from law school, it's difficult to know what happened next. Roberta thought that such a scenario was possible, but she also raised an alternate explanation. She said that Stanley was a skillful, successful salesman who enjoyed his work, and he was widely regarded as someone who "could sell manure back to the cows. Honest to God, he really could!" During the 1950s, he also pursued a number of independent business ventures and was frequently hired as a consultant.

When I asked: "What did Stanley do for fun when he wasn't engrossed in all this intense assassination research?" Roberta laughed and said: "This is a typical picture of my dad on a Sunday afternoon. He'd be in his study, which had a bookcase, a television, and a radio. And he'd have the TV on, maybe watching a Chicago White Sox game. And on the radio, he'd have another sporting event, and he's playing them both at the same time, OK? And then, in his hand would be a five-hundred-page book by Tolstoy, and he's reading it! Only, it probably wouldn't be Tolstoy; it would probably be something political. It was hysterical. That's the mental picture I have of my father. He was always like that; he always had a book on his lap."

*   *   *

Once Roberta's parent's realized that their only child wasn't returning home, they decided to join her. In December 1964, Ethel briefly remained in Chicago to tie up loose ends while Stanley flew to LA. He finally resurfaced in the public arena when the first ad for *Murder Most Foul!* appeared in a December 1, 1967 edition of the *Los Angeles Free Press*, an underground paper that was affectionately referred to as the "Freep" (a publication that MacArthur would have found more "foreign" and "alien" to his mentality than Japan itself). Although he would never again receive the high-profile accolades sparked by his first book, the publication of *Murder Most Foul!* did not go unnoticed. Ever aware of the need for publicity (especially for a self-published title), on the inside cover of the paperback Marks featured reviewers' blurbs from ten periodicals, including *Police Journal*, *West German Press*, *Midwest Book Syndicate*, *Law Journal*, *Pacific Coast Book Review*, *India Press Summation*, *Northeast Review*, *Naval Quarterly*, and *Marine 'Scope*. (As far as I can tell, none of these reviews are preserved online.) And somehow, he also managed to get *Murder Most Foul!* mentioned in the mainstream press. A journalist with the *San Francisco Examiner* included a listing of the title in his December 24, 1967 column: "Donald Stanley on Books–New and Notable." ("A Los Angeles attorney and author gets in on the Kennedy assassination furors with a paperback listing of 975 questions and answers.") Even in 1967, getting a self-published book mentioned in the mainstream media would not have been easy.

The following year, on January 12, 1968, *The Berkeley Barb* (an underground paper known for its combination of psychedelia and radical politics) featured a half-page review of *Murder Most Foul!* that can still be accessed online. The treatment is a bit "lite" but sympathetic. In the spirit of the times, the reviewer uses the term "mind-blowing"; compares *MMF* to William Manchester's *Death of a President* (referring to the latter as an "epic rationalization that Oswald killed Kennedy"); and ends with a suggestion: "read Marks' book and toss and turn the rest of the night."[88]

Perhaps hoping to kick-start *MMF*, Stanley placed ads in three subsequent editions of the Freep, all the way into February 1968. One includes a shipping address on North Laurel Avenue, which Roberta confirmed was her father's first LA apartment, where he received and processed orders for his book. One is tempted to speculate that Dylan, or one of his associates, may have first become aware of *MMF* as a result of scanning through these popular countercultural papers.

The following month, Elliot Mintz, an "underground DJ" at KPFK radio in LA, produced "a special, in-depth probe of new developments concerning the assassination of John F. Kennedy and the investigation by New Orleans District Attorney Jim Garrison." A brochure describing the program mentions an interview with Stanley, as well as interviews with prominent JFK researchers such as Harold Weisberg, Penn Jones, Maggie Field, and Ray Marcus; and a "Round table discussion with assassination experts." Comedian-activist Mort Sahl was also included in the show.[89]

A year after the assassination of Dr. King and fifteen months after the murder of Bobby Kennedy, Stanley published *Two Days of Infamy: November 22, 1963; September 28, 1964* (the latter "date of infamy" being the day the WC released its report). In this March 1969 text, Marks was already using the term "conspirators" when referring to the assassinations of these great leaders. And he adds:

> The tremendous implication of the Commission's finding that conspirators may assassinate future presidents with impunity can be seen in the various political murders since the assassination of President Kennedy. For if the right-wing forces can murder with impunity then that practice may have to be taken by the left-wing forces. A Martin Luther King threatened

no one with violence; neither did Senator Robert F. Kennedy; nor does a George McGovern or a Gene McCarthy, or a Ted Kennedy; but as long as the Commission's philosophy remains in our history books the political assassinations will continue … For if those conspirators can murder two Kennedys, they can, with impunity, murder another Kennedy, a Humphrey, a Javits …

History has proven that, once assassination has become the weapon to change the government, the style and form of government preceding the assassination falls beneath the hard-nailed boots of the assassins. Both Right and Left favor no democratic spirit in the people. The cold of Siberia and the gas ovens of the concentration camps have proved it.…

The tragedy of the Warren Commission is that they helped set those boots on the road to the destruction of American democracy.[90]

Indeed, Stanley was one of the first American researchers to draw a connection between the plotters of the JFK, MLK, and RFK assassinations, all of which helped to destroy the spirit of the Sixties: "All three were murdered as the end result of three interrelated conspiracies."[91] This represents a very early point in time to be reaching such a conclusion: one that can now be stated beyond any "reasonable doubt." One of the ways he arrived at this was to do precisely what Jim Garrison always recommended: study the reoccurring patterns.

In February 1970, Stanley's published his third assassination-related study, *Coup d'État! Three Murders That Changed the Course of History. President Kennedy, Reverend King, Senator R. F. Kennedy*. In the penultimate chapter of *Coup d'État!*, titled "Three Trials," he writes:

The outstanding characteristic of Lee Harvey Oswald, Sirhan B. Sirhan, and James Earl Ray is the fact that all three of them, although of very poor families and earning very poor wages, could travel around the country with no visible funds. Who gave Oswald the money to travel from New Orleans, to Dallas, to Los Angeles, to Mexico, and everywhere he wanted to go? How did James Earl Ray obtain the various sums of money to travel around the United States, secure a fake passport, go to

London[,] then Portugal[,] and then back to London? He was supposed to have left a trail of robberies but[,] for some strange reason, the FBI was never able to catch up to that trail. Of course, there also seemed to be no witnesses who identified Ray as the robber. As to Sirhan B. Sirhan, he also seemed to travel.[92]

That's just the chapter's opening paragraph; there's plenty more.

On February 13, 1970, the Freep hosted an article titled: "Assassination Story Slowly Disintegrates,"[93] which prominently features material from *Coup d'État!* The story focuses on how Dallas Police Chief Jesse Curry, who had publicly supported the WC, was now admitting that he'd given a press conference shortly after the assassination during which he'd stated that none of Oswald's fingerprints or palm prints had ever been found on the rifle, and that there weren't any witnesses who could place Oswald "at the same sixth-floor window prior, during, or after the president's murder." And, as if providing a hermetic foreshadowing of the Dylan–Marks connection that will emerge decades later, an ad for D.A. Pennebaker's film, *Bob Dylan: Don't Look Back*, is displayed right below the article's closing paragraphs.

As early as 1970, Marks was already discussing the connection between the assassination and JFK's foreign policy in places other than Vietnam, Cuba, or the USSR. In the second paragraph of *Coup d'État!,* he writes:

> The reasons for his murder can be traced to his conduct of his internal and external program. His ideas for a Test Ban on the use of atomic weapons, his groping and initial steps toward Red China, his attempt to secure a détente with the Soviet Union, and even his slight ... step to bring some small normalization between Cuba and the United States met with tremendous opposition. Opposition came not from the great majority of the people but from the military, economic, and fascist groups.

How many researchers in 1970 even *thought* about JFK's China policy? Once again, the author is prescient. A bright light was later shone on this topic by Roger Hilsman, an adviser to President Kennedy. Hilsman had served in the OSS as a guerrilla leader in the Pacific theatre; he later served as Assistant Secretary of State for Far Eastern Affairs under President Johnson. In a 1969 interview, Hilsman said that, as far back as 1961, Kennedy had informed him that he wanted to move toward a diplomatic recognition of Red China.[94]

Part III: The Usurpation of Humanism by Terrorism

As mentioned earlier, seven months after the publication of *MMF*, in 1968 *NOLA Express* published a conversation with Mark Lane, who was then assisting Jim Garrison on the Clay Shaw case. In the interview, Lane states unequivocally that "The CIA … killed President Kennedy." Two months later, during the closing moments of the California Democratic Primary, and shortly before Senator Robert Kennedy was slain in the Ambassador Hotel, Lane was being interviewed by a TV station in Washington, DC. When asked why RFK had not spoken out against the findings of the Warren Commission, Lane claimed that Robert Kennedy had sent several of his "emissaries" to discreetly meet with District Attorney Jim Garrison:

> Robert Kennedy did not believe the conclusions of the Warren Commission and agreed with Garrison that a conspiracy had taken the life of President Kennedy. Robert Kennedy, they said, would investigate the assassination of his brother thoroughly if he were elected president and would vigorously prosecute those responsible. The essential purpose of the visits was to "reassure" Garrison that, despite his public utterances, Robert Kennedy very firmly held a different private view. Garrison asked why Senator Kennedy felt it necessary to suppress his dissent. Each emissary answered with the same phrase: He [Robert Kennedy] knows that there are guns between him and the White House."[95]

In the course of my research I discovered an even more startling interview conducted with Jim Garrison by Art Kevin of WHJ radio in Los Angeles: a journalist who had clearly earned Garrison's trust. (Kevin had been broadcasting live from the Ambassador Hotel during the murder of RFK.)[96] Their conversation appears to be preserved in print in only two places. The first document I chanced upon was a July 3, 1968 edition of the *Great Speckled Bird*, an underground paper from Atlanta, which features an abridged version of Garrison's remarks. A subsequent search unearthed what appears to an unabridged transcript published in a *Liberation News Service* dispatch on

June 25, 1968, under the heading: "Garrison says: 'Any leader who speaks out effectively against the war will be assassinated." In the interview, Garrison also affirms the statement attributed to him a few days earlier by Mark Lane:

Art Kevin begins by asking, "Is that a true statement by Mark Lane?" Garrison replies: "Yes. That's essentially true; the only thing is, I would use different words in a few senses. For example, 'emissaries.' We had mutual friends that came down to visit from time to time, and, as a result, I finally came to understand Senator Kennedy's silence. He was silent, it became apparent, because he realized the power that lay behind the forces that killed his brother." Garrison adds that these mutual friends had visited separately, not together.

"One of them did ... when I brought up the question of [Kennedy's] continued silence, point it out that [there] were these forces still active in America, the same forces that killed his brother–that Bobby Kennedy, as he put it–was very much aware that there were many guns between him and the White House. And the way he put it, I think it was Bobby Kennedy's quotation–from him." After making a few additional remarks, Garrison reiterates: "The phrase 'many guns between Senator Kennedy and the White House' was indeed told to me by one of his friends and appears to have originally come from him [RFK]."

When Kevin follows up by asking, "Did you in any way seek contact with Senator Kennedy?" Garrison replies: "I told them ... I was going to lean over backwards not to seek him because there were some elements of the press, not all the press, but there were some elements of the press that had smeared me, and I didn't want any of the smear to rub off on him in any case. And ... by then, I recognized his problem of keeping at arm's length from this particular issue until he became President. So I made a point of not seeking it, but there was kind of, you might say, casual liaison behind the scenes."

Then Garrison goes a big step further. What follows may represent the first time that the district attorney publicly proposed a link between the murders of JFK, MLK, and RFK, when he says that Senator Kennedy "knew of this force in America which is disposing of any individuals who are opposed to the Vietnam war, our involvement with the Vietnam war, or any sort of involvement in the Cold War." Garrison thus draws a clear, unambiguous connection between the assassinations and the opposition to the Vietnam War and Cold War mentality. This would be further expanded upon in Garrison's first book about JFK's murder, *A Heritage of Stone*. And what he means by the word *disposing* will be made crystal clear in a moment.

Garrison is then asked about a quote issued by RFK's press secretary, Frank Mankiewicz, whose reaction to Lane's statement seemed to cast uncertainty on Lane's assertion that Robert Kennedy's associates had visited Garrison. Fortunately, this provokes Garrison to make a response that contains even more specific details about what actually occurred. After reiterating that he was told "Bobby Kennedy was well aware that there were many guns between him and the White House ... this is why he did not publicly go into the matter of precisely what forces killed his brother until the time came later on," he adds that there were three men selected by RFK to deliver this message and that each one visited Garrison separately, on three different occasions. One was from New York City, one from New York State, and a third man travelled from the West Coast.

Kevin then asks what he fittingly calls "A $64 question ... are you prepared to say that the same elements responsible for the death of John F. Kennedy were responsible for the deaths of Senator Robert F. Kennedy and perhaps even Martin Luther King?"

Garrison answers with six unambiguous words: "Well, you can remove the *perhaps*." What follows is both an affirmation of this dire reality and an insightful remark regarding the principal motivation behind JFK's desire to lead our nation:

> I don't think there's any question about the fact that the same forces removed everyone. Every one of these men were humanists. They were concerned about the human race. They were not racist in the slightest way; and above all, they were opposed to the evolution of America into an imperialist empire-seeking warfare state. Which it has become, I'm afraid. And

now there aren't too many, now there aren't too many leaders left to talk out loud against the war in Vietnam. They're eliminating them, one by one. Always a "lone" assassin.

Humanism was certainly not the motivating force of JFK's Cold War opponents, the power-elite puppet masters. (Hold this thought about *humanism*, for we shall return to it momentarily.) Equally important, Garrison raises the fact that inspirational antiwar figures were being liquidated systematically, and that the modus operandi was always the same. This point cannot be emphasized enough, because beyond any particular details (which often cause researchers to get lost in a labyrinth), Garrison warns us to search for a broader *pattern*. He also recognized part of this same pattern when it appeared in the guise of witness tampering and fraudulent testimony delivered at the Clay Shaw trial.

Garrison then puts a final touch on this "bigger picture" perspective when he's asked if the truth is ever going to emerge–either in regard to the Shaw case or the assassinations as a whole. In response, he widens the lens to include this panoramic view: "The truth was not as difficult to come across, [or] for us to find, as it is to communicate." Thus, already by 1968, Garrison was aware that the American media was functioning simply to censor, suppress, and malign him. He continues: "We know the truth, I think quite precisely, but to communicate it is almost impossible because of the steady brainwashing now from the administration, [and] from some organs of the press…. The truth is, to put it simply … it begins with the time … that Jack Kennedy was stopping the Cold War and getting ready to dismantle the CIA. By then, the CIA was too powerful to dismantle, and it dismantled him, instead."

He concludes by condemning the Agency's role in the assassination of Dr. King:

> Any leader in this country who speaks out effectively against the war in Asia or against the continuation of the Cold War machine or against the continued development of power by the military war complex, will be assassinated. And it will be

announced that it was by a lone assassin. Many months ago I said even if a President was elected and he tried to stop the Cold War and end Vietnam and tried to achieve genuine peace, that he'd be assassinated. And that's still true. And it's just a matter of a professional cover, which is no problem for the CIA because they work on it beforehand and then all you see is the lone assassin.

One final point I might make is–you see it already coming up to the surface in the case of Ray, the man who is charged with killing Martin Luther King, although it's still not clear that he was the professional shooter for the Central Intelligence Agency. But you can see from this pattern that the CIA is involved in this too, just as they were with John F. Kennedy. And if you became a successful political leader and you spoke out effectively against the war in Vietnam, they'd kill you, too. But it would be announced that it was a lone assassin and evidence would be produced and most of the people in the country would never be allowed to see any of the details.

Garrison provides a clear connection between the recurring pattern and the question of "why," which can be answered only by obtaining that broader perspective garnered through a more holistic vantage point. He completes the portrait by being one of the first to connect the deaths of the Kennedy brothers to that of the great civil rights leader, Dr. King.

By now, it wasn't just the CIA that was paying attention to Garrison's revelations. On January 16, 1969, the Pulitzer-prize winning *Philadelphia Evening Bulletin*, which was once the largest circulating evening paper in the country, published a short piece titled: "Soviet Accuses CIA in U.S. Assassinations." Sourced from a UPI dispatch datelined from Moscow, it reads:

An influential Soviet newspaper asserted yesterday that President Kennedy, the Rev. Martin Luther King, Jr., and Sen. Robert F. Kennedy were all victims of "dark conspiracies" backed by the Central Intelligence Agency.

The weekly Literary Gazette, organ of the Soviet Writers Union, backed its "conspiracy theory" with excerpts from an interview given by New Orleans District Attorney Jim Garrison to an unidentified American newspaper.

"Similarity of scripts imposed on the public cannot but alert those who watch events connected with these three assassinations," the Soviet newspaper said. "We are talking here about a conscious attempt to impose on the American public opinion the definite versions of the assassinations."

By the second paragraph, one can almost hear the Wurlitzer spin and the disc plop into place with the tune "A Mere Conspiracy Theory" blaring from the turntable. Instead of sourcing Garrison's remarks from the original American newspaper interview, the UPI and the obliging *Philadelphia Evening Bulletin* obliquely tie them to the Soviet media in what appears to be an attempt to discredit such "dark conspiracies." But, as would often happen in the Seventies, the truth would leak out edgewise. Indeed, it's a sad commentary on American media when a paper produced under the watchful, ever-censorious gaze of the USSR can still produce a better two-line analysis of what actually occurred in our country than any domestic media dared to do. For there certainly was a "similarity of scripts imposed on the public," as well as a "conscious attempt to impose on the American public opinion the definite versions of the assassinations." When virtually every major paper reports virtually the same thing, viewed in the same way, and "analyzed" into the same conclusion, isn't that a conspiracy of thought? And this was precisely the obstacle Garrison found himself up against and which Marks saw so clearly back in 1967. Where did I find such a juicy morsel … Newspapers.com? No; in fact, it's part of Garrison's declassified CIA file, accessible at the official CIA web site, and graced with a stamp reading: "Approved for release 2004 October 28th." Thirty-five years to declassify a story clipped from one of the nation's largest circulating papers. What were they so worried about? One can only imagine what remains classified.

Many of the somber conclusions that Garrison was beginning to draw during this period would be further explored in an interview he conducted in March 1969, with a European publication. For, by this point, he was fed up with being misquoted or ignored by American mainstream media. For example, in regard to the censorious American news outlets, he says: "It has not been possible for a long time to make any public statement to the national press in America without having it distorted or completely misunderstood." Or dutifully clipped and filed into his CIA folder. In a one-sentence summary that would be hard to surpass for incisiveness, Garrison adds that the actual function of both the Warren Commission and the FBI's investigation was to "conceal the involvement of United States intelligence agents in the murder of John Kennedy."

*   *   *

This might be as good a place as any to comment on the phrase "murder most foul" and how the media first decided to spin it in relation to JFK.

As can be gleaned from his titles on religion, history, and politics, Marks was a well-read, highly cultured autodidact. He was undoubtedly aware of the Shakespearian reference to the term "murder most foul." It's also likely that he'd seen Walter Lippmann's article, "Murder Most Foul," published on November 26, 1963. Lippmann (whom Marks cites in another context in *MMF*) was one of the most famous journalists in America. He was also closely associated with the CIA's clandestine propaganda machine, Operation Mockingbird. While Lippmann publically supported the findings of the WC, privately, he told a friend that JFK had probably been killed as the result of a conspiracy. In an act of ultimate irony as well as abject obsequious, in this same "Murder Most Foul" article, Lippmann states: "But I do have much hope in the healing arts of Lyndon Johnson."[97] Johnson, the very man who nearly tore the country in two over a bloodbath he imposed on a small country 8,568 away named Vietnam. And as usual, the media played its part in this deviant act:

In a deceptively worded front-page article authored by another journalist in the *New York Times* on November 24, Americans were informed that "President Johnson reaffirms today the policy objectives of his predecessor regarding South Vietnam. He called upon all government agencies to support that policy with full unity of purpose. This was disclosed ... after a meeting between President Johnson and Henry Cabot Lodge, United States Ambassador to South Vietnam." Lodge, whom Kennedy had come to regard as a reactionary war hawk and obstructionist: one who'd secretly supported a coup against South Vietnamese President Diem, earning JFK's enduring wrath and fury. As a result, Kennedy decided to recall Lodge and planned to fire him on November 24, 1963. Thus, President Johnson wasn't reaffirming Kennedy's policy; he was plowing it over. The keynote to this deception resides in the paragraph that follows: "The meeting lasted nearly an hour. It was described as being devoted to a full review of the conclusions reached by participants in a strategy conference on South Vietnam held in Honolulu last Wednesday." What the "Newspaper of Record" failed to tell its readers was that Kennedy had arranged this crucial meeting in Hawaii to push for an even faster exit strategy from Vietnam: something the conference transcripts make abundantly clear.

To complete the picture, we must consult the Congressional Record for December 4, 1963. After a congressman from Michigan read the full text of Lippmann's "Murder Most Foul" deception into the record, this was followed by another article that was also made part of the official record: a piece by Joseph Alsop, a man whom many consider to be a Master of Ceremonies for the High Cabal of the Economic Elite. Donald Gibson calls Alsop "one of the country's best-known columnists and one of the most important promoters of Establishment policies." Indeed, for decades, Alsop possessed an unerring manner of appearing on the chessboard at just the right time. And this includes his conversation with LBJ on November 25, 1963, when Alsop convinced Johnson to form not an "investigative body" but one that would produce "a public report on the death of the president."[98] This was the seed for what later became the Warren Commission. On November 27, Alsop penned a marvelous fiction printed by the *New York Herald Tribune* in which he had the gall to claim that "false friends" of President Kennedy as well as "false friends" of Vice President Johnson "did everything in their power to poison the Kennedy–Johnson relationship," adding: "It is a tribute to the character of both men that the attempt always failed."[99] Fiction, indeed; for there was never any love lost between these two adversaries. (Were Jacqueline Kennedy and RFK to be considered "false friends" of the president? Each reserved some of their finest venom for LBJ.) Clearly, the purpose of this piece (so dutifully read into the record by an obliging congressman) was to endorse President Johnson and the decisions he would make that would soon rend the nation asunder.

*   *   *

One of the principal contributions that Dylan has made by releasing his song, "Murder Most Foul," is to remind his followers that what occurred in Dealey Plaza is akin to a magic trick.[100] But lest we forget, Part One of Jim Garrison's first book about the assassination, *A Heritage of Stone*, was titled "Illusion." ("Our invisible government begins and ends with deception.")[101] The former district attorney was already referring to this illusion when, in his 1969 interview, he said: "The problem is essentially one of perceiving reality[,] and the American people thus far have been unable to obtain a clear view of reality with regard to the assassination of President Kennedy and with regard to American foreign policy." Garrison also reminds us that we must ask: What is the purpose of this (black) magic?

"The government," says Garrison, "has elaborate machinery to continue to maintain the insulation of the people from reality." By 1969, Garrison had come to the conclusion that the so-called "news magazines of the country are in the service not of the people of the country but of their military hardware advertisers– most of whose millions in advertising is concentrated in the 'news' magazines. Their presentations of any foreign relations issue or any question of military requirements for years has been colored by the necessity that their conclusions be harmonious with the interests of the war machine." Addressing the contemporaneous quagmire in Vietnam, he adds: "It is not true that we are in Vietnam in great force because we are fighting for democracy. We are in Vietnam, and have lost more than 35,000 men there, because it is a source of economic and power benefits for the warfare conglomerate which dominates the government."

Thus, "perpetual war" equals profit *à perpétuité* for the military hardware producers. It also ensures that they remain in power. "Geopolitical conflicts" are in reality merely markets for the war business, which Garrison calls "a death machine." "The nuclear capabilities of the United States and Russia canceled each other out years ago–and the military establishment of each knows this ... What is going on now is a game–a game played by the warfare interests of each country ... so that the warfare interest can perpetuate their power." John Kenneth Galbraith said essentially the same thing when, years later, he wrote: "The arms race became a strongly cooperative effort between the military establishments of the two countries, each doing what brought revenues, influence, and power to the other."[102] Garrison concludes his 1969 interview with the statement: "It was because of President Kennedy's repeatedly demonstrated tendency to view foreign relations idealistically, rather than in terms of power, that he had to be executed by the intelligence apparatus of the American warfare complex. The transition from a government of the people to a warfare state could not have been completed without his removal."

Although Cold Warriors had been pushing Kennedy toward total war with Soviet Union in 1961 (before the "parody" of a so-called nuclear parity had been achieved), by 1963 even the military's talking heads on the Joint Chiefs of Staff must have realized that such a conflict was no longer feasible. And so, from 1968 to 1970, when Garrison was describing the Cold War ramifications of Kennedy's removal, he's really talking about proxy wars in places such as Vietnam: not a direct conflict with Russia. As he wisely states in *A Heritage of Stone*, in Kennedy's final years there still remained "Asia with its undeveloped nations and its millions of poorly fed and poorly clothed humans. Here there was enough grist for the mill of the military superstate to keep it busy for years. It is the first rule of imperialism that unrest anywhere is not merely a breach of the general peace but it is in all probability secretly sponsored by the enemy. Like dinosaurs discovering new feeding grounds, the Pentagon and the CIA had gradually turned much of their attention from Europe to the new promise of Asia. The CIA, in particular, was already deeply involved in activities in South Vietnam and in Laos."[103]

At the moment Garrison was being interviewed in 1969, the war machine was grossing "eighty-billion dollars a year in America." The "resource wars" conducted in subsequent decades in places such as Afghanistan and Iraq continued in the same vein (adding to the till the profits of stolen oil and precious mineral rights); and the reasons for Kennedy's removal can be seen just as clearly when we analyze the foreign policy agenda of most of the presidents who have followed in his wake.

One could add here that JFK's foreign policy views were driven not only by idealism but by humanism. Recall what Garrison said earlier about the leading figures who were felled by the Sixties assassinations: "Every one of these men were humanists." In opposition to this humanist sensibility, Garrison would posit a covert, thinly veiled inhumanity that came to characterize the American government and the jingoistic war hawks who were in charge of its operation. He arrives at this simply by following the money trail. Not many folks were doing that in 1969; and his choice of the term *warfare state*–referring to *corporate welfare*– drives home the point.

Garrison's remarks about the defense industry's need to maintain a fear-filled foreign policy narrative, via the corporate media, are as relevant today as they ever were. They also provide a cogent answer to the question, Why was Kennedy killed?

*   *   *

In conclusion, I would like to tie these remarks about humanism into a fabric woven by Stanley Marks. Beginning in 1972, the Markses collaborated on several books about the intersecting topics of secular and religious history. To view this in proper context, one should bear in mind that the Seventies hosted the publication of many woolly-eyed books about Eastern mysticism and New Age "spirituality," many of which conveniently provided *divertissement* from the more pressing political problems of the day. As if to effect a counterpoint to this, Marks began to publish works on the history of religion that never neglected to present his subject in the context of a broader political dimension. To cite a few examples, *Three Days of Judgment* (1981), a play about religion "written in the form of a trial," "takes the reader from the desert of Sinai to the present where the CIA … became involved in the Vatican politics of selecting the last three Popes." The final page of this text reproduces a declassified "Information Report" from the CIA. A footnote featured in *Jews, Judaism and the United States* (1976) decries the use of "mind-controlling drugs" by both the U.S. and USSR. And in *Judaism Looks at Christianity* (1986), Stanley's opening gambit reads: "Pauline Christianity and Soviet Communism are two scorpions locked in a nuclear bottle of their own making! Each knowing that both die regardless of which one uses its stinger first[,] for the convulsions of the dying will destroy the one who struck first."[104] How ingenious to highlight the crypto-religious nature of all political "isms"[105] as well as to remind us that politicians, whose goals are often far from ethical or transparent, may use preachin' as a form of propaganda. Indeed, Marks reserves some of his sharpest invective for the "Christian" Fundamentalist poseurs and their rhetoric, which was then being channeled from Reagan's White House.

Just as Stanley's writings about religion were political, his political books often feature exposés on the abuse of spirituality. In *A Year in the Lives of the Damned! Reagan, Reaganism, 1986*, he nails it in a single sentence when he bemoans a president who "fully accepts the Fundamentalist Scripture which states that since no human being will live after 'Armageddon,' the present generation has no need for education, employment, medicine, clothing, food, and shelter." In this text from 1988, he offers us a direct glimpse into his political philosophy and allegiance. First, he quotes from President Roosevelt's 1937 Inaugural Address: "I see one-third of a nation ill-housed, ill-clad, ill-nourished…. The test of our progress is not whether we add more to the abundance of those who have much; it is whether we provide enough for those who have too little." Marks, an FDR New Dealer and a JFK

New Frontiersman, then concludes: "The goal set forth by President Roosevelt was converted under Reaganism to 'Suffer, little children, suffer!" thus "convert[ing] the American Dream into the American Nightmare." [106]

Rather remarkably, one of the Markses' volumes on religion received high praise from both Arnold Toynbee (a well-known British philosopher of history and author of the twelve-volume *A Study of History*; 1934–61) and Herbert Marcuse (a famous German-American philosopher and political theorist). In Marcuse's 1965 paper, "Socialist Humanism?" in words that are strangely reminiscent of JFK's American University speech (which also addresses issues of "ignorance, poverty, and disease"), Marcuse writes: "Humanism must remain ideology as long as society depends on continued poverty, arrested automation, mass media, prevented birth control, and on the creation and re-creation of masses ... and of mental and physical rearmament. These conditions and institutions are the social controls which sustain and extend the prevailing state of affairs."[107] For such ideas (all of which were compatible with those of Marks'), Marcuse became known as a "socialist humanist."

Toynbee's interest in the intertwining of secular history and spiritual values (and their codification in myth and religion), as well as his view of history as based on cyclical patterns rather than merely on economic forces, would have helped to form an intellectual bond between him and Stanley. In Toynbee's blurb for *Through Distorted Mirrors!* (which he calls a "remarkable tour de force"), he writes: "This small volume, small in relation to other histories, is more than history, for the Markses reveal why Judaism and its followers are, and were, necessary in this world."

Toynbee's endorsement is followed by that of Herbert Marcuse: "This book is not a history book, nor a religious book, nor a book relating to Law and Laws, nor a book dealing with political, social, and economic history. Rather, it is one that deals with Man's humanity toward Man and, at the same time, dealing with Man's inhumanity toward Man. A book that will stimulate and aggravate the reader."[108]

Man's humanity and inhumanity toward man; and an author who often stimulates and aggravates his reader: a better summation of what Stanley Marks believed in; what he fought for; and the style in which he chose to wage this battle could not have been articulated with greater clarity or precision. A belief in what man is capable of; of what narrow-mindedness he might fall prey to; and of how change must come through visions that inspire as well as through rhetoric that provokes are all things that were shared by the Kennedy brothers, the advocates Mark Lane and Jim Garrison, and by Stanley and Ethel Marks. Therefore, "humanism" might be the most fitting term with which to encapsulate much of this. And so, it's perhaps no coincidence that Garrison chose that word when he attempted to explain what was driving John Kennedy and why this humanist approach posed such a threat to the dark forces that finally swarmed round and closed in.

*   *   *

After November 22, 1963, the New Frontiersmen were largely shunted aside and exiled from government. (As Marks writes in his last JFK book, *Yes, Americans, A Conspiracy Murdered JFK!* "The prime function of the Warren Commission was to protect the transfer of power from President Kennedy's philosophy to those diametrically opposed.")[109] But in a classic example of "a return of the repressed," such "Frontiersmen" soon reappeared in a new form: as resolute researchers, many of them ordinary citizens, who refused to swallow the official lie and who took it upon themselves to delve into murky waters to discover hidden truths. Some were well-established professionals such as attorney Vincent Salandria, a member of the ACLU who also worked with organizations such as Women Against the War. Or Salandria's colleague, Sylvia Meagher, who was working at the U.N. as a research analyst for the World Health Organization. Another was Cyril Wecht, one of the nation's foremost forensic pathologists and a former president of both the American Academy of Forensic Science and the American College of Legal Medicine. And of course, without District Attorney Jim Garrison, the quest for truth would have been greatly waylaid. But many others were lesser known, everyday figures who became enraged over such a miscarriage of justice. To this group belong the likes of Penn Jones, Jim Marrs, Jim DiEugenio, Lisa Pease, and Stanley and Ethel Marks. I believe that JFK would have been grateful for their devotion to truth and justice, which always comes with a steep cost of personal sacrifice.

Just as *Murder Most Foul!* is more than just a dry, factual chronicle of Warren Commission misdeeds, the biography of Stanley Marks transcends the author's personal idiosyncrasies and, instead, reflects larger, macro political currents that comprise our twentieth-century zeitgeist. For one can easily see that, in many ways, Stanley's story is a story of our times.

A first-generation American who graduated from law school, he furthered his education by accumulating a 5,000 book library, conducted research with the approval of a Secretary of State, published a widely reviewed bestseller, taught at a remarkably avant-garde school, composed essays for an African American newspaper that played a key role in the Civil Rights Movement, served under General MacArthur in the Pacific, and was finally rewarded for such efforts by being blacklisted by that most un-American of institutions, HUAC. He later settled in LA with his wife and daughter and, undaunted, proceeded to self-publish at least twenty-two other books. On March 28, 1979, *Murder Most Foul!* was included in the Library of Congress's comprehensive JFK assassination index, *The Assassination of President John F. Kennedy: A Chronological Bibliography*. On the same day, the House of Representatives Select Subcommittee on Assassinations issued its report, which cited five assassination-related titles authored by Marks.[110]

Murder Most Foul! and *Coup d'État!* also came to the attention of two other prominent researchers. In the May 1, 1972 edition of his mimeographed "Truth Letter," Joachim Joesten (whom Jim DiEugenio calls "one of the most overlooked and valuable writers on the JFK case in the early days") paid Stanley a compliment of sorts. After chancing upon an essay written by a right-wing John Birch Society member who concludes that JFK was killed by a government-sponsored assassination, Joesten remarks: "To my knowledge, nobody but Jim Garrison (and an obscure West Coast writer named Stanley J. Marks) has ever endorsed before my unswerving contention that the murder of John F. Kennedy was nothing short of a camouflaged *coup d'état*."[111] But as we saw earlier, with the March 1969 appearance of *Two Days of Infamy* and the February 1970 publication of *Coup d'État!*, Marks had gone a step further, because he was one of the first to conclude that there was a connection between the assassinations of JFK, MLK, and RFK, as well as the "assassination" of Jack Ruby (who died under mysterious circumstances) and Lee Oswald (who was killed not only by a bullet, but, as Marks doesn't fail to notice, by the mouth-to-mouth "resuscitation" performed upon him right after he was shot, which only hastened his death by increasing blood loss). By the end of 1970, Marks also authored *A Time to Die, A Time to Cry*: "A three-act play concerning the three murders that changed the course of history." Although it remains impossible to find a copy of this text even indexed in a library, it is mentioned in Tom Miller's *The Assassination Please Almanac* (1977): "A three-act play, performance unknown." And although it's listed beside eight other JFK-related plays in Miller's *Almanac*, it's the only one that deals with all three major assassinations.[112]

Finally, in a later edition of his multivolume *Forgive My Grief* series, Penn Jones enthusiastically cites two of Marks' titles: "We urge you to read the new bestseller, *Future Shock* by Alan Toffler; and *Watch What We Do ... Not What We Say* [1971] by Stanley J. Marks ... Both will frighten you, but they are important books. That is, if you care which way we are going." In another volume of *Forgive My Grief*, Penn cites Marks quoting RFK: "'Those who refuse to struggle remain "free" only as slaves.' A Robert Kennedy remark quoted in *Two Days of Infamy* by Stanley J. Marks."[113]

And a letter recently discovered in Roberta Marks' archive reveals that, on March 12, 1973, the JFK Library contacted Stanley (through the office of the U.S. General Services Administration) with a request to purchase a copy of *Murder Most Foul!* for their collection.

*   *   *

Six months after his eighty-fifth birthday, Stanley Marks passed away in Los Angeles in 1999. He was survived by his wife and daughter, whose names often appear on the dedication pages of his books. (Ethel and Roberta's nicknames–Butch and Corky–also appear on the dedication page of *Murder Most Foul!*) Ethel died three years later, in Marina Del Rey. Their ashes were scattered at sea, off the coast of Los Angeles County. Over the last twenty years their work has continued to fall into obscurity, but with the release of Dylan's "Murder Most Foul" interest in the Markses has gradually been reawakened.

After just one week, Dylan's song rose in popularity to become the number one download in the Rock Digital Song Sales chart (with 10,000 purchases). And in less than a month, there were an additional 220,000 hits on the official Youtube "Murder Most Foul" channel. This has resulted in renewed interest about the assassination as well as reviving curiosity about the 1967 publication of *Murder Most Foul!* On April 2, 2020, the *Forward* newspaper featured an article about the song "MMF" that briefly mentions the possibility of a connection to Stanley's book. This represents the first time in over fifty years that Marks' name has again been featured in any mainstream press. The author, Seth Rogovoy, concludes: "It is likely that Dylan read the book; he has a long history of writing songs inspired by his reading."

Although I don't believe it's possible to prove conclusively that Dylan was aware of Marks' work, we can at least make an educated guess. And indeed, the place to look is Dylan's history of songwriting techniques. Dylan is known to be a voracious reader and researcher. As one example, he haunts library archives and reads firsthand accounts and newspaper stories from the Civil War era. And as I learned from my colleague, Jim Lampos, "Not only does he research deeply; it does it by himself. Therefore, it's likely that he absorbed as much as he possibly could in preparation for this song (and the results illustrate this). He's also known to have a particular love of memorabilia from the 1940s–1960s, including paperbacks, magazines, and newspapers, which he collects." Thus, he may have chanced upon one of the ads for

MMF in the underground press or upon one of the articles about Stanley's assassination research. "It's also an established fact that Dylan not only knows his Shakespeare; the marginalia of his early manuscripts contain numerous notes about the Bard. Therefore," Jim added, "it's possible that seeing the title of Marks' book may have set off a creative spark that triggered the song itself. And while Marks is more of a polemicist than Dylan ever was (since the singer instead relies on poetic expression), with this particular song Dylan certainly shares Marks' visceral rage. 'MMF' is by far the most polemical of his songs, with 'Masters of War' coming in a close second. Although his lyrics are usually clear in terms of narrative, they do possess an artful manner of defying a singular, set interpretation. Yet, atypically, the polemical 'MMF' features some rather direct statements."

Lastly, the Q&A format of Marks' *MMF* may have appealed to Dylan for a number of reasons. Dylan's song lyrics often resemble a collage, with scraps of information assembled from here and there, then juxtaposed in a manner that results in a surreal contrast of elements. The Q&A format of *MMF* provides a list of information that could easy be skimmed, allowing an artist to select various tidbits and then reassemble them into a new vision.

*   *   *

Hopefully, more may soon be uncovered about Stanley and Ethel Marks, who often liked to refer to themselves as a "twenty-first century Renaissance couple."

Perhaps, their time has finally come.

Epilogue:

A letter from Roberta Marks to Rob Couteau,
May 27, 2020:

"Finished reading the first draft of your essay late yesterday. Damn fine piece. Unlike a lot of my dad's writing, I could understand what you were saying. Strangely, what has interested me the most is Garrison. I need to get hold of the Kennedy film. I actually cannot believe I am saying this. I have to admit seeing my dad through your eyes has made me want to pick up *MMF* and take a look at it more carefully. And it is very apparent to me now how forward thinking my dad was. But much of what my dad said about the future was so depressing that I tuned him out. Who wants to hear this when you are in your twenties with your whole life in front of you?

Now in my seventies, seeing what the world, and especially America, has become, it saddens me to say he was right. In a way, I am glad that he and my mother are no longer alive during these horrifying times with our totally corrupt government."

———————————————

Primary sources obtained for this piece include certified marriage- and death certificates; Federal Census records; and first-edition copies and Library of Congress records of the Marks' books. Most importantly, I wish to thank Roberta Marks for kindly providing many valuable tips as I attempted to unravel the sometimes confusing threads of her father's intriguing life. Roberta also shared many wonderful stories, photos, and documents.

Ethel Milgrom and Stanley Marks, circa 1936

Yearbook photo, John Marshall Law School

Yearbook photo: "Debater's Forum," John Marshall Law School (standing third from the left)

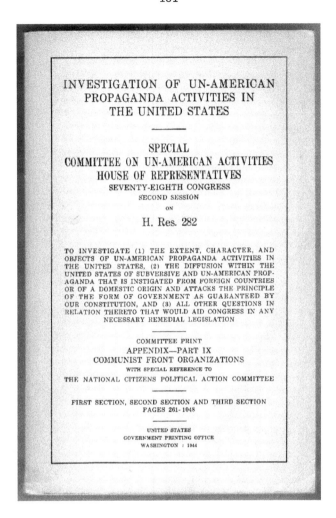

INVESTIGATION OF UN-AMERICAN
PROPAGANDA ACTIVITIES IN
THE UNITED STATES

SPECIAL
COMMITTEE ON UN-AMERICAN ACTIVITIES
HOUSE OF REPRESENTATIVES
SEVENTY-EIGHTH CONGRESS
SECOND SESSION
ON

H. Res. 282

TO INVESTIGATE (1) THE EXTENT, CHARACTER, AND
OBJECTS OF UN-AMERICAN PROPAGANDA ACTIVITIES IN
THE UNITED STATES, (2) THE DIFFUSION WITHIN THE
UNITED STATES OF SUBVERSIVE AND UN-AMERICAN PROP-
AGANDA THAT IS INSTIGATED FROM FOREIGN COUNTRIES
OR OF A DOMESTIC ORIGIN AND ATTACKS THE PRINCIPLE
OF THE FORM OF GOVERNMENT AS GUARANTEED BY
OUR CONSTITUTION, AND (3) ALL OTHER QUESTIONS IN
RELATION THERETO THAT WOULD AID CONGRESS IN ANY
NECESSARY REMEDIAL LEGISLATION

COMMITTEE PRINT
APPENDIX—PART IX
COMMUNIST FRONT ORGANIZATIONS
WITH SPECIAL REFERENCE TO
THE NATIONAL CITIZENS POLITICAL ACTION COMMITTEE

FIRST SECTION, SECOND SECTION AND THIRD SECTION
PAGES 261- 1048

UNITED STATES
GOVERNMENT PRINTING OFFICE
WASHINGTON : 1944

HUAC report from 1944

Stanley J Marks appears on three separate pages in this diabolical document. His crimes include working as an instructor at the progressive Abraham Lincoln School; composing "articles for labor papers"; and "having written favorably about the Soviet Union" (since *The Bear That Walks Like a Man: A Diplomatic and Military Analysis of Soviet Russia* highlights the positive role of our Soviet ally during World War II). The HUAC report includes an entire chapter on the Abraham Lincoln School and notes that it "makes a special effort to cater to members of trade unions."

**Photo of Stanley J. Marks from a feature article
in the April 12, 1945 edition of *Camp Hood News***

In April 1945 six newspapers in Texas published articles on Army Private Marks, who was then completing a massive tome, *History of the U.S. Army and Military Science*, commissioned by the Army. The first article appeared in the *Camp Hood News*. It says that besides utilizing State Department files, Stanley also obtained documents from the Soviet Embassy and the British Consulate in Chicago. It adds that he worked on *The Bear That Walks Like a Man* four or five hours a night, five nights a week … for three and a half years"; and that the profits enabled him to purchase "a nice home."

January 25, 1962: President Kennedy at an award ceremony of the National Newspaper Publishers Association (formerly the National Negro Publishers Association), founded by John H. Sengstacke, publisher of the *Chicago Defender*. Sengstacke stands beside the president, the fourth figure from the left.

During spring and summer of 1943, Marks published a dozen essays in the *Chicago Defender*, one of the most celebrated African American newspapers in America. The *Defender* played a key role in encouraging Blacks to leave the South and join "The Great Migration" to the North, to work in Chicago's factories. During WWII it also promoted the "Double V Campaign": a proposed "Dual Victory" over both foreign *and* domestic "enemies" who remained opposed to racial equality and justice for all, thus incurring the wrath of J. Edgar Hoover, who tried to convince FDR to prosecute its editors for treason. President Roosevelt was pressured to prosecute or suppress the Black press by U.S. postal examiners, the Office of Censorship, the Office of Facts and Figures (a federal propaganda agency), and the Office of War Information.

107

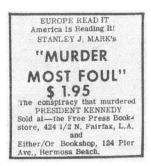

**MMF ad in the *Los Angeles Free Press*,
December 23, 1967**

Murder Most Foul! represents a very early and largely unprecedented polemical attack against the official story promulgated by the Warren Commission and its lackeys in the corporate media. While most of the Q&A's comprising the first part of *MMF* serve to puncture holes in the WC Report, there are also passages that go well beyond the usual framework of early critiques, leading contemporary researchers to say that the text is "rocket miles" ahead of its time. In his stirring conclusion, Marks issues a warning that that no other researcher was prescient enough to envision: a growing disbelief in the Warren Report would engender a cynicism that would eventually snowball and endanger the future spirit of the nation. Marks was also prescient in his analysis of how the Power Elite would attempt to besmirch the reputation of District Attorney Garrison through the manipulation of the media; and the author compares Garrison's plight to that of St. George battling the dragon.

UNITED STATES OF AMERICA
GENERAL SERVICES ADMINISTRATION

National Archives and Records Service
John F. Kennedy Library
380 Trapelo Road
Waltham, Massachusetts 02154

Telephone: 617 223-7250

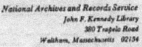
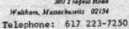

March 12, 1973

Bureau of International Affairs
6769 W. Lexington Avenue
Los Angeles, CA 90038

Gentlemen:

The Kennedy Library is interested in acquiring the
book listed below from your company. Please consider
this letter our order and bill us accordingly.

      Marks, Stanley J.
          MURDER MOST FOUL. 1967

Our purchase order number is: JB-NLK-147. If
you would be kind enough to send the book and
invoice to my attention, it would be much appreciated.

Thank you in advance for your cooperation in this
matter.

Sincerely,

Joan Baronian

JOAN BARONIAN
Purchasing Agent

Keep Freedom in Your Future With U.S. Savings Bonds

In 1973, the John F. Kennedy Library contacted Marks with a request
to purchase a copy of *Murder Most Foul!* for their collection.

Select Bibliography

Books

Cousins, Norman. *The Improbable Triumvirate: John F. Kennedy, Pope John, Nikita Khrushchev*. New York: W. W. Norton, 1972.

Davy, William. *Let Justice Be Done: New Light on the Jim Garrison Investigation*. UK, Bristol: Jordan Publishing, 2011.

DiEugenio, James. *Destiny Betrayed: JFK, Cuba, and the Garrison Case. Second Edition*. New York: Skyhorse Publishing, 2012.
– *The JFK Assassination*. New York: Skyhorse Publishing, 2018.

DiEugenio, James; Pease, Lisa, eds. *The Assassinations: Probe Magazine on JFK, MLK, RFK and Malcolm X*. Port Townsend, WA: Feral House, 2003.

Douglass, James W. *JFK and the Unspeakable. Why He Died and Why It Matters*. New York: Simon and Schuster, 2010.

Fonzi, Gaeton. *The Last Investigation. What Insiders Know About the Assassination of JFK*. New York: Skyhorse Publishing, 2016.

Ganser, Daniele. *NATO's Secret Armies: Operation Gladio and Terrorism in Western Europe*. New York: Routledge, 2005.

Garrison, Jim. *A Heritage of Stone*. New York: Berkley Publishing, 1970.
– *On The Trail of the Assassins*. New York: Warner Books, 1991.

Gibson, Donald. *Battling Wall Street*. New York: Sheridan Square Press, 2014.
– *The Kennedy Assassination Cover-Up*. Huntington, New York: Nova Science Publishers, 2000.

Goldberg, Danny. *In Search of the Lost Chord: 1967 and the Hippie Idea*. Brooklyn, New York: Akashic Books, 2017.

Hurt, Henry. *Reasonable Doubt*. New York: Henry Holt and Company, 1987.

Hyman, Mal Jay, *Burying the Lead: The Media and the JFK Assassination*. Walterville, OR: Trine Day, 2008.

Joesten, Joachim. *Oswald: Assassin or Fall Guy?* Winnipeg, Canada: Iconoclassic Books, 2012.

Kantor, Seth. *The Ruby Cover-Up*. New York: Kensington Publishing, 1978.

Kelin, John. *Praise from a Future Generation: The Assassination of John F. Kennedy and the First Generation Critics of the Warren Report*. San Antonio, TX: Wings Press, 2007.

Lane, Mark. *Citizen Lane. Defending Our Rights in the Courts, the Capital, and the Streets*. Chicago: Chicago Review Press, 2012.
– *Plausible Denial. Was the CIA Involved in the Assassination of JFK?* New York: Thunder's Mouth Press, 1991.
– *Rush to Judgment*. New York: Holt, Rinehart, and Winston, 1966.

Law, William Matson. *In the Eye of History: Disclosures in the JFK Assassination Medical Evidence. Expanded Edition*. Walterville, OR: Trine Day, 2015.

Lee, Martin A.; Shlain, Bruce. *Acid Dreams: The Complete Social History of LSD: The CIA, the Sixties, and Beyond*. New York: Grove Weidenfeld, 1992.

Marrs, Jim. *Crossfire. The Plot That Killed Kennedy*. New York: Simon and Schuster, 1989.

McBride, Joseph. *Into the Nightmare: My Search for the Killers of President John F. Kennedy and Officer J. D. Tippit.* Berkeley, CA: Hightower Press, 2013.

McKnight, Gerald D. *Breach of Trust: How the Warren Commission Failed the Nation And Why.* Lawrence, KS: University Press of Kansas, 2005.

Meagher, Sylvia. *Accessories After the Fact.* New York: Skyhorse Publishing, 2013.

Miller, Tom. *The Assassination Please Almanac.* Chicago: Henry Regnery Company, 1977.

Newman, John. *Oswald and the CIA: The Documented Truth About the Unknown Relationship between the U.S. Government and the Alleged Killer of JFK.* New York: Skyhorse, 2008.

Palamara, Vincent. *Survivor's Guilt: The Secret Service and the Failure to Protect President Kennedy* (Walterville, OR: Trine Day, 2013).

Pease, Lisa. *A Lie Too Big to Fail: The Real History of the Assassination of Robert F. Kennedy.* Port Townsend, WA: Feral House, 2018.

Popkin, Richard. *The Second Oswald.* New York: Avon Books, 1966.

Potash, John L. *Drugs as Weapons Against Us.* Walterville, OR: Trine Day, 2015.

Prouty, L. Fletcher. *The Secret Team.* New York: Skyhorse Publishing, 2008.

Riedel, Bruce. *JFK's Forgotten Crisis: Tibet, the CIA, and the Sino-Indian War*. Washington, DC: Brookings Institution Press, 2017.

Rocksborough-Smith, Ian. *Black Public History in Chicago: Civil Rights Activism from World War II into the Cold War*. Champaign, IL: University of Illinois Press, 2018.

Salandria, Vincent. *False Mystery*. Louisville, CO: Square Deal Press, 2004.

Saunders, Frances Stonor. *The Cultural Cold War: The CIA and the World of Arts and Letters*. New York: The New Press, 2001.

Schlesinger Jr., Arthur M. *A Thousand Days: John F. Kennedy in the White House*. Boston: Houghton Mifflin, 1965.
– *Robert Kennedy and His Times*. London: Andre Deutch Limited, 1978.

Scott, Peter Dale. *Deep Politics and the Death of JFK*. London: University of California Press, 1993.

Smith, Matthew. *The Second Plot*. Edinburgh, UK: Mainstream Publishing, 1992.

Talbot, David. *The Devil's Chessboard: Allen Dulles, the CIA, and the Rise of America's Secret Government*. New York: HarperCollins, 2015.

Theoharis, Athan; Cox, John Stuart. *The Boss: J. Edgar Hoover and the Great American Inquisition*. Philadelphia: Temple University Press, 1969.

Washburn, Patrick S. *A Question of Sedition: The Federal Government's Investigation of the Black Press During World War II*. New York: Oxford University Press, 1986.

Willan, Philip. *Puppetmasters: The Political Use of Terrorism in Italy*. Lincoln, NE: Author's Choice Books, 1991.

Journals and Periodicals

"Archives of Terror Discovered." *National Geographic Society*, December 22, 1992, nationalgeographic.org.

"Assassination Story Slowly Disintegrates." *Los Angeles Free Press*, February 18, 1920, p. 20.

"Camp Hood Man Authority on Military Tactics." *Llano News* (Llano, TX), Apr. 19, 1944, p. 11.

Davy, William. "'Shoot Him Down': NBC, the CIA and Jim Garrison." September 27, 2013, kennedysandking.com.

DiEugenio, James. "Beware: The Douglas / Janney / Simkin Silver Bullets." April 15, 2008, kennedysandking.com.
– "The JFK Assassination in the Press & the Public Eye." August 18, 2017, ourhiddenhistory.org.
– "The Dylan / Kennedy Sensation." March 30, 2020, kennedysandking.com.

Douglass, James W. "The Converging Martyrdom of Malcolm and Martin." March 29, 2006, ratical.org.
– "The Murder and Martyrdom of Malcolm X." February 21, 2002, kennedysandking.com.

Fife, Darlene. "Interview with Mark Lane." *NOLA Express*, April 1968, pp. 4-7.

Fonzi, Gaeton. "The Warren Commission, the Truth, and Arlen Specter." *Greater Philadelphia Magazine*, August 1, 1966, pp. 38-45, 79-88, 91.

Ganser, Daniele. "Terrorism in Western Europe: An Approach to NATO's Secret Stay-Behind Armies." *Orbis: A Journal of World Affairs*, p. 74, fpri.org/orbis.

"How Bush's grandfather helped Hitler's rise to power," *Guardian* newspaper, September 25, 2004.

Joesten, Joachim. "Truth Letter." (Gutenberg, Germany; mimeographed newsletter), 1 May 1972, p. 4.

Kevin, Art. "Any leader who speaks out effectively against the war will be assassinated." *Great Speckled Bird.*
– "Garrison says: 'Any leader who speaks out effectively against the war will be assassinated.'" *Liberation News Service.*

Lane, Mark. "Oswald Innocent?–A Lawyer's Brief. A Report to the Warren Commission." *National Guardian* newsweekly, December 19, 1963.
– "R. F. Kennedy Seeks Garrison Before End." *Los Angeles Free Press*, June 21, 1968, p. 3, 23.

Le Flem, Michael. "Mal Hyman, Burying the Lead: The Media and the JFK Assassination." May 3, 2019, kennedysandking.com.
– "Through a Glass Darkly: An MK-ULTRA Primer." July 16, 2018, kennedysandking.com.

Lippmann, Walter. "Murder Most Foul." *New York Herald Tribune*, November 26, 1963.

Mintz, Elliot. "Looking Out." *Los Angeles Free Press*, March 1, 1968, p. 24.

Morley, Jefferson. "CIA Reveals Name of Former Spy–and He's Still Alive." *Newsweek*, May 15, 2018, newsweek.com.

Norton, Ben. "Victims of Operation Condor, by Country." May 28, 2015, bennorton.com.

"Red Teachers on Faculty of Lincoln School." *Chicago Tribune*, October 12, 1943, pp. 1, 12.

Review of Stanley J. Marks' *Murder Most Foul!* (unsigned and untitled). *Berkeley Barb*, January 12, 1968, p. 10.

"Salesman Author Making Plans for Second Book Soon." *The Billboard: The World's Foremost Amusement Weekly* (Cincinnati, OH), March 13, 1943, p. 73.

"Subversive Groups–Duck 'Em." *The Billboard: The World's Foremost Amusement Weekly*, September 2, 1950, pp. 5, 11.

Turner, Hugo. "Sullivan & Cromwell: The Dulles Brothers, Corporate Power and the Birth of the CIA." *Internationalist 360°*, September 4, 2018, libya360.wordpress.com.

"U.S. Media Can Lick Red Lie, Sarnoff Says." *The Billboard: The World's Foremost Amusement Weekly*, September 2, 1950, pp. 1, 6.

Warner, Ken. "Big Bargains in Rifles." *Mechanix Illustrated*. October 1964, pp. 89-91, 152-153.

Published Government Documents

"Affiliation or Association with Organizations Having Interests in Conflict with Those of the United States." NSA Memorandum Number 120-26. June 3, 1953. ia801304.us.archive.org/18/items/41747169078636/4174716-9078636.pdf.

Appendix to Hearings, Select Subcommittee on Assassinations. Volume 12. Washington, DC. U.S. Government Printing Office, 1979.

"Dispatch: Countering Criticism of the Warren Report." CIA Record Number 104-10418-10431. April 1, 1967, maryferrell.org.

"Diary Notes," CIA Records Document Number (FOIA) / ESDN (CREST): CIA-RDP72-00341R000100120110-8. July 19, 1967, cia.gov/library/readingroom/docs/CIA-RDP72-00341R 000100120110-8.pdf.

Congressional Record: Proceedings and Debates of the United States Congress. Washington, DC. U.S. Government Printing Office, 1963, p. A7396.

Fourth Report of the Senate Fact-Finding Committee On Un-American Activities: Communist Front Organizations. The California Senate, Sacramento, CA, 1948, p. 95.

Investigation of Un-American Propaganda Activities in the United States, App. Part IX pages 261-1048. Washington, DC. U.S. Government Printing Office, 1944, pp. 296, 297, 303.

Khrushchev, Nikita. "Department of State Telegram Transmitting Letter from Chairman Khrushchev to President Kennedy, Moscow, October 26, 1962, 7 p.m." John F. Kennedy library and museum "Cuban Missile Crisis" web page, jfklibrary.org.

Lane, Mark. FBI file NO 100-17689. August 12, 1993, documents.theblackvault.com/documents/jfk/NARA-Oct2017 /2018/docid-32212202.pdf.

Mulhollan, Paige E. "Interview of Roger Hilsman." National Archives and Records Service Lyndon Baines Johnson Library Association for Diplomatic Studies and Training Foreign Affairs Oral History Project, May 15, 1969, Library of Congress, loc.gov/item/ mfdipbib000512.

Sarnoff, David; Dulles, Allen. "Letter To (Sanitized) From Allen W. Dulles." December 17, 1957, cia.gov/library/reading-room/document/cia-rdp80r0173 1 r00 0700010018-9.

The Assassination of President John F. Kennedy: A Chronological Bibliography. Library Congress, March 28, 1979.

Unpublished Dissertations and Papers

Galbraith, John Kenneth. "The United States and the Soviet Union: Change and the Vested Interest in Tension." Unpublished typescript, circa 1987-89, jfklibrary.org.

Interviews

Marks, Roberta. May 18, May 25, 2020; June 1, June 14, 2020: telephone conversations.

Films

Nelson, Stanley (director). *The Black Press: Soldiers Without Swords* (1999).

Radio Broadcasts

"Interview: Stanley Marks, author of *Murder Most Foul!*" From "A Shot Rang Out," a special eight-hour program on the JFK assassination produced by Elliot Mintz for KPFK Radio, Los Angeles, March 3, 1968. Program described and Marks listed as a guest in Mintz's article, "Looking Out," *Los Angeles Free Press*, March 1, 1968, p. 24. (Uncertain if Mintz was the interviewer.)

Books by Stanley J. Marks

Since the Markses' works on religion contain a powerful political dimension, they have also been included here.

The Bear That Walks Like a Man: A Diplomatic and Military Analysis of Soviet Russia (Dorrance and Company, 1943).

History of the U.S. Army and Military Science. (Circa 1945; most likely extant only in manuscript form in a U.S. military archive.)

Murder Most Foul! The Conspiracy That Murdered President Kennedy: 975 Questions & Answers (Los Angeles: Bureau of International Affairs, September 1967).

Two Days of Infamy: November 22, 1963; September 28, 1964 (Los Angeles: Bureau of International Affairs, March 1969). "A textbook for government agents, lawyers, professors, and students analyzing the methods of the Warren Commission." "An analytical and legal study."

Coup d'État! Three Murders That Changed the Course of History. President Kennedy, Reverend King, Senator R. F. Kennedy (Los Angeles: Bureau of International Affairs, February 1970).

A Time to Die, A Time to Cry (Los Angeles: Bureau of International Affairs, late 1970). "A three-act play concerning the three murders that changed the course of history: President Kennedy, Martin Luther King, and Senator Robert F. Kennedy." (Originally copyrighted February 19, 1968 under the title "A Murder Most Foul; or, A Time to Die, A Time to Cry" and described as: "A three-act play that reveals how a Chief of State was assassinated." See *Catalog of Copyright Entries: Third series*. Library of Congress Copyright Office, 1971.) By 1981 this had been retitled *Murders Most Foul! or A Time to Die, A Time to Cry* (also renamed *A Time to Die: No Time to Cry!*) and was described as "A three-act play relating to the past, present, and future of the figures and events surrounding the murders of President Kennedy, Martin Luther King, and Senator Robert F. Kennedy."

American Dream, American Nightmare (Los Angeles: Bureau of International Affairs, 1971).

Watch What We Do ... Not What We Say! (Los Angeles: Bureau of International Affairs, 1971). "An account of the present trend of the Nixon–Agnew–Mitchell–Southern strategy axis to the possibility of Orwell's '1984' being accomplished by 1972" (from the title page). Also described elsewhere as "guidebook" on Watergate.

Through Distorted Mirrors! The Impact of Monotheism–One God–Upon Modern World Civilization, by Stanley and Ethel Marks (Los Angeles: Bureau of International Affairs, 1972). "A brief history of the Jewish people."

A Time to Die: No Time to Cry! or The Four-hour War A.K.A. World War III (Pasadena, CA: Bureau of International Affairs 1980). "A one-act, two-scene play dealing with reasons why nuclear war is inevitable." This is a new piece that borrows its title from the author's earlier work. Relying "heavily" on documents and statements made by Congressional leaders, the drama is largely a critique of the Carter Doctrine (which justified the use of military force in the Persian Gulf). The play is set entirely in the War Rooms of the Pentagon and Kremlin. The final page of this publication includes a bibliography and a suggestion: "If the world is still 'teetering on the brink,' relax and read something more relaxing." The first book underneath this sentence is Philip Agee's *Inside the Company: CIA Diary*.

Three Days of Judgment! by Stanley J. and Ethel Marks (Bureau of International Affairs, March 1981). "A three-act play." "A mystery-detective story, written in the form of a trial, that deals with religion" as well as with the CIA and Vatican politics.

The Two Christs or the Decline and Fall of Christianity, by Stanley J. and Ethel Marks (Los Angeles: Bureau of International Affairs, September 1983). *The Two Christs* is based on secret Vatican documents that became available to the public in 1981, some of which expose the Church's dealings with Mussolini, Franco, and Hitler. The author discusses the establishment of Christianity in the Roman Empire as well as the Reagan–Weinberger doctrine of a preventative nuclear first strike against the USSR. Published in the fall of 1983, Marks also explores the contemporaneous fears of nuclear apocalypse and Armageddon, and the possibility of extermination through the use of nuclear weapons and the widespread use of toxic materials.

Judaism Looks at Christianity, 7 B.C.E.–1986, by Stanley J. and Ethel Marks (San Marino, CA: Bureau of International Affairs, 1986). "A bugle call summoning the American populace to withstand the insidious messages used by the 're-born' fundamentalist leaders that appeal for a nuclear war against the 'evil empire.'"

A Year in the Lives of the Damned! Reagan, Reaganism, 1986 (San Marino, CA: Bureau of International Affairs, 1988). "The format is written in the form of a diary; each month is a chapter."

Jews Judaism and the United States or the Impact of Judaism upon the American People, by Stanley J. and Ethel M. Marks (San Marino, CA: Bureau of International Affairs, 1990).

Yes, Americans, A Conspiracy Murdered JFK!, by Stanley J. and Ethel M. Marks (San Marino, CA: Bureau of International Affairs, June 1992).

The Defeat, Dishonor, and Disgrace! The Reagan–Bush Regimes: 1981-1993, by Stanley J. Marks (Bureau of International Affairs, 1993).

If This be Treason...! (San Marino, CA: Bureau of International Affairs, 1996). "The truth of how citizens Reagan, Bush, Casey, and their friends betrayed and destroyed the Carter administration in the 1980 presidential election." "Dedicated to those who seek the spirit of truth and the spirit of freedom."

Justice for Whom? or, Is Justice for WASPs Only? How the WASP Justice System Worked in Five Trials (Los Angeles: Bureau of International Affairs, 1996). ["Five Americans" (including Oswald) "whose criminal or civil trials engaged the attention of millions of people."]

Judgment Day! A Play in Three Acts (registered for copyright in 1997). As of this writing, it is not known whether this is an original play or a retitling and reworking of one of Marks' earlier dramatic pieces.

Beginning in 1974, the Markses also authored at least five guide books on stock and business investment. Contrary to legend, assassination research never pays the bills–unless it tows an "official line."

Essays Published by SJM

Review of *One World* by Wendell Willkie. *Chicago Defender*, April 24, 1943, p. 15.

"War and Warfare" weekly column. Nine articles published in the *Chicago Defender*, May 1, 1943–July 10, 1943.

Review of *The Thousand Year Conspiracy* by Paul Winkler. *Chicago Defender*, May 1, 1943, p. 15.

Review of *Germany's Master Plan* by Borkin and Welsh; and *The Coming Showdown* by Carl Dreher. *Chicago Defender*, May 8, 1943, p. 15.

Review of *Between Thunder and the Sun* by Vincent Sheean; and *Jake Home* by Ruth McKenney. *Chicago Defender*, May 15, 1943, p. 15.

Review of *Capricornia* by Xavier Herbert; and *A Latin American Speaks* by Luis Quintanilla. *Chicago Defender*, 22 May 1943, p. 15.

Review of *Round Trip to Russia* by Walter Graebner; and *Free Men of America* by Ezequiel Padilla. *Chicago Defender*, May 29, 1943, p. 15.

Review of *Journey Among Warriors* by Eve Curie. *Chicago Defender*, June 5, 1943, p. 15.

Review of *Brothers Under the Skin* by Carey McWilliams; *Combined Operations: The Official Story of the Commandos* by Hilary St. George Saunders; and *We Can Win This War* by W. F. Kernan. *Chicago Defender*, June 12, 1943, p. 15.

Review of *The Autobiography of a Curmudgeon* by Harold Ickes. *Chicago Defender*, June 19, 1943, p. 15.

Review of *Moscow Dateline* by Henry C. Cassidy; *Mother Russia* by Maurice Hindus; and *Pursuit of Freedom* by Chicago Civil Liberties Committee. *Chicago Defender*, June 26, 1943, p. 15.

Review of *Attack Can Win in '43* by Max Werner. *Chicago Defender*, July 3, 1943, p. 15.

"An Ode to the Mothers of the 'Chosen People." *California Jewish Voice*, from his feature newspaper column, "All Things Considered." December 31, 1971, p. 15. (Reproduced on p. 306 of SJM's book, *Through Distorted Mirrors!*)

Diogenes weekly political newsletter (self-published), 1984, 1988, 1990.

Selected Reviews of the Works of SJM

–*The Bear That Walks Like a Man*:

"New Facts about Russia." *Hartford Courant*, February 28, 1943, p. 14.

Vagg, Norris W. "A Forceful Espousal of Russia's Cause." *Democrat and Chronicle* (Rochester, NY), February 28, 1943, p. 11.

Indianapolis News, March 4, 1943, p. 6.

Jordan-Smith, Paul. "Data Concerning Russia Compiled." *Los Angeles Times*, March 7, 1943, p. 45.

Kahl, Norman. *Sunday Star*, March 7, 1943.

"New Books–United Press Reviews." Evening Herald (Shenandoah, PA), March 13, 1943, p. 2.

"Salesman Author Making Plans for Second Book Soon." *The Billboard: The World's Foremost Amusement Weekly* (Cincinnati, OH), March 13, 1943, p. 73.

"Red Review." *St. Joseph News–Press* (St. Joseph, MO), March 14, 1943, p. 12B.

Burns, J. Robert. "Russian Military Strength Is Discussed in Book by Marks." *Arizona Daily Star* (Tucson, AZ), March 21, 1943, p. 6.

Hirons, Ted. *The Union* (San Diego, CA), March 21, 1943.

Smith, Harold. "Two Books on Soviet Fighters–Only One is Worth Reading." *The Worker* (New York), March 21, 1943, p. 12.

"The Star's Book Corner." *Muncie Sunday Star* (Muncie, Indiana), March 21, 1943, p. 6.

O'Rourke, John T. "Little Known Aspects of Red Policy Revealed." *Washington Daily News* (DC), March 24, 1943.

"Partisan Account of Russia's Fight." *Kansas City Star*, March 27, 1943.

Cudahy, John. "A Recital of Russia's List of Grievances." *Chicago Tribune*, March 28, 1943, p. E16.

Loewinsohn, Joseph. "Revelation of Might of Russia Confounds Critics of That Nation." *Atlanta Constitution* (Atlanta, GA), April 4, 1943, p. 7.

The Enquirer (Cincinnati, OH), May 1, 1943, p. 7.

Barnes, Harry Elmer. "The Victor, Vanquished, and Vanishing." *The Progressive* (Madison, WI), May 10, 1943.

The Christian Science Monitor, May 29, 1943.

Navy News, June 1943.

Woolbert, Robert Gale. "Capsule Review: *The Bear That Walks Like a Man*." *Foreign Affairs*, July 1, 1943.

Seely, Charles S. "Light on the Soviet Union." *People's Worker*, July 9, 1943.

Seely, Charles S. "'The Bear That Walks Like a Man' Brings War Understanding." *The Worker* (New York), August 15, 1943, p. 12.

Hollis, Eva E. "Russian Bear." *Salt Lake Tribune* (Salt Lake City, UT), December 12, 1943, p. 2.

Parker, Adele. *Capitol Hill Times* (Seattle, WA), February 24, 1944.

–*Murder Most Foul!*:

Review of *Murder Most Foul!* (unsigned and untitled). *Berkeley Barb*, January 12, 1968, p. 10.

Stanley, Donald. "Donald Stanley on Books–New and Notable," *San Francisco Examiner*, December 25, 1967, p. 35.

Biographical Articles on SJM

Moore, Bill. "So You Want to Write a Best Seller–It's all in the Contacts, Brother." *Camp Hood News*, (Killeen, TX), April 12, 1943.

"Army Private is Army Authority." *Victoria Advocate* (Victoria, TX), April 15, 1945, p. 8.

"Army Writer at Camp Hood." *Fort Worth Star–Telegram* (Fort Worth, TX), April 15, 1945, section 1, p. 2.

"Colonels Don't Tell This Private Much." *Kilgore News Herald* (Kilgore, TX), April 15, 1945, p. 6.

"This Rookie 'Knows It All.'" *Taylor Daily Press* (Taylor, TX), April 15, 1945, p. 7.

"Camp Hood Man Authority on Military Tactics." *Llano News* (Llano, TX), April 19, 1944, p. 11.

"Stanley Jacob Marks." *Who Was Who in America*. New Providence, NJ: Marquis Who's Who LLC, 2004, pp. 161-162.

Notes for *An Introduction to the Life and Work of Stanley J. Marks*

[1] Sylvia Meagher, *Accessories After the Fact: The Warren Commission, the Authorities & the Report on the JFK Assassination* (New York: Skyhorse Publishing, 2013). As a *modus operandi*, Vincent Salandria, Mark Lane, Sylvia Meagher, and Stanley Marks turn the tables on government officials by using their own documents against them. The first edition of *Accessories* was published at the end of November 1967, about two months after the publication of *Murder Most Foul!*

[2] Sylvia Meagher, *Accessories After the Fact* (New York: Skyhorse Publishing, 2013), p. xxiii.

[3] John Kelin, *Praise from a Future Generation: The Assassination of John F. Kennedy and the First Generation Critics of the Warren Report*. San Antonio, (TX: Wings Press, 2007), p. 282, citing a memo reproduced by the Assassination Records Review Board, ARRB Record Number 1801005110092.

[4] Stanley J. and Ethel M. Marks, *Yes, Americans, A Conspiracy Murdered JFK!* (San Marino, CA: Bureau of International Affairs, June 1992), p. ii.

[5] See Mark Lane, *Rush to Judgment* (1966) and *Plausible Denial* (1991).

[6] Ken Warner, "Big Bargains in Rifles," *Mechanix Illustrated*, October 1964, pp. 89-91, 152-153.

[7] Mark Lane called attention to this discrepancy as early as December 1963: "Just after the arrest of Oswald, Dallas law enforcement officials announced that they had found the murder weapon. Wade and his associates studied the rifle. It was shown to the television audience repeatedly as some enforcement

official carried it high in the air. After hours of examination Wade said without hesitation that 'the murder weapon was a German Mauser.'" See Mark Lane, "Oswald Innocent?–A Lawyer's Brief. A Report to the Warren Commission," *National Guardian* newsweekly, December 19, 1963.

[8] Oswald was the Fair Play for Cuba Committee's only New Orleans member–and a self-appointed one at that. His entrée upon the world stage after Kennedy's death served to put an end to the national FPCC in the U.S. just one month later (an organization that once boasted support from authors such as Truman Capote, Allen Ginsberg, and Jean-Paul Sartre). See James DiEugenio, *Destiny Betrayed: JFK, Cuba, and the Garrison Case. Second Edition* (New York: Skyhorse Publishing, 2012), p. 158-159.

[9] See Jefferson Morley, "CIA Reveals Name of Former Spy–and He's Still Alive." *Newsweek*, May 15, 2018, newsweek.com.

[10] In 1940 the song was banned by the BBC and censured by the American Society of Composers.

[11] Henry Wade was the D.A. of Dallas during the Kennedy assassination. Seven years after his death in 2001, his reputation finally came under scrutiny. According to an NBC News report sourced from the AP, "Nineteen convictions–three for murder and the rest involving rape or burglary–won by Wade and two successors who trained under him have been overturned after DNA evidence exonerated the defendants. About 250 more cases are under review…. No other county in America–and almost no state, for that matter–has freed more innocent people from prison in recent years than Dallas County, where Wade was DA from 1951 through 1986."

In 2008 Craig Watkins, who replaced Wade as D.A., claimed that under Wade "There was a cowboy kind of mentality and the reality is that kind of approach is archaic, racist, elitist and arrogant." The report adds: "The new DA and other Wade detractors say the cases won under Wade were riddled with shoddy investigations, evidence was ignored and defense lawyers were kept in the dark. They note that the promotion system under Wade rewarded prosecutors for high conviction rates." See "After Dallas DA's Death, 19 Convictions are Undone," *NBC News*, nbcnews.com.

[12] In *Accessories After the Fact*, Meagher falls hook, line, and sinker for the official drivel when she concludes: "as the Garrison investigation continued to unfold, it gave cause for increasingly serious misgivings about the validity of his evidence, the credibility of his witnesses, and the scrupulousness of his methods" (pp. 456–457). The cantankerous Harold Weisberg (author of *Whitewash*; 1966) actually claimed that Jim Garrison didn't conduct any real investigating in New Orleans. And Anthony Summers, author of *Conspiracy*, called the Garrison investigation "grotesque." In fact, Jim Garrison's work still represents a major cornerstone to the entire case.

[13] Jim Garrison, *A Heritage of Stone* (New York: G. P. Putnam's Sons, 1970), p. 90.

[14] Gaeton Fonzi, *The Last Investigation* (New York: Skyhorse Publishing, 2016), p. 29.

[15] From the Foreword of Salandria's book, *False Mystery* (Square Deal Press, 2004).

[16] John Kelin, *Praise from a Future Generation: The Assassination of John F. Kennedy and the First Generation Critics of the Warren Report*. San Antonio, (TX: Wings Press, 2007), p. 339, citing Salandria's interview with Joe McGinniss, "The Fine Edge of Believability," *The Philadelphia Inquirer*, January 6, 1967.

[17] Marks mistakenly renders Gaeton Fonzi as "J. Fonzi." The article in question is "The Warren Commission, The Truth, and

Arlen Specter," which appeared in the *Greater Philadelphia Magazine* on August 1, 1966.

[18] Stanley and Ethel Marks, *Yes, Americans, A Conspiracy Murdered JFK!* (San Marino, CA: Bureau of International Affairs, June 1992), p. 4.

[19] Richard H. Popkin, *The Second Oswald*, (New York: Avon Books, 1966), p. 95.

[20] See Henry Hurt, *Reasonable Doubt* (New York: Henry Holt and Company, 1987), "The French Connection," pp. 414-419. According to Hurt, it remains unclear whether this was actually Souètre or one of his OAS colleagues: an equally dangerous deserter named Michel Roux, who was known to be present in Fort Worth on November 22. (Souètre often used Roux's name as an alias). See also James DiEugenio, *Destiny Betrayed: JFK, Cuba, and the Garrison Case. Second Edition* (New York: Skyhorse Publishing, 2012), p. 27-28.

[21] Thanks to Jim DiEugenio for pointing this out during a Black Op Radio interview with Len Osanic, broadcast on April 2, 2020.

[22] A typo in the text renders the intended phrase (those who could talk would not talk) as: "those who could *walk* could not *walk*." (My italics.)

[23] CIA Record Number 104-10418-10431, titled "Dispatch: Countering Criticism of the Warren Report" January 4, 1967. Originally accessed at the Mary Ferrell web site, maryferrell.org.

[24] Gerald D. McKnight, *Breach of Trust: How the Warren Commission Failed the Nation And Why* (Lawrence, KS: University Press of Kansas, 2005), p. 365, citing an "FBI damage control tickler" released to Mark Allen in April 1965 as a result of a FOIA lawsuit launched by his lawyer, James Lesar.

[25] Stanley and Ethel Marks, *Yes, Americans, A Conspiracy Murdered JFK!* (San Marino, CA: Bureau of International Affairs, June 1992), p. 177.

[26] In April 1953, Allen Dulles "authorized Operation MK-ULTRA, the CIA's major drug- and mind control program during the Cold War. MK-ULTRA was the brainchild of Richard Helms." By 1954, scientists at the pharmaceutical firm Eli Lilly Company "assured the CIA that 'in a matter of months LSD would be available in tonnage quantities.'" Martin A. Lee; Bruce Shlain, *Acid Dreams: The Complete Social History of LSD: The CIA, the Sixties, and Beyond* (New York: Grove Weidenfeld, 1992), p. 27.

[27] On January 14, 1967, the first "Human Be-In," largely a psychedelic event, was held in San Francisco's Golden Gate Park. "In effect the goal was to psychedelicize the radical left." A few days later, the *Oracle* newspaper "hosted a hip summit conference focusing on 'the whole problem of whether to drop out or take over,' as philosopher Alan Watts put it. Watts was joined by Allen Ginsberg, Gary Snyder, and Timothy Leary, who made no bones about where he stood on the issue. In Leary's opinion the psychedelic and antiwar movements were completely incompatible. 'The choice is between being rebellious and being religious,' he declared." Has there ever been a greater clarification of how and why Sixties mysticism was used to put a damper on the burgeoning political movement of America's youth culture? "'Don't vote. Don't politic. Don't petition. You can't do *anything* about America politically.'... Leary's rap was such an affront to the radical community that at one point ... the editors of the *Berkeley Barb* urged antiwar activists to demonstrate against the acid guru." An excellent idea. Martin A. Lee; Bruce Shlain, *Acid Dreams: The Complete Social History of LSD: The CIA, the Sixties, and Beyond* (New York: Grove Weidenfeld, 1992), pp. 159, 166-167.

[28] *Jews, Judaism and the United States or the Impact of Judaism upon the American People*, by Stanley J. and Ethel M. Marks (San Marino, CA: Bureau of International Affairs, 1990), f. 2, p. 199.

[29] In his April 1968 *NOLA Express* interview from New Orleans, Mark Lane weighs in with the following post-assassination scenario: "The Commission decided it would compromise because those who planned the assassination envisioned planes taking off the next morning to bomb China or Cuba or Russia or hopefully all three. The president didn't want that to happen and the Commission was established to conceal the facts; and in concealing the facts, they also concealed any evidence of a conspiracy, including the conspiracy the CIA wanted them to fall upon–the evidence of a conspiracy of the Left involving foreign governments." See Lane's FBI file NO 100-17689 at: documents.theblackvault.com/documents/jfk/NARA-Oct2017/2018/docid-32212202.pdf.

[30] Joachim Joesten, *Oswald: Assassin or Fall Guy?* (Winnipeg, Canada: Iconoclassic Books, 2012), p. 42.

[31] For example, Fonzi reports that while the anti-Castro terrorist Antonio Veciana was employed by the U.S. Agency for International Development (AID), Veciana "traveled around Latin America … involving himself in propaganda ploys aimed at the character assassination of leading Communist politicians." See Gaeton Fonzi, *The Last Investigation* (New York: Skyhorse Publishing, 2016).

[32] See James DiEugenio, "Beware: The Douglas / Janney / Simkin Silver Bullets" (Kennedys and King, 2008) and "The Posthumous Assassination of JFK," DiEugenio *The Assassinations* (Los Angeles: Feral House, 2003), pp. 324-373. See also Donald McGovern's *Murder Orthodoxies: A Non-Conspiracist's View of Marilyn Monroe's Death* (Lulu Publishing Services, 2019).

[33] L. Fletcher Prouty, *The Secret Team* (New York: Skyhorse Publishing, 2008), p. xxx.

[34] Stanley and Ethel Marks, *Watch What We Do ... Not What We Say!* (Los Angeles: Bureau of International Affairs, 1971), pp. 164, 172-173.

[35] Kennedy forced Dulles to resign from the CIA on November 29, 1961. Exactly two years later–on November 29, 1963, the very anniversary of his firing–Dulles was chosen by President Johnson to serve on the Warren Commission. Many have wondered if the appointment on this "anniversary" was intentional and meant to send a message.

[36] The "pyramid model" discussed here actually came to light during an Italian Senate investigation into Propaganda Due (P2), a Masonic lodge whose members were linked to Gladio terrorist operations in Europe. In 1984, an Italian parliamentary commission of legal experts issued a report that "likened P2 to a pyramid with [P2 Mason Lucio Gelli] at the apex, but suggested that above Gelli there was another, inverted, pyramid containing the people responsible for the overall strategy [of tension] and who passed their orders down to the lower pyramid through Gelli." One commissioner informed author Philip Willan: "We have identified, above all, the American secret services as the occupant of the upper pyramid." See Philip Willan, *Puppetmasters: The Political Use of Terrorism in Italy* (Lincoln, NE: Author's Choice Books, 1991), pp. 49, 55. (See my September 10, 2019 interview with Willan, featured at KennedysandKing.com.)

[37] See "Archives of Terror Discovered," *National Geographic Society*, December 22, 1992, nationalgeographic.org. See also Ben Norton, "Victims of Operation Condor, by Country," May 28, 2015, bennorton.com.

[38] Stanley Marks, *Coup d'État! Three Murders That Changed the Course of History. President Kennedy, Reverend King, Senator R. F. Kennedy* (Los Angeles: Bureau of International Affairs, February 1970), pp. 156-157.

[39] James DiEugenio, *Destiny Betrayed: JFK, Cuba, and the Garrison Case. Second Edition* (New York: Skyhorse Publishing, 2012), p. 385.

[40] Stanley and Ethel Marks, *Watch What We Do ... Not What We Say!* (Los Angeles: Bureau of International Affairs, 1971), p. 157.

[41] *Two Days of Infamy: November 22, 1963; September 28, 1964* (Los Angeles: Bureau of International Affairs, March 1969), p. 159, 161.

[42] Stanley and Ethel Marks, *Yes, Americans, A Conspiracy Murdered JFK!* (San Marino, CA: Bureau of International Affairs, June 1992), p. 15.

[43] Roberta Marks believes that Stanley's work would have been better received if he'd sought outside editorial assistance, since her mother was by no means a professional editor. But when she suggested this to her father, he simply brushed the idea aside. She agreed that his need to maintain complete control over his final product was probably the main motivating factor behind establishing his own imprint.

[44] John Kenneth Galbraith, "The United States and the Soviet Union: Change and the Vested Interest in Tension." (Unpublished typescript, circa 1987-89, deposited at jfklibrary.org), p. 6.

[45] "Some have argued that FDR's administration was actively engaged in co-opting elements of the left, such as radical labor, writers, and academics. Although the basic structure of capitalism remained in place (which was FDR's goal), there were some

remarkable reforms that incorporated many left-wing demands. For example, the professionalism of the Federal Government was codified: from food inspection, to infrastructure projects, to national parks and theaters. And, last but not least, Roosevelt's wife, Eleanor, was a true blue-blood socialist who often pushed the president to the left." Historian Jim Lampos, private correspondence, April 26, 2020.

[46] "Salesman Author Making Plans for Second Book Soon," *The Billboard: The World's Foremost Amusement Weekly*, p. 78. Founded in 1894, *Billboard* focused on radio programming and the entertainment industry; it later morphed into the modern-day *Billboard*.

[47] "Department of State Telegram Transmitting Letter from Chairman Khrushchev to President Kennedy, Moscow, October 26, 1962, 7 p.m.," deposited at the John F. Kennedy library and museum "Cuban Missile Crisis" web page, jfklibrary.org.

[48] It's important to distinguish between factions within the CIA and not to regard the Agency as a singular, monolithic entity (in the sense of "the" CIA killed Kennedy). Garrison later referred to a particular nexus of power as a "warfare conglomerate." Gaeton Fonzi also has some choice–and highly accurate–terms for this group. For example, speaking of CIA operator David Philips, Fonzi says that Philips was "an active player in a small clique within the CIA hierarchy who were almost autonomous in their operational capabilities. He was the protégée of a brotherhood sprung from the Old Boys network of OSS veterans, who held the operational reins of the Agency." Fonzi also refers to this circle as a "tight-spun world of deepest Agency insiders"; the "Old-Boy Agency Loyalists"; the "brotherhood of insiders"; the "select inside players"; the "Old Boy network of American secret intelligence–the superspy fraternity that included Allen Dulles, William Casey, Richard Helms and E. Howard Hunt." See Fonzi's *The Last Investigation* (New York: Skyhorse Publishing, 2016). Such terms enable us to draw a distinction between the

notion of the Agency as an entity driven with a single purpose, on the one hand; and, on the other, the reality of more than one fiefdom, each driven by different goals.

[49] Arthur Pope, *Maxim Litvinoff* (London: Martin Secker and Warburg, 1943). The *New York Times* called Pope's Litvinoff biography "a remarkable feat of scholarship and research." (October 17, 1943, Book Review Section, page 12.)

Stanley Irving Wilson, *The Russian Treason Trials 1936-37-38: Their Relation to Soviet Preparedness Policies* (a thesis completed at the Department of Political Science, Stanford University, 1946, and deposited at the university library).

Transformation in Russian and Soviet Military History (Defense Technical Information Center, 1986).

[50] Ian Rocksborough-Smith, *Black Public History in Chicago: Civil Rights Activism from World War II into the Cold War* (Champaign, IL: University of Illinois Press, 2018) pp. 31-40.

[51] "Written in the language of the layman, this new column will give to *Chicago Defender* readers a realistic picture of how wars are fought, description of weapons, brilliant analysis of today's action at the front. It will serve as an introduction to the business of warfare for soldiers in training and men who expect to go into the army. Marks is a military expert who speaks the language of the man in the street."

[52] Stanley Marks, "War and Warfare," *The Chicago Defender* (National edition), May 1, 1943, p. 10.

[53] According to author Patrick Washburn, Hoover prepared "a lengthy wartime report" on African Americans, twenty-five pages of which "dealt with Black papers." See Washburn, *The African American Newspaper* (Northwestern University Press, 2006), p. xvii.

[54] However, in the documentary *The Black Press: Soldiers Without Swords* (1999), Sengstacke claims that he told Eleanor Roosevelt that he wanted to meet with Biddle. According to Patrick Washburn, "It probably never will be known for sure whether Mary McLeod Bethune or Eleanor Roosevelt set up the meeting with Francis Biddle in June 1942. There is no question that Sengstacke talked at various times with both women, and both clearly had the clout to talk to Biddle and suggest that he meet with Sengstacke. However, for two reasons, I would lean toward Bethune as the person who called Biddle and set up the meeting. First, the mention of Bethune doing it came in an interview with Sengstacke by me in 1983, which was almost forty-one years after his meeting with Biddle. Then, the statement by Sengstacke about Mrs. Roosevelt was made in the mid-1990s to the documentarian, which was more than fifty years after the meeting with Biddle. It is likely that Sengstacke remembered better what occurred forty-one years before than more than fifty years ago. Second, if you look at Sengstacke's statement in the documentary, he does not say that Mrs. Roosevelt set up the meeting. He merely said that he told her that he wanted to see Biddle. Because of those two things, I would say that McLeod set it up." (Patrick Washburn, private correspondence, August 5, 2020.) Thus, it's possible that both women played a role in some way.

[55] Patrick Washburn, *A Question of Sedition: The Federal Government's Investigation of the Black Press During World War II.* (New York: Oxford University Press, 1986), pp. 206-207.

[56] Patrick Washburn, *A Question of Sedition: The Federal Government's Investigation of the Black Press During World War II.* (New York: Oxford University Press, 1986), p. 226, f. 11, citing Steele.

[57] Patrick Washburn, *A Question of Sedition: The Federal Government's Investigation of the Black Press During World War II.* (New York: Oxford University Press, 1986), p. 185.

[58] David Beito, private correspondence, August 2, 2020.

[59] Stanley Marks, "Books," *The Chicago Defender* (National edition), April 24, 1943, p. 15.

[60] Stanley Marks, "Books," *The Chicago Defender* (National edition), May 8, 1943, p. 15.

[61] "How Bush's grandfather helped Hitler's rise to power," *Guardian* newspaper, September 25, 2004, theguardian.com.

[62] Hugo Turner, "Sullivan & Cromwell: The Dulles Brothers, Corporate Power, and the Birth of the CIA," as posted online by *Internationalist 360°* on September 4, 2018, libya360.word-press.com.

[63] David Talbot, *The Devil's Chessboard: Allen Dulles, the CIA, and the Rise of America's Secret Government* (New York: HarperCollins, 2015), p. 162.

[64] John Kenneth Galbraith, "The United States and the Soviet Union: Change and the Vested Interest in Tension." (Unpublished typescript, circa 1987-89, deposited at jfklibrary.org), pp. 5-6.

[65] Copies of most of Stanley's other books (with the exception of his theatrical plays) were carefully preserved by the author in the Library of Congress, while this one was not.

[66] "Camp Hood Man Authority on Military Tactics," *Llano News* (Llano, Texas), April 19, 1945, p. 11.

[67] One wonders if Stanley's contacts within the Democratic National Committee may have helped to bring the *Bear* to the attention of the mainstream press.

[68] A historian whose publications focus on the Revolutionary War period, Lampos is also author of a study on the 1973 Chilean coup, *Chile's Legal Revolution* (1984), originally a thesis sponsored by the noted British sociologist Ralph Miliband. In his most recent book, Lampos explores how the spread of scientific, proto-Enlightenment ideas weakened the model of kingship, whose authority was based merely on "divine right." See Jim Lampos, Michaelle Pearson, *Revolution in the Lymes: From the New Lights to the Sons of Liberty* (History Press, 2016). One could also argue that the problem has now reversed itself: Guided no longer by even a pretense of an enlightened humanism, our contemporary model of secular kingship (the presidency) is guided merely by the divine right of filthy lucre, in the form of corporate wealth.

[69] *Investigation of Un-American Propaganda Activities in the United States, App. Part IX pages 261-1048* (U.S. Government Printing Office, 1944). Marks is cited on pp. 296, 297, and 303.

[70] *The Bear That Walks Like a Man: A Diplomatic and Military Analysis of Soviet Russia* (Dorrance and Company, 1943), pp. 277-278.

[71] "Red Teachers on Faculty of Lincoln School," *Chicago Tribune*, October 12, 1943, pp. 1, 12.

[72] Peter Dale Scott, *Deep Politics and the Death of JFK* (London: University of California Press, 1993), p. 311.

[73] *Fourth Report of the Senate Fact-Finding Committee On Un-American Activities: Communist Front Organizations.* (The California Senate, Sacramento, CA, 1948), p. 95.

[74] "Subversive Groups–Duck 'Em," *The Billboard: The World's Foremost Amusement Weekly*, September 2, 1950, pp. 5, 11.

[75] NSA Memorandum Number 120-26: "Affiliation or Association with Organizations Having Interests in Conflict with Those of the United States," June 3, 1953, accessed in May 2020 at the Internet Archive: ia801304.us.archive.org/18/items/4174 7169078636/41747169078636.pdf. It's also possible that the Abraham Lincoln School was associated with the Abraham Lincoln Brigades, which had fought the good fight against Franco's dictatorship in Spain.

[76] "U.S. Media Can Lick Red Lie, Sarnoff Says," *The Billboard: The World's Foremost Amusement Weekly*, September 2, 1950, pp. 1, 6.

[77] Mal Jay Hyman, *Burying the Lead* (Walterville, OR: Trine Day, 2008), p. 68.

[78] The Sarnoff–Dulles correspondence from 1957 still remains partially redacted after sixty-three years. Most of it concerns their mutual pet project: the development of a propaganda network known as Radio Free Europe. See "Letter to (Sanitized) From Allen W. Dulles," December 17, 1957, cia.gov/library/reading-room/document/cia-rdp80r 01731r000700010018-9.

[79] Frank Wisner, the Agency's second Deputy Director of Plans (1951-59), boasted that the CIA's "Mighty Wurlitzer" was capable of playing "any tune." It was also known as "Wisner's Wurlitzer." Both terms refer to the CIA's "Propaganda Assets Inventory," an "official list … of conduits and individuals on which the Agency could rely." According to Frances Stonor Saunders, "the nickname reveals the Agency's perception of how these assets were expected to perform: at the push of a button, Wisner could play any tune he wished to hear." Frances Stonor Saunders, *The Cultural Cold War: The CIA and the World of Arts and Letters* (New York: The New Press, 2000), p. 72.

[80] Accessed in May 2020 at the CIA's Electronic Reading Room; Collection: General; CIA Records Document Number (FOIA) /

ESDN (CREST): CIA-RDP72-00341R000100120110-8. Direct link: www.cia.gov/library/readingroom/docs/CIA-RDP7200341R 000100120110-8.pdf.

[81] *Washington Post* journalist George Lardner, as quoted by Gaeton Fonzi in *The Last Investigation* (New York: Skyhorse Publishing, 2016).

[82] Lewis Rosenstiel, founder of Schenley Industries, served as liaison between the Meyer Lansky Mafia and Hoover. Clint Murchison, Sr., a close friend of Hoover's, was an infamous red baiter, a wealthy Texan-oil magnate, a political operator, and a Mob associate. He provided "free race-track holidays for Hoover at the $100 a day Del Charro (a princely sum in the 1950s)," a resort motel owned by Murchison. "Special guests" included Joe McCarthy, whom Scott calls "one of Clint Murchison, Sr.'s top congressional allies in red-baiting"; as well as Vice President Nixon, Senator John Connally, and Lewis Rosenstiel. Hoover's association with Murchison's mobbed-up set, as well as the financial improprieties that came as a result of Murchison's largesse, placed him in a compromised position: one vulnerable to blackmail. Peter Dale Scott, *Deep Politics and the Death of JFK* (London: University of California Press, 1993), pp. 207-208.

[83] Peter Dale Scott, *Deep Politics and the Death of JFK* (London: University of California Press, 1993), pp. 304, 310-312.

[84] Danny Goldberg, *In Search of the Lost Chord: 1967 and the Hippie Idea*, (Brooklyn, New York: Akashic Books, 2017), p. 66. In my February 27, 2018 interview with Goldberg, when I asked if he would agree that the Kennedys were, in many ways, well ahead of their time, he answered without hesitation: "Yes. I'm a fan of John Kennedy; I feel he's been underrated by history…. As a political leader, he's really underrated when they do these ratings of the presidents. He was only in office for three years. But the fact that there was not a war over the Cuban Missile Crisis is such a *monumental* achievement, especially given that,

from what I've read, the entire military wanted him to attack. And on civil rights, he took steps, in terms of moral leadership, that Eisenhower was never willing to take. The Test Ban Treaty was also a big deal. No one knows what he would have done in Vietnam, but I believe he wouldn't have done what Johnson did. After he died, his brothers were against the war. He had been to Vietnam as a young man; he knew that it was bullshit. And he'd already confronted the military; he wasn't going to be pushed around by them. So, that's what I choose to believe…. There's this whole revisionism of how great LBJ was. Look, he did some terrific things, largely because he had the legacy of the love for Kennedy and this wide margin of Democrats in both houses in Congress. He was New Deal guy, and he wanted to do the right thing on those issues. But without John Kennedy, there is no Great Society. I think you're right: Republicans in the right wing put a lot of energy into trying to tarnish Kennedy's legacy, and they succeeded."

Goldberg's previous roles include: president of Atlantic Records, Chairman of Warner Bros. Records, and CEO of Air America Radio. A devoted political advocate, he serves on the Board of Directors of The Nation Institute, The ACLU Foundation of Southern California, Americans for Peace Now, Brave New Films, and Public Citizen.

[85] John Laffin, *Brassey's Battles: 3,500 Years of Conflict, Campaigns and Wars from A-Z* (London: Brassey's Defence Publishers, 1986), p. 303.

[86] President Truman relieved MacArthur from his commands in 1951. In 1972, Truman told his biographer, Merle Miller: "I fired him because he wouldn't respect the authority of the President ... I didn't fire him because he was a dumb son of a bitch, although he was, but that's not against the law for generals. If it was, half to three-quarters of them would be in jail." Apparently, John Kennedy was not the only president to experience such trouble with his generals.

[87] Mark Lane, *Citizen Lane* (Chicago: Chicago Review Press, 2012), pp. 24-29.

[88] *Berkeley Barb*, January 12, 1968, p. 10 (unsigned and untitled).

[89] This information comes from a KPFK Radio programming pamphlet published in March 1968. Marks is also mentioned as a program guest in Mintz's article, "Looking Out," *Los Angeles Free Press*, March 1, 1968, p. 24. Mintz recently informed me that he has no recollection of ever interviewing Stanley, and so it's possible that the interview was conducted by another journalist but was later included in the broadcast.

[90] *Two Days of Infamy: November 22, 1963; September 28, 1964* (Los Angeles: Bureau of International Affairs, March 1969), p. 158. On various dust jackets Marks promotes it as "A textbook for government agents, lawyers, professors, and students analyzing the methods of the Warren Commission" and as "An analytical and legal study."

[91] *Two Days of Infamy: November 22, 1963; September 28, 1964* (Los Angeles: Bureau of International Affairs, March 1969), p. i.

[92] Stanley Marks, *Coup d'État! Three Murders That Changed the Course of History. President Kennedy, Reverend King, Senator R. F. Kennedy* (Los Angeles: Bureau of International Affairs, February 1970), p. 150.

[93] "Assassination Story Slowly Disintegrates," *Los Angeles Free Press*, February 18, 1920, p. 20.

[94] Hilsman was interviewed by Paige E. Mulhollan on May 15, 1969. Their talk is archived courtesy of the National Archives and Records Service, Lyndon Baines Johnson Library Association for Diplomatic Studies and Training, Foreign Affairs Oral History Project, Library of Congress, loc.gov/item/mfdipbib000512. See also former CIA analyst Bruce Riedel's

JFK's Forgotten Crisis: Tibet, the CIA, and the Sino-Indian War (Brookings Institution Press, 2015), which describes the clever maneuvering JFK managed with China (thanks largely to John Kenneth Galbraith, JFK's Ambassador to India) during the Sino Indian War (20 October–21 November, 1962), which occurred in the midst of the Cuban Missile Crisis.

[95] See also: Mark Lane, "R. F. Kennedy Seeks Garrison Before End," *Los Angeles Free Press*, June 21, 1968, p. 3.

[96] Art Kevin's Ambassador Hotel coverage was broadcast to the RKO network. According to Kevin's obituary, "He covered Cesar Chavez and his campaign for farm workers' rights, civil rights marches in the South, as well as the Vietnam War debates and demonstrations": causes that would have been viewed sympathetically by both Jim Garrison and the Kennedy brothers. See Myrna Oliver, "Art Kevin, 67; Veteran Radio Newsman," *Los Angeles Times*, August 22, 2002, latimes.com.

[97] Walter Lippmann, "Murder Most Foul," *New York Herald Tribune*, November 26, 1963. The term "cold war" did not gain wider traction until the publication of Lippmann's book, *The Cold War* (New York: Harper & Row, 1947).

[98] Donald Gibson, *The Kennedy Assassination Cover-Up* (Huntington, New York: 2000), pp. 58, 62.

[99] Congressional Record: Proceedings and Debates of the United States Congress (U.S. Government Printing Office, 1963), p. A7396.

[100] As mentioned by DiEugenio in "The Dylan / Kennedy Sensation," in her forensic analysis of the assassination, Milicent Cranor often referred to such "tricks." For instance, in her piece, "The Third Wound," she writes: "The location of the entrance wound was not only revised in 1968, but, as if by magic, a round metal fragment appeared that had not been described before."

Milicent Cranor, *Kennedy Assassination Chronicles* magazine, fall 1998, p. 20. And in *Breach of Trust*, Gerald McKnight refers to the single-bullet theory as "an exercise in magical thinking."

[101] Jim Garrison, *A Heritage of Stone* (New York: G. P. Putnam's Sons, 1970), p. 90.

[102] To illustrate a similar parallel of mutual reciprocity occurring on a nonmilitary, cultural level: at the same time that the Soviets had banned a short story written by the American science-fiction author Ray Bradbury, the FBI was monitoring Bradbury for speaking out against both McCarthyism and the fear tactics employed by politicians seeking reelection. This represents just one example of how a "cooperative effort" of the superpowers remained eerily in synch–even when it impacted on cultural affairs. Such efforts to control American culture were intentional and well organized. One of the most blasphemous phrases ever uttered by Allen Dulles was his Stalinesque declaration about controlling the sacred muse of modern art. As OSS veteran Lawrence de Neufville recalls: "I do remember hearing that Jock Whitney and Allen Dulles agreed that they had to do something about modern art ... So what did they do? They turned to the CIA."

Part of what they did was to promote Abstract Expressionism, since it was impossible to convey political messages with abstract blobs and drips of paint. Abby Rockefeller's Museum of Modern Art (MoMA), whose board of trustees was literally stuffed to the gills with CIA and former OSS men, and presided over by her sons Nelson ("Rocky") and David Rockefeller, was happy to oblige. According to Frances Saunders, who authored the most valuable and comprehensive book on the subject of the cultural cold war, MoMA was "operating at a remove from the CIA, and therefore offering a plausible disguise for its interests." Rocky called Abstract Expressionism "free enterprise painting," and he dutifully filled the family-owned Chase Manhattan Bank with a plethora of these exorbitantly priced drips and blobs (he'd amassed over 2,500 in his personal collection). Since Nelson was the point man in charge of Latin American intelligence during World War II, he had plenty of highly placed cronies to call upon to help direct policy and propaganda at MoMA.

As Frances Saunders reveals in her extensive chronicle, a quick look at the bastards in charge is rather telling. Mommy's Museum was replete with rascals such as Rockefeller's pal John ("Jock") Whitney, a president and chairman of the board, who was former OSS and who also served on the CIA's Psychological Strategy Board. William Burden, a Vanderbilt descendent who worked for Rocky's wartime intelligence group, was president of the CIA's Farfield Foundation; he later became MoMA's president. William Paley, a MoMA trustee, just happened to own CBS television network; and, as a favor to his bosom buddy Allen Dulles, he arranged for sheep-dipped agents to be "employed" at the station. Media mogul Henry Luce, founder of *Time* magazine (who once tried LSD and claimed to have communed with God on the golf course), also served as a MoMA trustee. *Time* was also notorious for providing cover for "journalists" who were actually agents.

Some of these shenanigans eventually leaked out. Saunders quotes a "seminal" 1974 *Artforum* piece by Eva Cockroft that states: "Links between cultural cold war politics and the success of Abstract Expressionism are by no means coincidental ... They were consciously forged at the time by some of the most influential figures controlling museum policies and advocating enlightened cold war tactics designed to woo European intellectuals."

Even Picasso, who'd never stepped foot into America, had a file opened on him by J. Edgar Hoover: a 187-page dossier that tracked his movements for over twenty-five years, beginning in 1945. Ever trained, like an owl, to keep his eyes pinned to either side of the cosmic duality, Picasso had once confessed: "If I wouldn't be a Communist, I'd be the worst kind of bourgeois." How this must have rankled and confused poor old J. Edgar. And the French Préfecture de police had the painter under surveillance ever since June 18, 1901. See Frances Stonor Saunders, *The Cultural Cold War: The CIA and the World of Arts and Letters*

(New York: The New Press, 2001), pp. 219-223; and John Kenneth Galbraith, "The United States and the Soviet Union: Change and the Vested Interest in Tension." (Unpublished typescript deposited at jfklibrary.org; circa 1987-89), p. 6.

[103] Jim Garrison, *A Heritage of Stone* (New York: G. P. Putnam's Sons, 1970), p. 127.

[104] Stanley J. and Ethel Marks, *Judaism Looks at Christianity, 7 B.C.E.–1986*, (San Marino, CA: Bureau of International Affairs, 1986), p. iv.

[105] Mircea Eliade, a noted scholar of comparative religion, coined the term *crypto-religious* to describe how "The 'irreligious' still behave religiously, even though they are not aware of the fact." Anything from a simple superstition to a fundamentalist reverence for a political system, including either capitalism or communism, could fall into this category. See Eliade, trans. Willard R. Trask, *The Sacred and the Profane* (New York: Harcourt Brace Jovanovich, 1959), p. 15.

[106] *A Year in the Lives of the Damned! Reagan, Reaganism, 1986* (San Marino, CA: Bureau of International Affairs, 1988), p. 1.

[107] Erich Fromm, ed., *Socialist Humanism: An International Symposium* (Garden City, New York: Doubleday, 1965), pp. 107-117.

[108] Stanley may have sent pre-publication copies of his book to other literary figures as well, who perhaps hesitated to respond to such a little known author. However, in the days before personal computers, self-published books were still taken a bit more seriously, and, for example, were more readily considered for circulation in libraries.

But there's also another consideration. By the 1960s, Toynbee's star had begun to fade. One of the reasons he may have felt compelled to offer a little-known author such a powerful endorsement is that, right after Marks discusses Toynbee's 1939 anti-Semitic remark–that the Jew is but a "fossil" of history–he then encourages the reader to accept Toynbee's 1959 apology for making such a short-sighted statement, adding: "One need only read Toynbee's ten volumes of history to understand how dramatically he had shifted his position 180 degrees between 1939 and 1959. He should be honored for having the courage to do so." He also refers to Toynbee and Oswald Spengler as "the two greatest history philosophers in the twentieth century." It's possible that, once Stanley had Toynbee's endorsement in hand, it may have helped him to secure one from Herbert Marcuse, who was deeply involved in the study of Jewish history and culture. See Stanley and Ethel Marks, *Through Distorted Mirrors! The Impact of Monotheism–One God–Upon Modern World Civilization*, by Stanley (Los Angeles: Bureau of International Affairs, 1972), p. 18-19.

The Markses' *Through Distorted Mirrors!* was also endorsed by Father Andrew M. Greeley (1928–2013), a celebrated Roman Catholic priest. A professor of sociology at the University of Chicago, Greeley authored over seventy academic texts. He was also a journalist who regularly contributed to the *Chicago Sun-Times* and *New York Times*, and a prolific novelist of popular fiction. In 1981, he published a bestselling novel, *The Cardinal Sins*, followed by other popular novels that were also considered to be "sexually explicit." Greeley countered such criticism by saying: "There's nothing wrong with sex" and adding: "Sexual love tells us something about God." The *National Catholic Register* later claimed that Greeley had "the dirtiest mind ever ordained." In the blurb he produced for the Markses' book, Greeley wrote: "If this book proves anything, it proves that Man must return to His fold if he is to have both a present–and a future." The Markses may have become acquainted with Greeley in the 1950s, since Greeley served as an assistant pastor at Christ the King parish in Chicago (1954–1964). During this period, Greeley also studied sociology at the University of Chicago, Stanley's alma mater.

[109] Stanley and Ethel Marks, *Yes, Americans, A Conspiracy Murdered JFK!* (San Marino, CA: Bureau of International Affairs, June 1992), p. 1.

[110] *The Assassination of President John F. Kennedy: A Chronological Bibliography*, Library Congress, March 28, 1979, p. 770. *Appendix to Hearings, Select Subcommittee on Assassinations*, March 28, 1979, volume 12, p. 695.

[111] Joesten had come upon an essay by Medford Evans published in the September 1970 issue of "American Opinion": an "organ of the right-wing John Birch Society." (The Birchers were known for their virulent hatred of JFK.) Joesten was greatly amused by the discovery that even a John Bircher might come round to the same conclusion shared by many on the left regarding the faulted Warren Commission. (Evans writes: "There is now a fairly general consensus that the Warren Commission Report is not the last word on the subject in a figurative sense, as it certainly is not in a literal sense.") Joesten goes on to say: "Evans presented a picture of the assassination that could have come from my pen except for a few minor disagreements on details." Even more surprisingly, Evans believed there was a connection between the assassinations of the Kennedy brothers. Joesten quotes Evans: "I think there is a feeling, too, that what happened in Los Angeles in June 1968 was a consequence of what had happened in Dallas nearly five years earlier–the *coup d'état* of November 22, 1963."
Joesten pauses here to note: "To my knowledge nobody but Jim Garrison (and an obscure West Coast writer named Stanley J. Marks) has ever endorsed before my unswerving contention that the murder of John F. Kennedy was nothing short of a camouflaged *coup d'état*." Joesten then adds an ironic coup de grâce: "It is gratifying that so much insight should have penetrated the ranks of the John Birch society–which, incidentally, ought to know what's what, for some of its top-flight members were involved in that very same *coup d'état*."
Joesten certainly knew a something about *coups d'état*: before becoming a *Newsweek* correspondent in the early Forties, he was

forced to flee Germany and the Gestapo under threat of persecution. America wasn't the only country where he encountered difficulties in publishing his books.

[112] Tom Miller; intro. Donald Freed, *The Assassination Please Almanac* (Chicago: Henry Regnery Company, 1977), p. 224.

[113] After his newspaper offices were destroyed by a suspicious fire, Penn Jones "was awarded the Elijah Parish Lovejoy Award for Courage in Journalism, presented annually by the Journalism Department of Southern Illinois University.... After Jones got the award he received congratulatory messages from several politicians, including President Kennedy." John Kelin, *Praise from a Future Generation: The Assassination of John F. Kennedy and the First Generation Critics of the Warren Report*. San Antonio, (TX: Wings Press, 2007), p. 108.

Murder Most Foul!

STANLEY J. MARKS

Murder Most Foul!

The Conspiracy That Murdered President Kennedy

975 Questions & Answers

Editor's Note

In this edition of *Murder Most Foul!* grammar has been standardized and corrected, and capitalization of words not normally capitalized are now presented in lower case (except for a passage in chapter thirteen, where such usage takes on special meaning). Since the first edition was based on a Photostat reproduction of a manuscript produced on a manual typewriter, the author indicated emphasis through the use of phrases typed EXCLUSIVELY in capitalized letters. In the present edition, this has been replaced with italicization. When numbers in the Q&A section were mistakenly repeated (e.g., question "509" followed by another question "509"), the insertion of an alphabet letter is now used to distinguish between them (e.g., "509a" followed by "509b").

Textual changes involving anything more complex, such untangling garbled syntax or inserting missing phrases, are indicated by brackets.

A select bibliography of works cited throughout the text has been added at the end, along with annotated footnotes and a general index. Otherwise, the original *Murder Most Foul!* is reproduced here without any substantial changes.

When citing passages from the Warren Commission Report or the twenty-one volume WC Hearings and Exhibits, the author uses the abbreviation "R" for the Report and "H" for the Hearings and Exhibits. Hence, the abbreviation "R81, 235" refers to the Warren Commission Report, pp. 81, 235, while "3H294-95" refers to the third volume of the Hearings and Exhibits, pp. 294-95. Some of the WC witness statements quoted by Marks are not verbatim transcripts but represent a condensation of their remarks.

Author's Preface

In attempting to formulate questions and answers, it is extremely difficult to form the classic pattern that is generally found in fiction and nonfiction books. The progression of the book is generally in a logical sequence and the reader is swept along in the author's portrayal of the events and characters.

However, in a question and answer book, and especially in regards to the murder of a president of the United States, both events and persons are so intertwined that the reader may become befuddled. Thus, at times, a few events and characters involved in the President Kennedy murder will appear in several sections of this small volume. The answer to a question may also bring to the mind of the reader other facts that have lain dormant in the hidden recesses of his mind until he has read the question and answers.

The contents of this book have been arranged in the manner of an attorney representing a client in a criminal court and in the manner that a district attorney would present his case against the alleged criminal. Thus, the reader has the opportunity of selecting any part of the book relating to a specific matter and locating the questions and the answers.

It is the proposal of this book to reveal the attempts of the Warren Commission to befuddle, delude, and deceive the American people who sincerely desire the answer to the question, "Who murdered President John F. Kennedy?" The Commission and the believers in the verdict rendered by the Warren Commission have given the impression that the Commission has the final word and no one has the right or privilege to dispute this word. The Commissioners seem to have forgotten that it was not the obligation of the American people to accept the Commission's report; rather it was the obligation of the Commission to "ascertain the truth and evaluate the facts." There was no Commission obligation to prove Lee Harvey Oswald the "sole and only murderer of President Kennedy."

TO

BUTCH and CORKY

Contents

MURDER

MOST

FOUL!

$1.95 (p/b)

The Conspiracy That Murdered President Kennedy.

975 Questions & Answers

By

STANLEY J. MARKS

Cover of the first paperback edition of *Murder Most Foul!*

-1-

TO DALLAS WE GO

1. Who was John F. Kennedy?
The 35th President of the United States of America.

2. Why was he flying to Dallas, Texas?
President Kennedy had been urged to fly to Texas by various members of the Democratic Party and attempt to solve the differences between the pro- and anti-Kennedy factions in Texas.

3. Who comprised the anti-Kennedy forces in Texas?
The power structure of Texas in the political, economic, social, and educational life was all anti-Kennedy. Governor Connally and his political associates were one hundred percent anti-Kennedy as were the Texas oil interests and their banker cohorts. Naturally, the police and educational forces, being under the absolute control of Governor Connally and his administration, were all anti-Kennedy. The entire communication media in Texas were bitterly anti-Kennedy and it was this type of media that willfully fanned the flames that led to the murder of President Kennedy.

4. What did the Texas citizens think of President Kennedy?
In the political campaign of 1960, Senator Johnson was attacked by a mob led by a U.S. congressman. In September 1963, the U.S. ambassador, Stevenson, was attacked and struck across the face and eyes. In both instances, the Dallas police permitted attacks to be made. The Dallas police chief admitted that both demonstrations were, in reality, a "full-scale riot" which would have led to the lynching of Ambassador Stevenson.

5. Did President Kennedy believe he would be fully protected?
Yes. He informed his associates that he relied upon the Secret Service.

6. Did President Kennedy or Governor Connally know the parade route?

No.

7. Was a map ever printed showing the *actual* parade route?

No. The *Dallas Morning News* of November 22, 1963, published a map of a route, but it was not used.

8. Did Oswald have any prior knowledge of the parade route?

No. The map found by the Dallas police [had] x's on it that were made by Mrs. Paine, his landlady in Irving, Texas. The marks were made by her to assist Oswald to find employment. R31-40.

9. What was improper pertaining to the selection of the route?

(1) The double detour compelled the motorcade to reduce its standard speed, under Secret Service regulations, from twenty-five miles per hour to between ten and twelve miles per hour.

(2) The double-detour route compelled a further slowing down when the president's automobile had to make, not one detour, but two detours, from Main Street down a short one-half block to Elm Street, and then a left turn on Elm Street, which then led to the triple underpass. This double detour brought the president's auto one hundred yards closer to two buildings: the Texas School Book Depository and the *Dal-Tex Building*.

10. Did the President's automobile ever come to a complete stop?

Yes. Contrary to Secret Service regulations. Motorcycle Officer Chaney informed the Dallas police chief that the president's auto would have come to a complete stop at the time the car cavalcade made its turn into Elm Street. Chaney's statement was hushed up. 3H266.

11. Did the Secret Service know of this double detour?

The Secret Service testified that they did not know of the double detour and simply followed the police chief's automobile.

12. Did the Dallas Police Department know the route? Yes. The *only* persons who knew the *actual* route were (1) the officials of the Dallas Police Department and (2) the murderers.

13. Is there any evidence to substantiate the above statement?
Yes. A statement by Dallas Chief of Police, J. Curry, printed in the November 22, 1963 issue of the *Dallas Morning News*: "*They* had to bring him through town.... A Secret Service man told me they didn't want that either."

14. What did the police chief mean by "*they*"?
Ask (1) the Warren Commission, which was frightened to ask the chief what he meant by "*They* had to bring him"; or ask the chief!

15. Who pressured the police chief to use a double detour?
Ask the police chief!

16. Where was the police chief at the time shots were fired?
Police Chief Curry was in the *lead* automobile about ninety feet in front of the presidential automobile. 4H461.

17. What circumstances surround the activity of the chief after he heard the shots ring out?
Amidst the tumult and shouting, and when the chief's automobile was near or approaching the triple underpass, the chief said that he, and only he, *knew* the shots came from the Book Depository Building.
But R. W. Youngblood, the Secret Service agent riding in the vice president's auto, testified that although the vice president's auto was less than forty-five feet from the same book building, he, Mr. Youngblood, did not know where the shots came [from]. But the police chief *knew*!

18. What did the police chief testify to under oath?
"To get someone up in the railroad yards and check those people."

19. Why the discrepancy?

Ask the police chief; the Commission did not want to know. 4H161.

20. Is there any evidence upholding the chief's testimony?

Yes. Sheriff Decker instructed "all available men from the jail and office to go to the railroad yard off Elm near the triple underpass."

21. What time was this?

The *Dallas Times Herald* reported the sheriff as saying 12:25 p.m. The police radio log upholds the 12:25 p.m. time; the Commission says 12:30 p.m.

22. Why did the sheriff order his men to the railroad yard?

This question was never asked; the sheriff never volunteered.

23. What time was the correct time of the murder?

The correct time, according to independent witnesses, was 12:25 p.m. not 12:30 p.m. The Dallas police broadcast announcing the shooting of the president was relayed to the *Dallas Times Herald* at 12:27 p.m.

24. Where was the reporter?

Sitting at the newspaper desk in the Dallas Police Station listening to the police radio broadcast the progress of the presidential motorcade. The reporter said the announcement was at 12:25 p.m.

25. What time is used by both Dallas newspapers?

The *Morning News* at 12:20 p.m.; the *Times-Herald* at 12:25 p.m. The time was repeated in both papers on November 23 and 24.

26. Did the Commission determine the reason for the discrepancies?

Of course not! Oswald, the patsy, was dead.

27. Did the police arrest any other person besides Oswald?
At least two, possibly as many as six.

28. Who disclosed one of the arrests?
The *Times Herald* of December 8, 1963 published the following:
"It was also learned that an early suspect in the assassination of President Kennedy was still in jail–but is no longer a suspect in the killing. The man, a thirty-one-year-old man, was arrested *minutes* after the killing when the police swarmed near the assassination scene. The *man was reported [to be] carrying a rifle*."

29a. Was there another arrest?
Yes. Patrolman W. Barker arrested a man who was pointed out to him by employees of the Texas School Book Depository. This man was taken to Sheriff Decker's office and booked on "Investigation to commit murder." The man was held on "city charges" until December 10 and then released.

29b. Was there another mysterious arrest?
Yes. A man, who was carrying a rifle in the Dal-Tex Building, was also arrested and taken to the police station. However, to this day, no one knows what happened to this man. The Altgens picture, not published by the Warren Commission, reveals a rifle poking out of the window of the second floor of this building. A Dallas TV commentator stated he saw this rifle from this building. The suppressed Secret Service survey proved the president was shot from this Dal-Tex Building; yet the murderer was in the Dallas jail and let free!

30. What did Sheriff Decker say to the press?
The sheriff stated that his investigators had *two eyewitnesses* to the shooting and they had seen the man with the rifle.

31. What happened?

The Commission never questioned the sheriff concerning this matter; nor did they call in the *Times Herald* reporter to ascertain the truth of the sheriff's statement. *Times Herald*, November 22.

32. Did the sheriff ask these two witnesses to identify Oswald?
No.

33. Did the Commission ask the sheriff why he had held a man incommunicado for a ten-day period?
No.

34. Where was the press when these three men were arrested?
Accepting handouts from the Dallas Police Department.

35. Did the Commission ask about these three men? Of course not. Why stir things up; they might uncover something.

36. What is the significance of these events?
The major significance is the cover up by the Dallas police and the sheriff's office relating to the investigation of these men. The reason why the Commission refused to delve into these arrests is, of course, speculation.

However, the thirty-one-year-old man matched the description of the man in the Dallas police broadcast! Yet, the Warren Commission did not deem it necessary to investigate this strange behavior of the police.

Another factor is that the same police broadcast stated that the man was "carrying a rifle." In addition, this man was captured in the area of the "railroad yards near the triple underpass" where the sheriff stated the shots were fired. Finally, the sheriff admitted to the press that he had two eyewitnesses to this rifleman.

From the testimony given to the Warren Commission, it is seen that the police had three riflemen: (1) the man arrested in the Dal-Tex Building; (2) the man arrested by Officer Barker; and (3) the man arrested by Sheriff Decker's deputies, and this man was seen carrying a rifle. *Everyone has disappeared; two of them were conspirators!*

37. What time were these men apprehended?
At approximately 12:45 p.m.

38. Would it be proper to say that the Dallas Police and Sheriff Department may have had two or three conspirators in jail and then released them long after the death of Oswald, thus keeping the press away from them so no pictures could have been taken?

The above could be the only logical answer! American citizens are not supposed to be kept in prison, incommunicado, for a period of ten days or more. Then [be] mysteriously released. There is *no* record of any habeas corpus proceeding being held by any Dallas court. These arrested men just vanished with the contrivance of the Dallas authorities.

39. Where were the "gentlemen of the press"?
Today, that is the question being asked by millions of people. These arrests were not made secretly, for the two Dallas newspapers reported the arrests but no reporter showed any initiative.

A reporter, as distinguished from a "news gatherer," would have smelled a rat, for everything was too convenient. A good police reporter would have known that Oswald could *not* have been the killer when the police announced that he had been captured through fingerprints found on the gun. How could Oswald have had his fingerprints taken to match a rifle's print when the gun was still in Washington, DC? A good police reporter would have known that Oswald's name was never mentioned in any police radio broadcast, so how did the police obtain his name?

-2-

THE COMMISSION

40. Who was Lee Harvey Oswald?

Lee Harvey Oswald was born on October 18, 1939. He served in the U.S. Marine Corps in the United States and Japan. Evidence is now accumulating that he was a minor cog in the CIA. He was trained as a radio technician and received a security Class A clearance in the Corps. Immediately prior to his discharge, Oswald applied for a passport to the USSR and received it from the U.S. State Department. Oswald failed in his first assignment as a CIA agent and requested a return to the United States. The CIA was able to convince the visa division of the State Department to grant a visa to Oswald and his Russian wife, Marina. Oswald then became, through the good offices of the CIA, involved with the Batista Cuban exiles. The CIA has a worldwide reputation of overthrowing democratic governments and the Batista Cubans were the CIA's "cup of tea." Oswald became the patsy in the Kennedy murder, but when he attempted to make a deal with Inspector Kelley of the U.S. Secret Service Oswald was doomed. Jack Ruby, a member of the conspiracy, shot Oswald with the connivance of several Dallas police officers. However, in law, Ruby only shot Oswald who, in turn, was murdered by at least one member of the Dallas Police Department. Ruby, in turn, was murdered by a disease known as "galloping cancer."

41. Where did Oswald reside on the day of the murder?

Oswald actually had two residences: (1) his family, consisting of his wife, Marina, and his two children and himself, rented a room from Mrs. Paine, in Irving, Texas; (2) his other abode was in the 1200 block on Berkeley Avenue[1] in Dallas, Texas.

---

[1] The address was 1026 N. Beckley.

42. How did Oswald obtain his job at the Book Depository?

Mrs. Paine, the landlady, asked Superintendent Truly to give Oswald a job and vouched for his reliability and honesty.

43. Did the FBI know where Oswald was employed?

Mrs. Paine informed FBI Agent Hosty of the Dallas office.

44. Was Oswald either an FBI agent or informer?

Yes, as to being an informant, as distinguished from being an agent. It is now known that *no one associated with the Warren Commission ever* read the FBI dossier on Oswald. *Nor has the FBI stated that he was not an* FBI informant. Just that he was *not* an agent or on the FBI payroll.

45. Was Oswald any type of an agent for the CIA?

The evidence is accumulating that the answer is "yes."

46. What is meant by "against the national interest"?

The Warren Commission has never defined this indefinable phrase. However, after the publication of the Warren "Report," many commentators and historians interpret that phrase to mean that whenever a future president is murdered his killers can escape capture and punishment if a future investigating committee decides their capture would be "against the national interest."

47. How was the Warren Commission created?

The Commission was created by President Johnson under Executive Order Number 11130, signed on November 29, 1963. This order was then approved by a joint resolution of Congress on December 13, 1963.

48. Was any *time* or *money* limit placed on the Commission?

No.

49. What powers were granted to the Commission?

The Commission had the right to subpoena witnesses, documents, papers, and any items necessary to "evaluate the facts" relating to a murder or conspiracy. Defiance could lead to a fine or jail sentence.

50. Did the witnesses have a right to an attorney?

Yes. In addition, any witness could claim this right under the Fifth Amendment, but the Commission then had the right to grant immunity.

51. Did any witness claim this right to an attorney?

Yes, two witnesses: Mrs. Marina Oswald and Mrs. Bledsoe.

52. Who were the members of the Warren Commission?

The chairman was Chief Justice Warren, Supreme Court; Senator Russell of Georgia; Senator Cooper of Kentucky; Congressman Ford and Boggs; A. Dulles, former director of the CIA; and J. McCloy, former World Bank head.

53. Was this a pro- or anti-President Kennedy lineup?

A definite anti-Kennedy tinge, as will be seen from their actions.

54. Is there any evidence in the "Report" to show an anti-Kennedy tinge?

Yes. The Commission permitted a man from the Birch Society to abuse the memory of President Kennedy. For more than a 132 pages of abuse is published by the Commission as its "tribute." This man's "testimony" was given more space than that given by Mrs. Jacqueline Kennedy, Governor Connally, Mrs. Connally, and Deputy Sheriff Weitzman combined. This John Birch officer testified that the American people should have mourned the death of Hitler but not that of President John F. Kennedy.

Not a single Commissioner or Commission aide raised his voice in protest.

This Commission, composed of "Americans who believed in the basic principles of American justice," did not accept, or permit, any official of the federal, state, or local governing body, or any private citizen, to insert in the "Report" or "Hearings" a statement showing the respect and love the American citizenry had for President Kennedy.

The Commission published this "eulogy of hate" under the imprimatur of the "Government of the United States," and the future school children will thus obtain the viewpoint of the Warren Commission regarding the president of the United States, John F. Kennedy.

55. What was the purpose of the Warren Commission?

According to Executive Order Number 11130, the Commission was to "satisfy itself that the truth is known as far as it can be discovered." The Commission was to "ascertain the truth and evaluate the evidence" so that the truth would be exposed to the world."

56. Did the Commission "ascertain the truth"?

No! How could the Commission find the "truth" when it refused to accept facts that would have brought forth the "truth"?

57. How was the Commission organized?

The General Counsel was J. Lee Rankin, former solicitor general of the United States; fourteen members acting as assistant counsel; and twelve staff members.

58. Was there a division of labor between the members or aides?

The prestige lawyers received $100 a day for consulting with the Commission; the aides received $75 a day, plus expenses. The main portion of the work fell upon the shoulders of the aides. The aides became known as "legal beagles," for they were neither nor "legal" or "beagles."

59. Did Executive Order Number 11130 limit the Commission to lawyers?

No! The disrepute of the modern lawyer is on a steady increase. Nor did the "work" of the lawyers of the Commission stifle this dislike for the legal profession. Never have so few demeaned so many!

The chief justice's theory that only lawyers should be selected to serve as aides was the ultimate in arrogance and a revelation of the contempt the lawyers had for the people of the United States.

60. How was the work of the Commission blueprinted?

The Commission decided that six basic issues were involved: (1) basic facts of the assassination; (2) the identity of the assassin; (3) Oswald's background and motives; (4) did Oswald have any conspirators; (5) death of Oswald; and (6) presidential protection.

61. What other basic issue should have been blueprinted?

Who murdered President John F. Kennedy?

62. Did the Commission know, *in advance*, that a conspiracy existed?

Yes. In possession of the Commission, *on the day it officially commenced its investigation* in January 1964, the Commission had these facts:

(1) The FBI official report that President Kennedy had been struck in the *back* and that there was no exit wound for that back wound, and another bullet struck the president in the head.

(2) The FBI official report that Governor Connally had been struck by an *independent bullet. This made* = three = bullets!

(3) The Secret Service report which *confirmed* the FBI official report. *Three bullets.*

(4) The Secret Service *survey* which *proved* that Oswald could *not* have fired those three bullets from the sixth-floor [of the] Depository Building.

(5) *The Secret Service reports are so destructive of the Commission's case against Oswald that the Commission has suppressed them.*

(6) The Commission had the official report of the doctors of Parkland Hospital which stated the president's neck wound was an *entry* one.

(7) The Commission had the *Secret Service report*, from the Houston Secret Service office, that Oswald had an FBI number.

(8) The Commission *knew* that Police Chief Curry of Dallas had stated, before a TV audience numbering in the millions, that *the police had no witness to identify any alleged killer*, including Oswald! This statement was made after Oswald was in custody.

(9) The Commission knew that the Dallas police and the Dallas Sheriff's Office had arrested a minimum of three men; that one of the men had been held incommunicado for a period of ten days; that another one had been arrested, with a rifle, in the Dal-Tex Building; and that another one had been arrested in an area, with a rifle, where the shots were fired.

(10) That the FBI reports, volume 1 and 5, raised more than a "reasonable doubt" concerning the bullets and the Italian rifle.

Based on only these ten points, a conspiracy had to exist.

63. Did any Commissioner write a book on the murder?

Yes. Congressman Ford wrote a book that sold for $6.95. He now says that persons writing about the Commission reveal a "lack of taste" if these persons attack the Warren Report. It reminds one of the story of the law student who, after five tries, passed the bar. His first proposal to the Bar Association was that the qualifications be raised!

64. How long did the Commission work?

From February 3, 1964 to September 6, 1964. Published September 28, 1964.

65. What is the value of the "Report"?

888 pages of words or "hearsay piled upon hearsay"!

66. How many "Hearings," witnesses, and affidavits were produced?

The FBI inundated the Commission with 25,000 reports; in fact, the FBI gave the Commission so many reports of its "investigations" that the FBI created a "fog" over the work of the Commission. It now seems to have been deliberate for, in a period of nine months, no group of fourteen lawyers could have read, digested, and analyzed each report to see what [effect] each report would have on an overall picture of the conspiracy.

A total of 552 witnesses were called before a "Hearing" session. However, a mere ninety-four witnesses were heard in a "session": that is, where at least one Commissioner attended.

It must be noted that where a Commissioner attended a session, the evidence that was most damaging to the Commission's case against Oswald was brought forth. Thus, it was Mr. Dulles' examination of Bonnie Ray Williams that proved Oswald was innocent of being the "sole and exclusive killer" of President Kennedy. His testimony that, from 12:00 noon to about 12:20 p.m. when he, Mr. Williams, was eating lunch on the *sixth* floor he saw no one or heard no one, proved Oswald's innocence!

Again, it was the examination of Policeman McDonald by Senator Cooper that proved Oswald's revolver did not fire the bullets that struck Officer Tippit. As will be shown later in this book, Senator Cooper *proved* the revolver taken from Oswald was not the one used!

67. What was the attendance record of the Commissioners?
Extremely poor! Senator Russell attended a *mere five meetings* while banker McCloy attended only sixteen meetings or sessions. The overall average was about forty percent. So little concern over the murder.

68. Did the seven members ever attend a session where all were there?
No.

69. How was the time of the Commission spent?
According to Mr. Epstein of *Inquest*, nearly forty-four percent was spent on the life of Oswald; twelve percent on his life in the USSR; and the balance trying to prove he was the "sole and exclusive murderer" of President Kennedy. They were not interested in "Who murdered President Kennedy"!

70. What did the Commission aides think about the Commission?
Again, referring to Mr. Epstein, the aides thought the Commission was a "joke"; a "farce"; a "nothing."

But the murder of President Kennedy was no joke!

71. What is the value of the books analyzing the Warren Commission?

The essence is to illuminate, for the American people, the darkness surrounding the work of the Commission. The books of most value would be: Weisberg's *Whitewash*, volumes 1 & 2; Lane's *Rush to Judgment*; Epstein's *Inquest*; and Marks' *Murder Most Foul!* Jones's *Forgive My Grief* deals with the strange deaths, in violation of all actuary insurance laws, of the witnesses who are involved in the Kennedy murder. George Thompson's *Quest for Truth* is valuable for its sketches and engineering drawings related to material facts of the murder. The value of all the books is found in the fact that the critics of the books attack the author, not the facts in their books.

72. What value were the NBC and CBS programs in 1967?

No value except that the programs revealed the awesome power of the FBI and CIA to compel the mass communication media to intercede on behalf of the Warren Commission. Both systems used "hearsay" to prove that Oswald was guilty; both systems used testimony "out of context" to prove Oswald guilty; and both systems proved that its interpretation of "freedom of the press" in 1967 is not Jefferson's of 1776! The CBS "rifle" tests and "bullet" tests were as phony as phony could be. CBS should have first read Hoover's testimony and letters!

73. How did Chief Justice Warren "protect" Oswald's rights?

He appointed Walter E. Craig, the president of the American Bar to represent "the alleged assassin and *his* family." However, at the conclusion of the statement appointing Mr. Craig, the chief justice admitted that Mr. Craig would only represent the widow, Mrs. Marina Oswald.

74. Why was Mr. Craig appointed?

Chief Justice Warren hailed Mr. Craig's appointment with the ringing phrase that Mr. Craig, an attorney, would advise the Commission as to whether or not the proceedings would conform to the "basic principles of American justice." The foreign press commented that it was strange that the chief justice had to accept the services of another attorney to keep the chief justice informed as to what was "American justice."

75. How did Mr. Craig perform his duty?

The facts speak for themselves. He attended exactly *two* sessions. He did so much for the "basic principles of American justice" that is name is not mentioned in the "Report."

76. Was hearsay evidence presented to the Commission?

Yes, despite the fact that hearsay evidence is inadmissible in any court of law, in any country. The statement by the chief justice that the Commission was not a judicial one is of no value when the facts reveal that his aides used legal tools in an attempt to suborn witnesses so that their testimony would uphold the Commission's theory.

An overwhelming majority of the statements obtained by the FBI and the Secret Service was hearsay. This is why the three-judge panel in New Orleans, during the Jim Garrison investigation, labeled the Warren Report "hearsay piled upon hearsay." This is also the reason why the NBC and CBS programs broadcasted in June and July 1967 were worthless.

77. How did the aides conduct themselves?

With the arrogance of a priest conducting an Inquisition! Never in American history has greater contempt been shown by the legal profession toward the American citizen. These "legal beagles," having the full power of the federal government behind them, glorified in their role to destroy the lives of other human beings.

There is now absolute proof that many of the interviews conducted by the "legal beagles" were not only illegal but threats were made to witnesses that if the witness did not change his testimony to conform to the Commission's theory, the witness would be charged with perjury.

It was not until June 8, 1964 that the chief justice elaborated on the powers of his "legal beagles." By that time, however, the

Commission had secured the type of testimony it desired. 5H254-58.

The whole investigation is covered with the smog of intimidation and perjury. Far too many lawyers in the United States seem to have the morals of a whore and the soul of a pimp.

-3-

RIFLES, RIFLES EVERYWHERE

78. Why was a "dead" Oswald better than a "live" Oswald?

The Dallas police, if Oswald had lived to be tried, would have had to explain to a jury composed of rational men: (1) a 7.65 German Mauser, (2) a 6.5 Italian Mannlicher-Carcano rifle!

79. According to the Commission, how many rifles were involved?

One.

80. But how many rifles are involved in the "Hearings"?

Two or more!

81. How is this proved?

By *comparing* the official "Report" Exhibit Number 139 with the AP official photograph. The AP photograph is authenticated by the Commission.

82. What are the discrepancies?

(1) The front sight of Exhibit Number 139 has a *tapered* sight.

(2) The AP authenticated photograph has a *round* site.

(3) The *front end* of the telescopic sight and Exhibit Number 139 is 4/16 of an inch *behind* the barrel.

(4) The front end of the AP photography is *directly in line*.

(5) In Exhibit 139, the rifle bolt is *even* to telescopic mount.

(6) In the AP photo the rifle bolt is *behind* the mount.

(7) In exhibit 139, the *rear* of the telescopic mouth is *slanted*.

(8) In the AP photo, the rear of the mount is *vertical*.

83. What does this mean?

That there were *several* 6.5 Italian Mannlicher-Carcano rifles floating around the Dallas Police Station!

84. Is there any corroborative evidence relating to a *German Mauser*?

Yes! Deputy Sheriff Weitzman, who saw and found the rifle, signed an affidavit on November 23, 1963, which stated that the rifle he found "was a 7.65 *Mauser* bolt-action equipped with a 4/18 scope, (with) a thick brownish black sling on it." R235; 19H507; 24H228.

85. Who was Deputy Sheriff Weitzman?

The background of Mr. Weitzman includes a degree in Civil Engineering; the owner for a number of years of a sporting goods shop where he purchased and sold all types of guns. To deprecate his evidence and remove its value, the Commission called it a rumor. R19; R489-92; 3H446.

86. Was his testimony substantiated by other independent witnesses?

Yes! By Deputies Boone and Mooney. In addition, by Captain Fritz and Lieutenant Day. Furthermore, FBI Agent Odum radioed the Dallas FBI Office that the rifle was a *German Mauser*. R81, 235, 646; 3H294-95.

87. What Dallas county officer upheld Deputy Sheriff Weitzman?

None other than *District Attorney Wade*. It must not be forgotten that Mr. Wade was a former FBI agent whose training included identification of all types of firearms. Mr. Wade, on November 22 and November 23, 1963, at a formal press conference said: "The murder weapon is a *German Mauser*." 26H829-31.

88. Did Deputies Weitzman or Boone identify Exhibit Number 139?

No! 7H105-09.

89. Why did the Commission refused to ask Deputy Sheriff Weitzman to identify the Commission's Exhibit Number 139?

For the obvious reason that the Commission had the deputy's affidavit of November 23, 1963 in their possession and the affidavit was in such detail that the deputy executing the affidavit would immediately know that Exhibition No. 139 was not the same rifle. 24H228.

As a matter of fact, the $75.00 a day "legal beagle" never asked Deputy Weitzman to identify Exhibit Number 139 even though the "rifle" was in the examination room while he was testifying! 7H105-09.

The Commission *knew* that Commission Exhibit Number 139 was *not* the rifle found at 1:22 p.m. on the sixth floor of the Book Depository Building.

90. Was Deputy Sheriff Boone asked to identify Exhibit Number 139?
Yes.

91. What evidence did he give?
He *refused* to identify the Italian Mannlicher-Carcano rifle as the one he found with Deputy Sheriff Weitzman. 3H204.

92. In a law court would the court permit the Commission the right to refuse to admit the Exhibit Number 139 to the jury?
No! The failure of the Commission to permit their own witness to identify the rifle would lead to an instant dismissal of the case with a verdict of "not guilty" entered on behalf of the alleged murderer. This is a basic rule of law under the principles of American jurisprudence.

Every law student knows this rule; however, the attorneys for the Commission were lawyers, not students, and everyone knows that few lawyers could pass a Bar Examination once they practice their "profession."

93. What words appeared on the rifle known as Commission Exhibit Number 139?
In large letters: "*MADE IN ITALY. CAL. 6.5.*" 3H390-92.

94. Is it true that Captain Fritz and Lieutenant Day "promptly" identified the "found" rifle as an Italian made Mannlicher-Carcano 6.5 rifle?

No! The Commission statement is false. A change from a 7.65 German Mauser to a 6.5 Italian Mannlicher-Carcano was made *after* the rifle had been removed from the sixth floor and was "switched" by someone in the Dallas Police Department. R79, 553-54, 654; 3H295; 4H202-49; 7H401-04; 15H145-54.

95. Did the FBI testify that the found rifle was a Mannlicher-Carcano?

No! Only that they had received such a rifle from the Dallas police.

96. Did any police agency testify that the rifle found by Deputies Weitzman and Boone was an Italian Mannlicher-Carcano 6.5 carbine?

No.

97a. Did the Commission prove that the "found" rifle was Exhibit Number 139?

No. Although the Commission twisted and turned and manufactured statements, there is absolutely *no* evidence to sustain the Commission's own self-serving statements. There is testimony, given under oath, that revealed that Captain Fritz of the Dallas Police Department promptly identified the rifle as a *German Mauser*. 3H295; 4H202-49, 264; 7H108, 403; 15H145.

It is a *fundamental rule of American law* that where a district attorney, in a murder trial, refuses to put into evidence and the record the alleged murder weapon used to commit the alleged murder, the court must issue a verdict of "not guilty" where the weapon is in the possession of the district attorney.

In the possession of the Commission was a rifle which they alleged was used to murder President Kennedy. Yet, when the police officer who found the weapon was in the examination room, the Commission refused to ask him to identify "their" weapon, known as Commission Exhibit Number 139, as the rifle he found at 1:22 p.m. on the sixth floor of the Depository.

This refusal, in conjunction with the refusal of the co-finder Deputy Sheriff Boone, to identify Commission Exhibit Number 139 as the rifle found on the sixth floor, is conclusive evidence, in the eyes of the law, that Commission Exhibit Number 139 *was not the rifle used, as alleged by the Commission, to murder President John F Kennedy.*

The reader, to verify the above statement, is referred to citations appearing to answers on pages 14, 15, and 16 of this book.

97b. Was Oswald telling the truth when he said he had seen a Mauser in the Book Depository Building where he was employed?

Yes. A Mr. Caster admitted that he had a "30.06 *Sporterized Mauser*" in the building prior to the day of the murder and that he had shown this Mauser to various employees. This *Mauser* had a telescopic sight. R601; 612.

98. Was there anything strange about this incident?

Yes. This is the *identical* type of rifle seen by Mr. Rowland whose testimony appears later in this book. Mr. Caster was cleared by the FBI.

99. Was there a possibility that another rifle was used in the murder?

Yes. Mr. D. Ryder, of Irving, Texas, a gun shop employee, testified before the Commission that he had mounted a telescopic sight for a man named "Oswald." His testimony was never discredited by the Commission although a Commission aide attempted to compel Mr. Ryder to change his testimony by use of an "off the cuff" interview. R315.

This is the first indication that a conspiracy existed.

100. Regarding the rifles, who is to be believed?

The matter of belief, under American law, is in the domain of the jury composed of rational people. Five experienced police officers, one FBI agent, and one district attorney who was a former FBI agent experienced in the identification of firearms, stated that the rifle found by Deputy Sheriffs Weitzman and Boone was a 7.65 *German Mauser*.

The Commission had *no* eyewitness who ever testified that the found rifle was a 6.5 Italian Mannlicher-Carcano rifle.

The Federal Bureau of Investigation was never asked whether or not the FBI *knew*, on its own personal knowledge, that the rifle found on the sixth floor by Deputies Weitzman and Boone, was in fact and in law, an Italian Mannlicher-Carcano rifle.

The only statement ever made by the FBI was that it had received an Italian Mannlicher-Carcano rifle from the Dallas Police Department.

101. What did the Warren Commission legally prove?

(1) That two rifles were found, but where *one* was found was not known! (2) That the rifle found by the two deputies was a *German Mauser*. (3) That Deputy Boone *refused* to identify the Italian rifle as the one he found with Deputy Weitzman. (4) Five policeman said it was a *German* Mauser rifle. (5) The Commission *refused* to permit Deputy Weitzman to identify Commission Exhibit Number 139. (6) The *Commission suppressed Deputy Weitzman's* November 23, 1963 affidavit from the "Report." (7) The FBI never testified that the Italian Mannlicher-Carcano rifle was *the* rifle used as the murder weapon used to kill President Kennedy.

102. Who changed the rifle from a *German Mauser* to an Italian rifle?

Someone in the Dallas Police Department who was involved in the conspiracy. The testimony clearly indicated a conspiracy.

103. What other essential fact was not explained by the Commission?

The discrepancies between the photographs showing Commission Exhibit Number 139 and the AP photograph. This is further proof that a minimum of two rifles were floating around the Dallas Police Department.

104. How many bullets did the Commission say Oswald possessed?

Four (4) bullets! The fact that *no* gun shop ever sells only four bullets never fazed the Warren Commission. Was someone using LSD or smoking bananas? Was this a *rational* investigation?

105. How many bullets were found by the police?

The police testified that they found three empty cartridge cases plus one live bullet in the rifle chamber. 3H28.

106. Where did Oswald obtain only four bullets?

This is the unsolved mystery. The FBI testified that they could not locate any gun shop who sold or gave Oswald any type of ammunition. Evidence also revealed that the ammunition for an Italian Mannlicher-Carcano rifle was last manufactured in 1944.

The Commission admitted (1) that Oswald *never* purchased any ammunition for the rifle he allegedly received from Klein's of Chicago. (2) Nor did he receive any ammunition *clip* with that rifle. (3) Nor was any type of ammunition found in his Irving or Dallas abode.

107. What did the FBI testify to regarding the cartridge cases and shell?

(1) The live bullet in the rifle chamber has "marks which were *not* identified with the rifle." (2) Three sets of marks were on the cartridge base which could *not* be found on the other two cases. (3) The third case (shell) "had been loaded into and extracted from [a] weapon at least twice." J. Edgar Hoover Letter to Commission. 26H449-50.

108. What other vital information was given by the FBI regarding bullets?

FBI ballistic Agent Frazier informed the Commission that the live bullet was a "full metal jacketed bullet of the military type" and that that bullet had a "rather *low* velocity." The Commission converted the word "low" to "high"! 3H399, 414.

109. What surprising testimony was given by Dallas Police Officer Lieutenant Day?

(1) That *one* of the shells was so deformed that it could *not* fit into the rifle. (2) No fingerprint, partial or full, was ever found on any of the three shells or live bullet. (3) No fingerprint, partial or full, was found on the ammunition clip, or rifle bolt. (4) Although Captain Fritz held the rifle in both hands, and pulled the trigger to eject the live bullet, *his fingerprints and his palm prints were not found*! 4H205; 253-55.

This amazing and incredible testimony was *not* analyzed by anyone in the newspaper or electronic business. The FBI report and testimony makes *no* mention of this "deformed" bullet nor of the lack of fingerprints. *Nor does the FBI state that the four bullets submitted to the Bureau* were the *identical* ones "found" by the Dallas police!

110. What is the meaning of Lieutenant Day's testimony?

That Lee Harvey Oswald and Captain Fritz should be enshrined in the Smithsonian Institute or the National Archives; they have *no* prints!

111. What did the Commission print regarding the *live* bullet?

"This type of cartridge is loaded with a full metal jacket, military type of bullet weighing 160-161 grains.... It is just under 1.2 inches long, and just over one-fourth inch in diameter." R555.

112. Did the Commission produce any evidence to support the above?

No. The American manufacturer of that type of bullet, the Western Cartridge Company, East Alton, Illinois, admitted that it last manufactured that type of bullet in 1944. See *Rush to Judgment*; *Quest for Truth*.

113. The Commission stated that those types of bullets were available?

The Commission said "Yes"; the FBI said "No"! No federal or state police agency ever located any mail-order house or gun shop that sold the type of bullet found in the chamber of the

Italian rifle that weighed 160-161 grains. No evidence supported the Commission.

114. How did the Dallas Police Department handle the shells?

In the same manner they handled the "found" rifle. Like a hot potato! Captain Fritz admitted that his department did not give the three shells to the FBI; only two of them. Then, at 1 a.m. (past the witching hour!) on November 28, *five days after the shells* were found, Captain Fritz gave the third shell, *plus Oswald's notebook*, to FBI Agent Drain. Why did Captain Fritz withhold a bullet? Why did he withhold Oswald's notebook? Why? Was the withheld bullet the deformed bullet? Was Oswald's notebook the *complete* notebook? 78404.

115. What was the significance of Mr. Hoover's letter to the Commission?

Mr. Hoover was informing the Commission, in a very polite manner, to "go slow." Since the bullets could not match the rifle, his letter could mean one of three things: (1) *Two* rifles were involved. (2) Thus, a conspiracy did exist. (3) The rifle submitted to the Bureau was a "plant" and a switch had been made. 26H449-50.

116. What other "red flag" warning was given by the FBI?

In the FBI report the Bureau never stated that Oswald *used* the rifle. The FBI repeatedly employed the word "*owned*." Owning a rifle does *not* presuppose the word "using" nor are they synonymous!

117. Was there another surprising statement in the FBI report?

Yes. The Bureau stated that the "gun barrel *may have been changed since April, 1963*" when the attempt was made on ex-Major General Walker.[2]

---

[2] In April 1961, Walker, a right-wing extremist, was accused of indoctrinating his troops with propaganda from the John Birch Society. As a result, JFK's Secretary of Defense Robert McNamara relieved Walker of his command and began an investigation. Shortly afterward

118. Where could anyone purchase the barrel of a 1940 rifle?

Ask the Commission! The implication of the FBI statement is staggering; yet the Commission calmly dismissed it. If evidence disturbed their "theory" they simply refused to believe the evidence.

119. Were any fingerprints found on the Italian rifle?

No! This was another FBI "red flag." The FBI testified that the gun given to them by the Dallas police was *received in a well-oiled condition.*" 4H20, 29.

120. Were any gloves or wiping material used by Oswald at any time?

No. The Commission admitted that Oswald, on the day of the murder, *never* had any gloves or wiping materials in his possession at *any time.* Yet, the rifle was in a "well-oiled condition"!

121. Where did the FBI differentiate between "*used*" and "*owned*"?

The FBI report, dated December 9, 1963. Paragraph 1: "All three (bullets or shells) had been fired in the rifle *owned* by Oswald! Paragraph 2: "It had been fired from the rifle *owned* by Oswald." Paragraph 3: "had been fired from the rifle *owned* by Oswald."

In the same report in discussing the Walker murder attempt, Section G: "belonging to Oswald"; and "It was not possible to determine whether or not this bullet was fired *from* Oswald's rifle."

General Walker resigned from the army, becoming the century's only U.S. general to do so. On April, 10, 1963, while seated at a desk in his Dallas residence, Walker was supposedly the target of an assassination attempt. Although Oswald had never been a suspect in the subsequent police investigation, an April 10, 1963 FBI report attempted to pin the blame for the Walker shooting on Oswald.

Thus, it can be readily seen that the use of the English language by the FBI was not a whim but carefully thought out.

Anyone reading the various letters sent to the Commission by the FBI is struck by the careful use of words. Some of the letters sent to the Commission by the FBI also revealed the fact that the Bureau *did not* answer the questions asked by the Commission. Yet, the Commission stated that the FBI answers conformed to the questions asked.

122. Is it possible to handle a "well-oiled rifle," plus four bullets, plus an ammunition clip, pull the bolt four times, and leave *no* prints?

Ask the FBI! Or ask any member of the armed services!

123. What was the internal condition of the Italian rifle?

No one knows. It is standard police procedure to examine a gun used in the commission of a crime. Tests can be made to determine whether or not the gun had been fired recently. However, neither the Commission nor the Dallas police wanted to know the answer.

124. Did the Dallas police use a paraffin test on Oswald?

Yes. The tests revealed nitrate deposits on his hands. Regarding his neck and cheeks, no traces whatsoever. Thus, in law, if the district attorney attempted to prove Oswald had used a firearm, he could only prove that Oswald had used a revolver, not a rifle. 4H276.

125. What did the Commission do regarding these paraffin tests?

The Commission correctly rejected the tests as being evidence against Oswald. Nitrate comes from all sorts of material, like toothpaste.

126. Why and how did the Commission attempt to prove Oswald had taken a rifle into the Depository on the day of the murder?

The Commission, under law, had to prove that Oswald carried a rifle into the Depository on the morning of November 22, 1963; for if he had no rifle, the Commission had no case.

127. According to the Commission, how did Oswald get a rifle in?

The Commission simply printed [a statement] which said that Oswald carried a rifle, which [he] had first disassembled, in a brown paper bag which he had made from wrapping paper and tape stolen from the shipping room.

128. Did the Commission prove their "self-serving" statement?
No, as the evidence will show.

129. Who were Mr. W. Frazier and Mrs. Randle?

Mr. Frazier was Oswald's neighbor in Irving, Texas and was also a fellow employee who occasionally drove Oswald to work in the mornings. Mrs. Randle was Mr. Frazier's sister and also a next-door neighbor. The uncontradicted testimony of these two people, given under oath, was the first step that destroyed the Commission's case vs. Oswald. 2H210-15; 7H53.

The conduct of the Commission's aides, attorneys who had sworn to uphold the "basic principles of American justice," is a revelation to both students and nonstudents of legal methods used in an attempt to secure "evidence" needed to support a "theory."

130. What occurred between Mr. Frazier and Oswald?

Mr. Frazier drove Oswald to work that morning and Oswald sat next to Mr. Frazier. Oswald placed a package on the back seat. 2H210.

131. Did Mr. Frazier ask Oswald the contents of the package?
Yes. Oswald said: "curtain rods." R131-34.

132. Did Mr. Frazier believe Oswald's statement?

Mr. Frazier testified: "Oswald never lied to me before, so I never had any reason to doubt his word." A sensible answer. 2H228.

133. Did Mrs. Randle see Oswald's package when he left with Frazier?
Yes. The package, not the contents. R131-34.

134. How did Mrs. Randle describe the bag?
She testified that the package was like a grocery bag, *not wrapping paper* like the exhibit shown to her by the Commission. 2H226-29; 239-44.

135. How large was the bag?
Mr. Frazier, under oath, said the bag was about 24 to 26 inches. Mrs. Randle said about twenty-eight inches. 2H226-29; 2H239-44.

136. How long was the disassembled rifle?
34.8 inches was the longest part. R133.

137. How did the Commission attempt to negate the Frazier-Randle truth?
By inventing and concocting their own "evidence."

138. Did the Commission substantiate their own "evidence."
How can a misrepresentation be substantiated?

139. Did the FBI substantiate Mr. Frazier's testimony? How?
The Bureau asked Mr. Frazier to show them how he determined the length of Oswald's package. On December 1, 1963, Frazier took the FBI agents to his automobile and showed them the space occupied by the package. The FBI agents measured the space and the agents testified to the Commission that the space was exactly twenty-seven inches! 2H21; 14H408-09.

140. How did Mrs. Randle substantiate her testimony?
After Mrs. Randle had *rejected* the Commission's paper bag as being *too large*, the Commission asked her to fold their bag to size. 2H248-50.

141. [To] what size did Mrs. Randle fold the Commission's "bag"?
To 28 1/2 inches! 2H210, 248-50; 14H408.

142. How long was the *stock* of the Italian rifle?
34.8 inches. R133.

143. What other testimony was given by Mrs. Randle?
That Oswald had grabbed the bag at the top.

144. How did Oswald carry this package into the building?
Mr. Frazier testified that he "cupped" it; that is, the bottom portion of the package was carried by Oswald by "cupping" it in his hand; the top of the package was *under* his armpit. 2H226-29, 239.

145. What does the testimony, in law, of Frazier–Randle prove?
That the *only eyewitnesses* to the package were telling the truth. The Commission, to disprove their testimony, simply had to go to the autopsy report on Oswald to find his measurements, from his armpit to his hand, cupped and uncupped. It was as simple as that!

146. Did the Commission do that simple thing?
Of course not! The autopsy would substantiate the witnesses.

147. Were Mr. Frazier and Mrs. Randle indicted for perjury?
No! How can the truth be perjury? R137.

148. Is there any other proof to substantiate their testimony?
Yes! The reader is referred to Commission Exhibit Numbers 142 and 1304. These exhibits, authenticated by the Commission, are pictures of the paper "bag" and reveal *no shape of a rifle or parts of a rifle*. R132; 16H513.

149. What did the Commission *conceal* from the American people?

The Commission did *not* inform the public: (1) That the paper bag shown to Mr. Frazier and Mrs. Randle *was an alleged replica*. FBI Agent Cadigan testified that this "bag" was *reconstructed from paper* and *tape* in the Dallas FBI office. (2) The actual paper bag container had been *destroyed* in the FBI Washington laboratory. (3) Mrs. Randle testified that the Commission's "bag" was too thick; that the bag used by Oswald was a "grocery" bag. In other words, the Commission was attempting to compel a witness, under oath, to accept as true, evidence that was false. This is "basic principles of American justice"? R136; 4H93; 16H513.

150. What other evidence did Agent Cadigan give to the Commission?

That the "bag" received by the FBI in Washington, DC, from the Dallas Police Department, *had no oil stains or rifle indentations*. This, despite the fact that the rifle was received in a "well-oiled condition." 4H97.

151. When Mr. Randle refused to commit perjury, what did the Commission do?

They *ordered* him to take a "lie test." To the dismay of the aides he passed with flying colors. 7H190; 21H602.

152. What, then, did the Commission do?

The Commission published a statement that Oswald had concealed the rifle, disassembled, in a paper bag and carried it into the Depository on the morning of November 22, 1963; then assembled the rifle in a hiding place never discovered by the Dallas police, the Secret Service, the CIA or the FBI, and calmly walked from the hiding place to the sixth-floor window.

153. Did any police agency substantiate the Commission in any aspect?

No! In fact, no one ever saw Oswald with a rifle at any time!

154. What was the implication of the FBI evidence as to the rifle?

This was another "red flag." The Bureau was implicitly asking the Commission: "How could a rifle 'in a well-oiled condition' leave *no oil stains on the inside and outside of a paper bag?*" How could a person handle a rifle in that condition and leave no fingerprints or palm prints except for one of each when the person allegedly carried that bag in a "cupped" position? Where were, the FBI was asking, Oswald's prints that should have been on the *top* of the bag where he had grabbed it? R135.

155. Did the FBI find the fingerprints of the police who found the bag?

Another red flag! The FBI did *not* find the fingerprints of Lieutenant Day or Detective Studebaker on the bag sent to them by the Dallas police. This in spite of the fact that both Lieutenant Day and Detective Studebaker handled it. An amazing department of police. R135, 556; 7H139.

156. What does this mean?

That Lieutenant Day and Detective Studebaker should join Lee Harvey Oswald and Captain Fritz in the Smithsonian Institute! Four new species of mankind!

157. Would a court of law accept Mr. Frazier's and Mrs. Randall's testimony?

Absolutely, yes! They are the *only* witnesses to the size of the paper bag, how it was carried, and how it was constructed. The destruction of the bag in the Washington FBI Laboratory, whether by negligence or by extreme use, was not the fault of Oswald. In law, secondary evidence would be admissible. Furthermore, Mr. Frazier's and Mrs. Randle's testimony was not impeached, but upheld by *both* the FBI and the factual tests. R134; 2H240; 4H93; 16H513.

158. Did the Commission try another method to "tie the bag" to Oswald?

The Commission stated that when the paper bag was found, it had pieces of fiber from the blanket which Oswald used to hide the rifle. 4H81, 87.

159. How did the Commission attempt to "prove" their statement?
By sending the fibers to the FBI Laboratory. 4H31.

160. Did the FBI sustain the Commission's statement?
No! The Bureau refused to testify that the fibers in the paper bag were the same as those in the blanket. R137; 4H81.

161. What did the Commission then do?
Politely implied that the FBI was incompetent and printed a statement in the "Report" that converted the FBI "No" to a "Yes"!

162. Did the Commission conceal a vital fact from the "Report"?
Yes. Buried *deep* in the "Hearings" is the fact that the fibers which were found on the rifle *did not match those in* (1) the blanket; or (2) *in the paper bag*. 4H87.

163. What did this mean?
It proved that the blanket was *not* used to conceal *that* rifle. Thus, another portion of the Commission's case was destroyed.

164. Then how did the Commission "prove" its statement?
The Commission simply inserted a sentence in its "Report" that Oswald used stolen wrapping paper and tape from the shipping room.

165. Was this a true statement?
No. Mr. Troy West, an employee for sixteen years, testified that at *no* time did Oswald ever take any paper or tape from the shipping room. R136.

166. How did Mr. West substantiate his testimony?
He gave the Commission a lesson in shipping room procedure. Mr. Troy pointed out that for Oswald to take the tape he would have had to dismantle the tape machine to obtain *dry tape*. If the

machine was not dismantled then the tape would have to go through the water. The Commission admitted that Oswald had not walked around with four to five feet of wet tape for two or three days prior to the murder. 6H356-63.

167. Did any evidence prove the rifle was in a "brown, paper bag"?

No. the FBI *refused* to testify that there was any rifle in the bag submitted to them by the Dallas Police Department. How could they? There were *no* rifle markings, abrasions, or scratches on the *inside* or *outside* of that bag; nor were there *any* fingerprints on the *top* of that bag; nor any *oil* stains; and nor did the fibers match. 4H97.

168. When was this "brown paper bag" found?

According to Captain Fritz, *after* the shells and rifle were found.

169. Did Deputy Sheriff's Weitzman, Boone, or Mooney see the bag?

No!

170. What was written on the tag that identified this bag?

"A handmade bag of wrapping paper and tape was found in the southeast corner of the building *within a few feet of the cartridge cases.* Found next to the sixth-floor window gun fired from. May have been used to carry gun. (Signed) Lieutenant J. C. Day." 4H266.

171. Was the day or time, or both, specified?

No! Contrary to *all* police procedure.

172. In a court of law, would the bag be admitted in evidence?

The district attorney would, and must, convince the court that the "bag" was actually found on the sixth floor *at* the area alleged plus the *time* and *day*.

The Commission and the district attorney would have to convince not only the judge but also a jury of rational people that

(1) a brown paper bag, 34.8 inches in length, lying within four feet from the spot where the shells and cartridges were found, *was not seen by* (a) three deputy sheriffs, (b) a police captain, and (c) FBI agents; (2) yet, these three deputy sheriffs found a rifle which was partially hidden by cartons; and (3) all these men searched the area and *none* of them, except Lieutenant Day and Detective Studebaker, saw the "brown paper bag." 7H137-50.

173. Were nonpolice personnel on the sixth floor at this time?

Believe it or not, when the rifle and cartridges were found, the sixth floor had *not* been sealed off. A flock of newspapermen had been permitted to circulate all over the building. The police admitted that *anyone* who said he was a newspaperman, or showed credentials, true or forged, were permitted to roam around the building! 4H623

174. How did this "bag" get to this area less than ten feet from the rifle?

It was a *plant*, pure and simple.

175. Who planted it?

One of the conspirators converted himself into a newspaperman. Just as Oswald appointed himself secretary of a nonexistent club.

176. Did Captain Fritz find the paper bag?

No, he testified he was not there when it was found.

177. Who "found" this bag?

A man who leaves no fingerprints, Lieutenant Day. 4H266-67.

But *no* one knows at what time or on what day. Nor did the FBI ever testify that the bag submitted to them was the one found!

178. Was there a brown paper bag?

In a court of law, *no*. The implication of the fact that *no* police officer or newspaper reporter ever saw that "bag" could only lead to the conclusion that the bag was a *plant*. This "bag" was planted by a conspirator who was on the sixth floor *after* the rifle and cartridges were found. This bag was lying on the floor in full view, according to the Warren Commission, of more than twenty-five persons searching for clues, yet it was not discovered until picked up by Lieutenant Day. 7H137-50; Commission Exhibit Number 729.

179. Were pictures taken of this area where the rifle and shells were found?
Yes, approximately fifty pictures were taken by the police.

180. Were any pictures taken of the bag?
No! The police photographer ran out of film.

181. Did Lieutenant Day replace the bag on the spot where he found it?
Of course not. He worked for the Dallas Police Department.

182. So what did the Commission do?
They simply drew "dotted" lines on the spot where Lieutenant Day says he found the brown paper bag.

183. Did any of the deputy sheriffs uphold the Commission?
No. None of them ever saw the brown paper bag.

184. When was the rifle found?
At 1:22 p.m. 2H293; 17H107; 19H507.

185. Why is this paper bag so essential to the Commission's case?
Without the bag, the Commission has no case. The Commission has admitted that *no person*, at any time on the day of the murder, saw Oswald with a rifle. Therefore, the Commission has to have Oswald carrying a rifle in a sealed package. As a famous philosopher once stated: "Once a person starts to lie, he cannot stop until the truth comes forth."
There is no court of law who would accept the Commission's statement relating to the finding of the bag and the size of the bag. This "bag" was *not* accepted by the only two witnesses who

saw the original package carried by Oswald. Uncontradicted testimony of Mr. Frazier and Mrs. Randle stated the bag was not more than twenty-eight inches; yet the "bag" given to them by the Commission was thirty-six inches in length. This "bag" shown to them *had been made*, not by the FBI Laboratory in Washington, DC, which had the *original bag*, but by the *FBI Bureau* in Dallas, Texas, *who admitted they made the Commission's bag to fit the measurements of the rifle*. This fact the Commission did not inform the American people of in their "Report." This fact was *concealed* and *suppressed*. The actual measurements of the package carried by Oswald *is known by the FBI Laboratory in Washington, DC*, and the Commission *never* asked the FBI Laboratory to testify to those measurements for the obvious reason that the Commission knew, prior to the examination of Mr. Frazier and Mrs. Randle, the size of the bag, which was that testified to by those two witnesses!

186. What conclusion can be drawn from this "bag" episode?
Is the reader a rational person; let him draw his conclusion.

187. Did the FBI find any fingerprints or palm prints on the rifle?
No. Not even a partial one.

188. Who testified to that fact?
FBI Agent Latona, with twenty-five-years fingerprinting experience. 4H20-24.

189. How did he answer this question: "So as of November 23, 1963 you have not found an identifiable print on Exhibit Number 139 (the rifle)"?
"No," answered Mr. Latona, "that is right." 4H23.

190. Why were *no* identifiable prints found by Mr. Latona?
Because he testified that: "The rifle was a cheap one, the wood so old, that *it would not take a print*, and the metal *not* the best, hence the rifle was *not* susceptible to a latent print." 4H23.

191. When did the Dallas police inform the FBI of a "palm print"?

Seven days *after* the murder. 4H23-25.

192. To contradict the FBI, what did the Commission do?

They trotted out their own bullpen fingerprint expert, Lieutenant Day.

193. What was his experience as a fingerprint expert?

He studied at the FBI school under FBI expert, Mr. Latona. 4H250.

194. What did the student discover?

Lieutenant Day said he "lifted a palm print on the underside of the wood stock of the rifle." R123.

195. What other world-shaking feat did Lieutenant Day discover?

When he made the "lift" he could still "see the palm print on the underside of the gun." R123.

196. What *new* rule of fingerprinting did the Commission and Day create?

The Commission stated: "The lifting (of the print) was so complete in this case that there was a *no trace of a print on the rifle* when examined by Latona." R123; 26H832.

197. Was the Commission statement true or false?

False, a lie. FBI Agent Latona, the Bureau's chief fingerprint expert for more than a quarter of a century testified, under oath, "that there was *no* trace of a palm print" on the rifle; and also swore that there was *no* indication that "any lifting had been done or that there had been an attempt on the part of anyone else to *process* the rifle." His sworn testimony can be found in: 4H20-24; 4H261.

198. What did Lieutenant Day "accomplish"?

Lieutenant Day shocked every police department in the world when he swore that the lifting of the print was so complete that *no* trace was found!

199. Was it possible for *anyone* to obtain a print from that rifle?
No! Lieutenant Day *never* contradicted Mr. Latona's testimony.

200. Did the Commission attempt to solve this contradiction?
Yes, Mr. Rankin, the general counsel, requested Mr. Hoover to solve this riddle of the "disappearing fingerprint or palm print." Mr. Hoover wrote to Lieutenant Day to put his new discovery in writing. As of the day this book was sent to the publisher, there has been no reply. 26H828-29.

201. Was Lieutenant Day or FBI Agent Latona charged with perjury?
No.

202. Why did the Commission use Lieutenant Day's statement?
It was the only way to "prove" Oswald "used" the "found" rifle. Again, without the "print" the Commission had no case. R122-24.

203. Did Lieutenant Day *positively* identify the "palm print" as Oswald's?
No! Buried *deep* in the "Hearings" is the admission by Lieutenant Day that he could not positively identify the palm print as Oswald's! 4H261-63.

204. Then *legally* there were *no* palm prints or fingerprints?
That is correct. In a court of law, an impartial judge would *not* have permitted Lieutenant Day to testify before a jury. Lieutenant Day admitted that *no* one saw or witnessed the "lifting" of the alleged palm print; only he "saw" that palm print. Furthermore, Lieutenant Day would be compelled to admit that under the regulations of the Dallas Police Department, he should have taken photographs of the alleged "palm print." The taking of photographs of prints is standard police procedure in *all* police

departments. The testimony of FBI fingerprint expert Latona was never contradicted by Lieutenant Day and the further fact that Lieutenant Day admitted he could *not* positively identify the palm print only he "saw" as Oswald's would prevent his testimony being given to a jury. 4H40; 26H832.

The American concept of government is that the government is guided by law, not men. A close analysis of the Commission's case against Lee Harvey Oswald regarding the rifle reveals that the Commission's case is not based either on fact or law.

There is absolutely *no* evidence that Oswald carried a rifle into the Book Depository on the morning of November 22, 1963. There is *no* evidence that he fired any rifle bullet at the president. There is *no* evidence that the bullet and shells were fired from *that* rifle. There is *no* evidence that the *rifle* found by *Weitzman was actually* the identical rifle sent to the FBI Laboratory in Washington, DC.

-4-

Maggie's Drawers!

205. What was the Commission's "conclusion" regarding Oswald's marksmanship?
He "possessed the capability with a rifle which would have enabled him to commit the assassination."

206. Did the Commission prove its "conclusion"?
No. They proved the fact he could not have the capability.

207. Was the rifle Oswald allegedly purchased a special one?
No. R304.

208. How old was this rifle?
Twenty-three years old.

209. What did Oswald receive with this rifle?
A telescopic sight, *no* ammunition; *no* ammunition clip.

210. What reputation did the 6.5 Mannlicher-Carcano enjoy?
A bad one. [See] *Mechanix Illustrated*, October 1964.

211. How did Oswald obtain the rifle from Klein's of Chicago?
According to the FBI, Oswald purchased the rifle for $19.95 and it was sent to his PO Box in Dallas; but ordered by "A. Hidell."

212. What does this mean?
That Oswald was a "patsy." He purchases a rifle under an assumed name of "A. Hidell" but turns around and has it sent to a PO Box under his real name. Oswald was a "red herring" in the conspiracy. R118-22.

213. Did the Commission investigate the destruction of the P.O. records?

No.

214. Why?

It would have led to several paths away from Oswald.

215. Was the statement "true" that "the rifle could fire accurately"?

No. A half-truth which is more damaging than an outright lie.

216. What testimony was given by FBI ballistic expert, Mr. Frazier?

He testified that three shims had to be inserted under the telescopic mount of the Italian Mannlicher-Carcano rifle and that the sight had to be completely *rebuilt*. 3H443-4. Statement in volume 17.

217. Were any shims, or any evidence of shims being used, found?

No. 3H443.

218. What astonishing evidence was "buried" by the Commission?

A statement, buried in volume 25, that the experts revealed that the telescopic sight was *adjusted for a left-handed man*. 25H799.

219. What information did Mr. Hoover give to the Commission?

That the rifle given to them by the Dallas police was a "right-handed, bolt-action, military rifle." FBI report, volume 5, paragraph B.

220. Could a right-handed man use a telescopic sight for a left hand?

No, not unless the Commission believes Oswald was cross-eyed.

221. What other information was given to the Commission by Mr. Frazier?

"... every time we changed the adjusting screws to move the crosshairs in the telescopic sight in one direction it also affected the movement of the point of impact in the other direction."

222. What does this testimony mean in relation to accuracy?

That Oswald did *not* fire those shots *nor* was the Italian rifle used to murder President Kennedy. Mr. Frazier, when making the tests for the Commission, was shooting at a stationary target. Thus, he could make the necessary adjustments by "twiddling" with the telescopic sight until the subject was in the "crosshairs" and then fired the gun.

However, and this is the vital distinction, President Kennedy was not only sitting in a moving automobile but he was also moving his body to wave to the crowd. Thus, the alleged rifleman on the sixth floor would have had to be constantly "twiddling" with the telescopic sight to bring the president within the "crosshairs."

There is *no* human being alive that can "twiddle" with a telescopic sight with one hand and fire a military rifle with the other.

Thus, Agent Frazier's testimony (Q. 221) was applicable only to a *stationary target* with the *further* proviso that three shims be used. 3H405, 443-44; 26H104.

223. Did Mr. Hoover support the Commission's "accuracy" statement?

No! He reaffirmed his agent's testimony. Mr. Hoover stated that the rifle given to the FBI by the Dallas police "could not be properly aligned with the target" *but* that it could be repaired so that it could fire accurately. 26H104.

The Director of the FBI was correct since the rifle was repaired but that does not alter the fact that the rifle, *at the time of alleged* shooting, was *defective* and, as Mr. Hoover so stated, was an inaccurate rifle. 26H104.

224. Thus, were not two important conditions omitted by the Commission?

Yes. For these two reasons the FBI *refused* to state that Oswald *used* the rifle and instead said he "owned" the rifle.

225. Did the telescopic sight have any value to a rifleman?

No! Mr. Frazier said the defect was "structural." 3H405; 26H104.

226. In law, what is the effect of Mr. Frasier's and Mr. Hoover's testimony?

The Commission's case *collapsed*. The rifle needed (a) three shims which were never found nor did the FBI ever testify that the rifle had shim scratches on it; (b) the telescopic sight was structurally inaccurate; and (c) the sight was for a *left-handed rifleman*. 15H799; 26H104!

227. What additional sensational testimony was given by Mr. Frazier?

That the Italian rifle was in such a shape that it was worthless as a firearm! His testimony: "No, sir; the lands and grooves were worn [...] the interior of the surface was roughened from corrosion [or] wear." [3H394.]

The Commission also buried the testimony of R. Simmons, firearms expert, who aided in the *repair* of the Italian rifle. 3H443; 26H104.

228. In a court of law, were the Commission's "conclusions" of any value?

Since the "conclusions" were not upheld by any proof, the "conclusions" had no value. The FBI qualified its alleged endorsement by stating that the tests to determine those conditions were *not* identical to the factual conditions which surrounded the condition of the rifle.

229. How long did it take for the killer to fire three shots?

The Commission said between 4.8 seconds and 5.6 seconds.

230. What did the Commission do to prove their "own" statement?

The Commission used the evidence of four men: FBI Agent Frazier; R. Simmons, chief of U.S. Army Weapons Evaluation Research Laboratory; Major E. Anderson, Marksmanship Branch, U.S. Marine Corps; and Major Sergeant Zahm, NCO in Charge of Marksmanship Training Unit, Quantico, Virginia, Marine Base.

231. What was the testimony of FBI Agent Frazier?

"From my own experience, in shooting over the years, when you shoot 175 or 260 feet away, which is less than a hundred yards, with a telescopic sight, you should have no difficulty in hitting your target ... I mean it requires no training to shoot a weapon with a telescopic sight once you know that you must put the crosshairs on the target and that is all that is necessary." (Tell that to the Marines!)

232. What facts did the Agent fail to state in his answer?

Mr. Frazier failed to add to his answer the facts that he was (1) talking about a *stationary target*; (2) that he was speaking of a telescopic sight fitted for a *right-handed man* but the Italian rifle was fitted for a left-handed rifleman; and (3) he used an accurate telescopic sight while the alleged rifleman used a sight that was "structurally defective." Let's not change the rules!

233. What was the testimony of R. Simmons, chief of U.S. Weapons Laboratory?

"... in order to achieve three hits, it would not be required that a man be an exceptional shot. A proficient man with a weapon, yes."

234. What was the testimony of Major Sergeant Zahm?

"... the shot that struck the president in the head at a distance of 265.3 feet was an 'easy' shot." R192, 11H306.

235. Who actually went to the firing range to prove his testimony?

Only FBI Agent Frazier and he failed in his tests.

236. How did the Commission obtain "evidence" from Major Anderson?

The Commission attempted to prove, by using only *hypothetical* questions given to Major Anderson and Major Sergeant Zahm, that the average serviceman could fire a defective rifle with sufficient accuracy to hit the neck and head of a person twisting his body while riding in an automobile traveling between the speed of ten to twelve miles an hour at a growing distance between 175 feet to 265 feet away, from the height of sixty feet, through the branches of a tree which permitted the rifleman only .8 of a second to sight and pull the trigger for the first shot.

Neither the sergeant nor the major went on the range to prove it!

237. Were tests actually conducted by the Commission?
Yes, on November 27, 1963.

238. What did the tests prove?
That Lee H. Oswald was the world's greatest marksman.

239. Who were the riflemen and what were the results?
Mr. Frazier: three shots fired in six seconds.
Mr. Killion: three shots fired in nine seconds.
Mr. Cunningham: three shots fired in eight seconds. 3H403-05.

240. What did the tests prove?
That the Commission was living in a dream world. *None of the experts* fired three shots in the *maximum time limit* of 5.6 seconds.

241. Did any of the experts hit the *aiming point*?
No. They all missed. They hit to the right of the point. 3H403-05.

242. What evidence did the Commission conceal from the "Report"?

The vital fact that the *target was placed only* forty-five feet away. The president's car was between 175 to 265 feet away. 3H403-05.

243. What did the tests prove?

That three of the Commission's own experts, with nine shots, could not hit a stationary target forty-five feet away; but Oswald, with *no* target practice in a period of three years, could hit a target, moving, from not less than 175 feet away at a sixty-foot angle. 3H403-07.

244. What else did the tests prove?

The time limit of 5.6 seconds was impossible. 3H403-05.

245. Did Mr. Frazier conduct a further test?

Yes, by pulling the *bolt* of the rifle he averaged 4.7 seconds. He admitted that during this test he did not aim the rifle at anything.

246. Was the Commission satisfied with these tests?

No, and the Commission instructed the FBI to hold further tests. The FBI again selected Mr. Frazier as their best rifleman.

247. What was the result of this second test?

This test, held on March 16, 1964, was a failure. Using the same rifle and again using a stationary target, he averaged 6.2 seconds. 3H407.

248. Did Mr. Frazier hit the target?

No. Every shot was a 5" x 5"; that is, each shot was five inches to the right of the aiming point and five inches high. Five misses! 4H406.

249. Did the FBI Agent give any explanation for his failures?

Mr. Frazier said the inaccuracy [was] due to "an uncorrectable mechanical deficiency in the telescopic sight." 3H406.

250. What did the Commission now do to prove Oswald's marksmanship?

Naturally, they ordered new tests with new riflemen. 3H441.

251. Who did the Commission select for their final conclusive test?

Three riflemen who held the rank of Master Rifleman from the National Rifle Association. The *final* authority regarding marksmanship.

252. What would a law court say about this final test?

That the [tests] were as phony as plastic baloney! 3H444-47.

253. What were the conditions of the tests?

(1) Each rifleman was placed on a thirty-foot platform; the sixth floor was sixty-feet high. Thus, the *angle* of fire was wrong, by fifty percent.

(2) Each rifleman shot at a *stationary* target located at a distance equal to the distance from the building to the automobile.

254. What was the result of this final test?

Each rifleman fired six shots. *All* eighteen shots failed to hit the target area of the back, neck and head! 3H446-47; 17H261-62.

255. Why were these tests inadmissible in a law court?

(1) The riflemen had all the time they desired to pull the trigger for the first shot. R193.

(2) The Commission admitted that the sixth-floor killer had only eight-tenths of a second to fire his first shot. R98, 105.

(3) The president's car was in motion, the test was not. R98.

(4) The riflemen used an *accurate* rifle and scope! 3H443; 16H104.

256. What additional fact was concealed from the "Report"?

They concealed the fact that the riflemen, during the "dry" run, feared to pull the trigger because they believed the firing pin would break! 3H447.

257. What did all these tests prove?

That the rifle was a worthless weapon and that it was not the weapon used to murder the president of the United States.

258. What Soviet defector was used as a witness by the Commission?

None other than a former Soviet secret service officer.

259. What did this defector testify to regarding Oswald's marksmanship?

He testified that "Oswald was an extremely poor shot and it was necessary for the persons who accompanied him on hunting trips to provide him with game."

260. Was this ex-Soviet secret service agent lying?

Under American law, since the ex-agent was a Commission witness, his testimony, uncontradicted, is acceptable as being the truth. This witness, who defected after Oswald had returned to the United States, brought with him files from his agency. He knew all about Oswald while Oswald was in the Soviet Union, plus the fact that Soviet intelligence considered Oswald to be a CIA agent.

261. Did this ex-agent say that Oswald was a Communist Party member?

No.

262. Who was this former Soviet secret service agent?

The person was Yuri Nosenko, who fled the USSR in February 1964. His testimony is suppressed. It is known as Document Number 434, National Archives.

263. Did the Commission inadvertently prove that Oswald did not purchase the Italian rifle given to the FBI by the Dallas police?

Yes!

264. How?

By accepting Mrs. Marina Oswald's testimony that she first saw a rifle in February 1963. Mrs. Oswald said: "… that it (the rifle) was always either in a corner, standing up in a corner, or on the Shelf." She also testified that the rifle in their home had *no* telescopic sight. 1H13-21.

265. Where can this evidence be found?

In the National Archives, Commission Basic Material Number 344. Even assuming Mrs. M. Oswald's date is incorrect, her testimony that the rifle in her home had *no* telescopic sight was never impeached.

266. What does her testimony imply?

That there were more than two rifles involved, and that the Ryder testimony stating that he had mounted a telescopic sight for a man named "Oswald" is correct. 11H224-231, 245-53; 22H531.

267. Since Mrs. Oswald's testimony destroyed the "rifle" evidence against her husband, what did the Commission then do?

They created a new theory of law called the "Three F's."

268. What are the three F's?

Fact, fiction, and fancy.

269. How was the Three F's theory used by the Commission?

(1) They used the testimony of Postal Inspector Holmes to "prove" Oswald had received a 6.5 Mannlicher-Carcano rifle from Klein's.

(2) This inspector was like the proverbial pile in China. He was all over the place, conveniently selected, by the Commission.

(3) He was also the witness who testified that the three shots fired at President Kennedy took between twenty and thirty seconds. 7H291.

(4) He testified that Oswald *owned* the PO Box to which the rifle was to be delivered; he did *not* see the rifle delivered. R118.

(5) He could not explain why the post office destroyed evidence regarding postal regulations to box rentals.

(6) He testified that the Klein advertisement used by Oswald to purchase the Italian rifle was in the November 1963 *Field & Stream*.

(7) The Commission, however, stated that "Klein's" received Oswald's order on March 13, 1963, which order was clipped to a coupon from the February 1963 issue of *American Rifleman*.

(8) But the February 1963 issue of *American Rifleman* does *not* contain an advertisement from Klein's offering that Italian rifle.

(9) That same advertisement listed no rifle at $12.78.

Thus, how could Oswald clip a coupon for a rifle that was *not* advertised? Holmes Exhibit Number 2.

270. What do the above nine points prove?
The juxtaposition of fact and fiction!

271. Where is "fancy"?
"Fancy" that the public would swallow the above.

272. To whom was the rifle sent?
"A. Hidell."

273. To what PO Box owner?
Oswald's rented post office box. 17H636, 677-78.

274. How could a package sent to "A. Hidell" be in Oswald's box?
Ask the post office.

275. Was this a violation of postal regulations?
Yes, Regulation Number 355, Section 111 (B), paragraph 4.

276. What admission was made by Inspector Holmes?
"No other person than Oswald was authorized to receive mail" from Oswald's post office box. R119.

277. Did Oswald authorize any person to receive his mail?

No. The FBI, Secret Service, and Dallas police could not find any.

278. Did the Commission or any government agency produce any witness that saw Oswald pick up any kind of package from his PO Box?
No.

279. What does this imply?
That since *no* P.O. employee ever identified Oswald, any person could have used Oswald's name to pick up a package addressed to "A. Hidell." The person would simply present the package form and obtain the package. R118-21.

280. Then what is the use of a name on a PO Box?
Ask the postal authorities.

281. Did the Commission find evidence that Oswald collected a package containing an Italian Mannlicher-Carcano rifle from Klein's?
No.

282. In law, what did the Commission prove?
Nothing. This is correct for the Commission produced not one single iota of evidence that connected Oswald with the Italian rifle. The Commission proved that Klein's accepted an order from an "A. Hidell" in Oswald's handwriting. But did they, because Q. 269 suggests that they could not accept an order not published in a national magazine. But, assuming Klein's filled the order. The order was filled and given to the truck driver at the Klein's shipping room. From here on, there is no evidence of any delivery to (1) the post office box in Oswald's name; (2) to Oswald himself. In a court of law, the Commission proved nothing.

283. How did the Commission attempt to prove Oswald's marksmanship?
They delved into his history as a U.S. Marine.

284. What did the Commission publish regarding his marksmanship?

The Commission considered Oswald's Marine Corps record and based on this record said that Oswald, on November 22, 1963, used a worthless rifle, with a telescopic sight set for a left-handed man, with a rifle that had to be rebuilt, fired three shots from this rifle and hit a man that was sixty feet down and 275 feet away. He was the only man to do this!

285. Did the Commission prove its statement?
No.

286. What did the Marine Corps think of Oswald's marksmanship?
The Corps flatly stated he was a "poor shot." 19H16.

287. What was his highest score?
212. R191.

288. Did the Corps think this was an "excellent" score?
No. Oswald's record was *below* his fellow marines. 19H16-18.

289. What was Oswald's record when he received his discharge?
190! Worse than when he started! 19H16-18.

290. What was Oswald's M.O. specialty?
Radio, radar, and electronics.

291. Did the Commission prove that Oswald used the Italian rifle for target practice?
No. The Commission admitted this fact.

292. Did Mrs. Marina Oswald ever see her husband target practicing?
No.

293. Did *any* person ever see Oswald target practicing?
No.

294. Then how did the Commission *prove* Oswald's "proficiency"?
By simply printing a statement that Oswald became "proficient" by working the bolt of his rifle as his wife stated she saw him do it. R128, 192, 645.

295. What new military practice did the Warren Commission create?
All members of the Armed Services should work the bolt of the rifles and this will make them "marksman" and "sharpshooters"!

296. What did the Commission actually prove to a jury?
That the FBI received a rifle from the Dallas Police Department. The FBI then proved that the rifle was worthless and inaccurate. 3H443.

-5-

Till Death Do Us Part

297. Who used the hammer and nails on Lee Harvey Oswald?
His wife, Mrs. Marina Oswald.

298. How was her testimony obtained?
By threats, intimidation, and bribery.

299. Who did these things?
Every government agency involved.

300. Was Mrs. Marina Oswald in the United States legally?
No, she lied when she said she had never been a Communist member.

301. Is she subject to deportation?
Yes, under the then and present government immigration laws.

302. Did the Commission have the right to "waive" that law?
No, they could only grant immunity from prosecution.

303. Was Mrs. Oswald threatened by means other than deportation?
Yes, for there is an implication that during her incarceration she was threatened with the loss of her children. 1H78; 18H541-47.

304. Is this legal in the United States of America?
Yes. There have been several cases of this new "humane" tactic. In Illinois, during the Sixties, a mother of two minor children desired to return to her homeland, Yugoslavia. The judge permitted the mother to only take the younger child but placed the older child in an orphanage. His reasoning was that the thirteen-year-old knew the dangers of communism!

305. Would this decision be upheld by the U.S. Supreme Court?

Yes. In 1966 the U.S. Supreme Court approved an Iowa Supreme Court decision that any child may be removed from natural parents if those parents lived a "bohemian life." The parents were artists!

Following this decision to its logical conclusion, any judge may now remove children from their natural parents based on the interpretation of "bohemian." The children of an artist, author, songwriter, or sculptor can now be removed from their parents.

The courts accelerated Orwell's *1984* to 1964.

306. What other method did the Commission use to "convict" Oswald?

The Commission permitted Mrs. Oswald to condemn her husband in a national TV broadcast by saying by saying: "Facts tell me Lee shot Kennedy."

307. How much money has Mrs. Oswald earned or received?

By the end of 1964 close to $190,000.00. 1H469; 2H132; 5H604.

308. Who approved her "business and financial" advisor?

Lee Rankin, general counsel; Department of Justice, Attorney General Katzenbach.

309. What advice did Mr. Katzenbach give to Mrs. Oswald?

"To talk to no one but federal investigations."–*New York Times*.

310. What did Mrs. Oswald testify regarding the FBI?

She testified: "If I didn't want to answer (the questions) that they told me that if I wanted to live in this country, I would have to help in this matter, even though they were often irrelevant. That is the FBI." 1H78-90.

311. Were there any threats to deport her?

Yes. Commission Exhibit Number 344, National Archives.

312. Was Mrs. Oswald in "protective custody"?
This is Chief Justice Warren's remark after her testimony: "We can understand Mrs. Oswald's desire to live a perfectly normal life with *her* children ... but she may feel free from this moment on, that she is under no protection ..." 1H79; 7H325; 18H541-47, 642. National Archives Number 344.

313. What other "evidence" did Mrs. Oswald give to the Commission?
That her husband attempted to murder Richard Nixon.

314. Did the Commission accept her "evidence"?
No. Even fools sometimes know when they are being taken!

315. What other "evidence" did Mrs. Oswald give to the Commission?
That Oswald attempted to murder ex-General Walker on April 10, 1963.

316. Were there any witnesses to the Walker incident?
Yes.

317. What were the police told?
The witness informed the police that immediately after the shooting he saw two men, one carrying a rifle, run away from the site.

318. What other vital evidence did he give to the police?
Each man got into a different auto and drove away. 26H437-38.

319. Did Oswald know how to drive?
No.

320. What evidence did the police find at the Walker home?
A .30 slug that could not be ballistically tested.

321. What did the FBI report to the Commission about this slug?

That the .30 slug was the same as a 7.65 bullet which *cannot* be discharged from a 6.5 Mannlicher-Carcano rifle! 3H424-40.

322. How did the Commission attempt to negate the FBI statement?

From the Dallas Police Department witness bullpen came forth Chief of Dallas Police Detectives, Stevenson, who said that the bullet came from the Italian rifle ... "in all probability." 3H429.

323. What was the Commission attempting to achieve?

A reading of the "Report" and the "Hearings" revealed that whenever the Commission obtained evidence that conflicted with their theory, the Commission simply called in another agency in an attempt to negate the testimony given by the original agency. The Commission then published the testimony of the agency closest to the theory.

324. What did the Commission prove in the Walker case?

That the FBI Laboratory, costing millions of dollars, was (1) incompetent; or (2) issuing "phony" tests.

325. Since Oswald did not drive, how did he get to Walker's home?

Mrs. Oswald said he returned by using the bus line.

326. She did not answer the question, so how did he?

Using a "flying saucer"! This answer is as good as any.

327. Was the rifle fully assembled when "Oswald" made this attempt?

Mrs. Oswald said the rifle was assembled when in the blanket.

328. Did the FBI, the Secret Service or the Dallas police locate any witness to connect with this incident?

No.

329. Where did "Oswald" carry the rifle?

As he never attempted to murder Walker he carried no rifle.

330. Why did the Commission attempt to connect Oswald with Walker?

The Commission was attempting to foist upon the world the impression that Oswald was a psychotic who had the urge to kill; thus the more persons he killed, or attempted to kill, the greater the impact upon world opinion to accept the Commission's "conclusions."

331. Could Oswald be found guilty for the Walker incident?
No!

-6-

THE MAN WHO WAS NOT THERE!

332. What was the police radio broadcast, at 12:43 p.m., regarding the description of the man wanted as a suspect?

"9-513[:] 'The wanted man in this (the Kennedy murder) is a slender white male about thirty, five-foot ten inches, 165 pounds, carrying what looked to be a .30-.30, or some type of Winchester.' 9-531[:] 'Yes, a rifle.' 531-9[:] 'Any clothing description?' 9-531[:] 'Current witness can't remember.'"

333. What is the code reference?

"9" is Inspector Sawyer of the Dallas police. "531" is police headquarters. Sawyer Exhibit Number A, volume 21.

334. Did another call go out to the Dallas police force?

Yes, a code 3 which said: "Hold as a suspect, a white male approximately thirty, slender build, five-foot nine inches, weight 165 pounds." 17H401.

335. Did the police ever broadcast Oswald's name and description?

Never. The Commission admitted this fact. R236.

336. Was District Attorney Wade's statement, on November 24, true, that a "description and *name* of Oswald went out to the police?" 26H819-29.

This was false. He was trying to sway public opinion. R236.

337. Captain Gannaway of the Dallas police informed the press that Oswald was wanted because (1) Oswald missed a roll call; and (2) Mr. Truly could not account for his absence. Was this true?

No. A falsity; for *no* roll call was ever made after President Kennedy was murdered since many of the employees left the building. R156; 3H187; 6H321; 7H382-86; 22H632, 655-56.

338. Captain Fritz said that the police were seeking Oswald because they had found the rifle on the sixth floor. Is this true?
No! The rifle was *not* discovered until 1:22 p.m. and the police broadcast was at 12:45 p.m. and did not contain any description of the clothes or person. *New York Times*, November 24, 1963; 3H294; 23H843-44.

339. Did the police rely upon Oswald's fingerprints or palm print?
No! The rifle was not found until 1:22 p.m.

340. Was any clothing description of any kind broadcasted?
No! 6H321; 21H392-93.

341. How did the police "know" that Oswald was the killer?
The Commission never answered this question and never sought to obtain the answer. The Commission admitted that at *no* time, from 12:20 p.m. until Oswald was in the police station was there any evidence to connect Oswald with the murder. The police just "knew"!

342. Did any federal agency or Dallas police authority testify to the identity of the person giving the 12:45 p.m. broadcast?
No!

343. Did the 12:45 p.m. broadcast, code 3, apply to Officer Tippit?
No. To all policemen *except* Officer Tippit! 17H397; 23H843-44.

344. Was he given any specific instructions?
Yes. To move into the Oak Cliff area. One block from Ruby. 17H401.

345. Did Tippit acknowledge this code 3?
The evidence is conflicting. 17H379 vs. 23H444; 17H901; 23H840-50.

346. How many policemen in the Dallas Police Department?
About 1,700 men and women.

347. Did any of them locate any man described by the broadcast?
Yes, in a city of 800,000, was Officer Tippit.

348. Then Oswald was the only man fitting that description?
Yes. Oswald was the only man in Dallas who was (1) white, (2) thirty years old, (3) slender build, (4) five-foot nine inches, and 165 pounds.

349. Was Oswald the *only* white male of that description in Dallas?
Believe it or not, *yes*, so sayeth the Dallas Police Department.

350. Would a rational person believe the above statement?
Rational people do not deal with the Dallas Police Department.

351. What time did Oswald leave his Beckley Avenue room?
The Commission stated at 1:00 p.m. and [that he] walked "briskly" to the Tippit murder site. R163.

352. Is that a correct statement?
No.

353. Why?
Mrs. E. Roberts, the housekeeper, testified that Oswald left his room and she saw him waiting at a bus stop. The time was 1:04 p.m. R158, 163.

354. Did the Commission conduct a test to determine the walking time?

Yes. A "brisk" walk took seventeen minutes, forty-five seconds. 6H434.

355. According to the police "call" sheet when were they notified?
1:16 p.m.

356. Based on the "call" sheet, could Oswald have killed Tippit?
No! He would have arrived one minute, forty-five-seconds *late*.

357. Why did the Commission conceal this fact from the "Report"?
It would have proved Oswald innocent of the Tippit murder.

358. What is the distance between Oswald's room and the murder site?
Nine-tenths of a mile; slightly more than a seven-furlough race.

359. Did the Commission ever contradict Mrs. Roberts' time?
No. Therefore Oswald was at the bus stop at 1:04 p.m. 7H439.

360. Would a court of law accept Mrs. Roberts' testimony?
Yes. The Commission produced no conflicting evidence.

361. Is there any other evidence to substantiate her evidence?
Yes. The fact that Oswald was (1) not a racehorse; (2) was not an athlete who could run nine-tenths of a mile in four minutes; (3) the world's mile record is now three minutes, fifty-three seconds; (4) the Commission tester took seventeen minutes, forty-five seconds.

362. Is Mrs. Roberts supported by any additional testimony?
In the fact that Officer Tippit was murdered between 1:06-1:08 p.m.!

363. Who proved the time of Officer Tippit's murder?
The *Commission*. 3H306; 24H215.

364. How did the Commission do this?

By admitting it relied upon the sworn testimony of Mrs. H. Markham.

365. What time did Mrs. Markham swear she saw the murder of Tippit?

1:06 p.m. 3H306; 24H215.

366. Where was Oswald?

According to the Commission running from the bus stop, at 1:04 p.m., at a world record speed for nine-tenths of a mile, to murder Officer Tippit!

367. What did this event make Oswald?

On this day: (1) the greatest marksman; (2) the fastest runner!

368. Did Oswald get there in time?

According to the testimony he never got to the Tippit site.

369. Did any witnesses substantiate Mrs. Markham's testimony?

Yes, two men: Mr. Benavides and Mr. Bowley. R484, 447-48; 24H202.

370. What did Mr. Bowley see and what was the time element?

Mr. Bowley, under oath, said that at 1:10 p.m. he saw Officer Tippit "next to the left front wheel of the squad car, *on the street.*"

371. What did he do when he saw this scene?

Mr. Bowley took the auto's police "mike" from a man trying to raise police headquarters and said: "A policeman has been shot. He is lying out there in the street. I think he is dead." 23H857-58; 24H202.

372. Who was the man he took the "mike" from?

Mr. Benavides, who admitted he did not know how to operate it.

373. Did the police "call" sheet substantiate Mr. Bowley?
Yes. 23H857-58.

374. What time did the police log that his call?
Between 1:15 and 1:16 p.m.

375. Did Mr. Benavides substantiate Mr. Bowley's call?
Yes.

376. Where was Mr. Benavides when the shooting took place?
He was sitting in his truck fifteen to twenty [feet] away from Tippit's auto. When the killer fled, he got out of his truck. 4H444-48.

377. How can the time 1:06 and 1:16 p.m. be explained?
Mrs. Markham's time of 1:06 p.m. and Mr. Bowley's time of 1:10 p.m. is *not* in conflict. Nor does the police call sheet of 1:16 p.m. conflict with the other two time elements.

A court of law would accept Mrs. Markham's time since she witnessed the shooting and the Commission *accepted* her evidence as true. The court would also accept Mr. Bowley's time of 1:10 p.m. since he arrived at the scene and Officer Tippit was lying on the street. Thus, the shooting had already occurred and Mr. Bowley's evidence corroborated Mrs. Markham's that the shooting had occurred *prior* to his coming onto the scene.

The police "time" of 1:15 or 1:16 p.m. simply means that the police received a call at that time which informed them that a police officer had been killed. The police simply "logged" the time they were notified, not the time when the shooting took place.

The Commission was in a quandary for if they accepted Mrs. Roberts' testimony, which they had to do under the laws of evidence, Oswald could not have been on the scene at 1:06 or 1:10 p.m. Thus, the Commission had to *move up the time* to 1:16 p.m. by deceiving the American public that Tippit had been murdered at 1:16 p.m. The Commission fraudulently relied upon the police "log" which only stated the time as to when they received the Bowley call.

The Commission *suppressed the Bowley affidavit* from the "Report," but it can be found in 24H202.

The CBS four-hour report on the Warren Commission *also conveniently overlooked* this vital affidavit.[3] However, this was only one of the factors overlooked by that broadcasting system!

378. Who identified Oswald as the murder of Officer Tippit?
No one! No person legally identified Oswald.

379. Did Mr. Bowley?
No. When he arrived at 1:10 p.m. the killer had fled.

380. Did Mr. Benavides?
No! He was less than twenty feet away when he saw the killer.

381. What description of the killer did he give to the police?
The killer was (1) dark-complexioned; and (2) had curly hair.

382. Did the police use this description over the police radio?
Yes. This was broadcasted at 1:32 p.m. 6H452; 17H416.

383. As Mr. Benavides had seen the killer did the police ask him to view the police lineup which contained Lee Harvey Oswald?
Of course not. The police *seem to know* that it was Oswald they wanted and since Mr. Benavides had already given them a description that *did not match Oswald*, they did not ask him or let him. R166.

384. However, did Mr. Benavides testify before the Commission?
Yes. He swore that he could not identify Oswald. 6H452.

---

[3] Marks is referring here to the June 25-28, 1967 *CBS New Inquiry: The Warren Report.*

385. How did Mrs. H. Markham describe the murderer?

He had *bushy hair*, wore a *white* shirt, and a *white jacket*. "He was not a very big man; he was *short* as well as I can remember."

386. What type of shirt was Oswald wearing when he left his room?

A brown shirt.

387. What type of jacket?

A *tan* jacket

388. What was Mrs. Markham's physical condition at the Oswald lineup?

According to Detective Leavelle she was "in an *absolute state of shock*" and was unable to view the lineup. Captain Fritz admitted to the Commission she was sick and *unable to give any physical description*. Thus, any statement she made at the lineup was illegal. 4H212; 7H262.

389. What testimony would a law court give to a jury?

The description given to the police at the murder site would be part of the "res gestae"[4] and not subject to any kind of pressure. Her "identification" of Oswald was a travesty of justice, made in a "state of shock." 20H577; 24H316.

390. What famous picture substantiated her testimony?

---

[4] According to the Cornell Law School Legal Encyclopedia (online), this Latin phrase (meaning "things done" or "things transacted") refers to "the events or circumstances at issue, as well as other events that are contemporaneous with or related to them. Courts previously employed this term in order to admit otherwise inadmissible hearsay. The term has since been put to disuse by scholars and legislators. In evidence law, for example, the Federal Rules of Evidence, Rules 803(1) ['present sense impression'], 803(2) ['excited utterance'], 803(3) ['declaration of existing physical condition'], and 803(4) ['declaration of past physical condition'] now specifically encompass and limit what was previously used as *res gestae*."

The USIS[5] picture with showed Oswald at the time of the arrest wearing a "*tan*" shirt, hair combed, light complexion.

391. Did the Commission also state that they had twelve other witnesses?
Yes. Twelve witnesses. R166.

392. Did these 12 Witnesses identify Oswald?
No. The Commission relied mainly upon Mrs. Davis and Mr. Scoggins.

393. What did Mr. Scoggins testify to the Commission?
(1) He saw a man "who never looked at him (Scoggins)" but he did not see Mrs. Markham. (2) He was able to select Oswald from the illegal lineup; but (3) when an FBI or Secret Service agent asked him to [pick out] Oswald's 8" x 12" face from other similar photographs, he picked another face as the murderer! 3H327, 335, 337. Mr. Scoggins admitted he did not see or hear Mrs. Markham at the time of the shooting. 3H333-37.

394. Did Miss Davis identify Oswald?
Legally, no! To the Dallas police at the murder scene, Miss Davis informed them that she did *not* see his face or his *physical* features. She made a definite statement to the police, recorded by them, that she could *not* identify the killer. However, when she was called before the Commission, some ninety days later, she remembered Oswald and said she saw him at the scene. 3H345; 4H449-50.

395. In a court of law how would a judge rule on the contradiction?
Her first statement would be given priority since that statement would be considered part of the "res gestae."

396. Were any other witnesses selected to identify Oswald?

---

[5] A possible reference to the United States Information Agency.

Yes. The Commission admitted that they relied upon four witnesses who selected Oswald from a picture two to four months later.

397. How can the Commission's case vs. Oswald be characterized?

What the witnesses said was not heard; what the Commission "heard" was not said. The evidence did not support the "Report."

398. What illegal conduct did the Commission accept as evidence?

The gross illegal conduct of the Dallas police in the method of identification lineups. The Dallas police violated every rule of law enunciated by the U.S. Supreme Court regarding identification of alleged criminals. Nowhere in the "Report" is there any statement by the Chief Justice of the United States, Mr. Warren, condemning this illegality. Not only was the conduct of the police illegal; but the moral crime of not condemning this practice so as to infer the guilt of Oswald, is of far greater magnitude.

399. Under legal procedures was Oswald legally identified?

No, not unless the Commission overruled the U.S. Supreme Court!

400. Why do police departments all over the world consider the Tippit murder case a "mystery within a mystery"?

For the exciting reason that the number of shots do not match the number of bullets in the body; and the number of shells found beside the body; and the fact that there are *either more bullet holes than bullets extracted from the body* or *more bullets and less holes!*

401. How many shots did Mrs. Markham and Mr. Benavides hear?

Three shots. R165-66.

402. How many bullets were recovered from Tippit's body?

The Commission says *four*. Four bullets. R172.

403. How many bullets did the Dallas police say hit Tippit?
Three, only three! 24H253.

404. Then how could the police obtain four bullets from three holes?
That is what other police departments would like to know!

405. Did the Commission request the autopsy report on Tippit?
This is another mystery. To solve it the Commission need only to have asked the police autopsy physician or subpoenaed its records. *However, there is no official Tippit autopsy report!* Why?

406. Did the Commission imply that more than three shots were fired?
Yes, they imply five shots! 3H473.

407. *What important Secret Service report was suppressed?*
Secret Service Document Number 563. Commission File Number 87. December 11, 1963.

408. Why was this document suppressed in the "Report" and "Hearings"?
The Secret Service uncovered evidence which implicated, impliedly, put simply, some Dallas policemen were involved in Tippit's murder.

409. Was Tippet impressed by the broadcast of the wanted man?
No. Tippit, without drawing his gun from his holster, simply got out of his squad car and calmly walked toward him.

410. Would a jury of rational men believe that any policeman would approach the suspected murderer of President Kennedy in this fashion?
That is what the Commission would have everyone believe.

411. Did Officer Tippit know this man he approached?
If he did not, then he certainly believed he had nothing to fear.

412. How many shells or cartridges were found?
Four.

413. Who found them?
Mr. Benavides found two, and one each by the Davis sisters.
R168, 3H445.

414. What was the caliber of the revolver taken from Oswald?
A .38 revolver.

415. What kind of shells or cartridges were discovered?
Several types! Included was a shell not capable of being
discharged from a .38 revolver. An *automatic shell!* R171-72;
17H417-20.

416. Was Oswald's revolver tested to see if it had been used?
No!

417. What is the meaning of this failure to test his revolver?
It is standard police procedure, *except* in Dallas, to always
examine a firearm to see if it has been recently discharged and
whether or not the weapon is capable of discharging bullets.
Owners of firearms know that bullets leave traces of firing and it
is a presumption of law that if there are no firing tracers then the
weapon has not been used. According to the Commission,
Oswald *had no time* to do anything from 1:16 to 1:45 [or] to
clean a revolver. The presumption must be, in law, that Oswald's
gun was not a weapon used to murder Officer Tippit.

418. What happened to the four bullets "found" in Tippit's
body and the four shells given to the police by the witnesses who
found them?
The police, under oath, testified that they had *mixed up* the
bullets and shells in such a way that *no* positive identification

could be made. Negligence or conspiracy? 4H449-50; 7H68-69; 24H415.

419. Did the police submit any bullet to the FBI for identification?
The police first *withheld* three bullets and gave only *one* to the Bureau, known as "Q or C"-13. 3H474-75; Commission Exhibit Number 602.

420. When were the remaining three bullets forwarded to the FBI?
March, 1964. More than ninety days after the murder.

421. Were those "bullets" the identical ones taken from Tippit?
No one knows. The FBI only said they received the "bullets."

422. Did the policemen, who had originally obtained the four bullets, testify that they were *identical* to the ones found at the scene or from Tippit's body?
No. The policemen contradicted each other. 3H343-46; 6H448-51; 7H271-76; 24H415.

423. Did the police testify that the shells were fired from the revolver "taken" from Oswald at the Texas Theatre?
No! Contradictions again! 3H465-67; 3H511-12.

424. What did the FBI ballistic examination report say?
"It was *not* possible from an examination and comparison of these bullets to determine whether or not they had been fired–these bullets themselves–had been fired from *one* weapon or whether or not they had been fired from *Oswald's* revolver." R171-72; 3H473.

425. What other evidence did the FBI present to the Commission?
The FBI stated (1) three of the four bullets were manufactured by the Winchester–Western Corporation; (2) the fourth bullet was a Remington–Peters; (3) only two shells of the three bullets were

found; and (4) two shells of one bullet were found. R171-72; 3H473.

426. What is the implication of the above?

That the FBI believed (1) Tippit had been shot with more than [one] revolver; or (2) that some of the bullets given to them by the Dallas police may *not* have been taken from Tippit's body.

427. What document did the Commission *suppress* from the FBI?

None other than a letter from Mr. J. Edgar Hoover in File Number 87, Document Number 774. Mr. Hoover stated that the bullets sent to the FBI Laboratory were too mutilated to be tested. Three of the four bullets were too mutilated to be tested and the fourth one, stated Mr. Hoover, may have come from the revolver, from Oswald's pockets, or the U.S. Secret Service. File 87, Commission Document Number 774.

428. Did the FBI support the Commission regarding the bullets?

No! In fact, this was another "red flag" to the Commission. Mr. Hoover was saying much more than what he was writing. By answering the negative he was affirming a positive. Mr. Hoover was telling the Commission to obtain positive evidence that the revolver taken from Oswald was the revolver used in the killing; he was telling them that the FBI could not be used to testify to facts they knew nothing about, that is, where those bullets came from.

429. How could one bullet leave two shells?

Ask the Warren Commission.

430. What was the Commission's theory?

Tippet was shot at five times. 3H473.

431. Did any witness testify that they heard five shots?

No. Only the Commission and its staff heard the five shots.

432. Did the Commission give an answer?

They *invented* a solution stating that the murderer had fired five shots; but admitted they could not discover the fifth bullet.

433. What was wrong with the Commission's solution?

Their "solution" brought up questions they could not answer: (1) how could one revolver fire (a) different shells; (b) different bullets; (2) leave only four shells when five bullets were fired?

434a. What fact destroyed their solution?

The fact that a. 38 revolver could *not* fire a .38 *automatic shell*.

434b. What is the implication if the Commission's solution is correct?

If five shots were fired, then two guns are involved, a revolver and an automatic pistol. If two are involved, then a conspiracy existed. If five shots were involved but only three heard, then one of the guns used a silencer.

435. Why did the Commission publish this unacceptable solution?

Even without the five shots, the evidence points to two guns being used. No matter how the Commission struggled they could not overcome the .38 automatic shell which could *not* have been fired from Oswald's revolver, whether it be the one allegedly "taken" from him at the Texas Theatre or the one the Dallas police presented to the Commission.

436. Is there any evidence that *two* men, *not* Oswald, murdered Tippit?

Yes. Mrs. Acquilla Clemons was interviewed by the FBI and stated that she saw *two* men murder Officer Tippit.

437. When did her statement appear?

In the magazine *New Leader*, the October 12, 1964 issue.

438. Was she known to the Commission?

Yes, but she was not called before the Commission nor did any aide go and interview her at her home. She was threatened by the Dallas police *not* to discuss her evidence to anyone. She was, however, interviewed by the FBI, and the fact that the Commission, in its "Speculation" and "Finding" section, admitted that they knew of the "rumor" is self-proof that they had knowledge.

The reason the Commission did not desire her testimony is due to the fact that she could prove a conspiracy by what she saw.

439. Is this true?

It would be true regarding the Commission's statement that they never heard of Mrs. Clemons only if the FBI never informed the Commission of her existence. However, her evidence is proved by other witnesses, so the Commission must be condemned, at the minimum, for gross negligence.

440. How many shots did she hear?

Three shots. *New Leader*, October 12, 1964. G&P Nash interview.[6]

441. What did she see?

Two men shooting at Officer Tippit and, when he fell to the ground, each fled in a different direction.

442. Was her statement substantiated by other witnesses?

Besides Mrs. Markham and Mr. Benavides, Mr. and Mrs. Wright.

443. How did Mr. and Mrs. Wright become involved?

The Commission avoided calling for their testimony. R449-50.

444. Where does their statement appear?

In the *New Leader*, October 12, 1964 and the *New York Times*, same date.

---

[6] George and Patricia Nash.

445. What did Mr. Wright say?

He heard *three* shots and he ran from his home to the outside. He saw a man run from Tippit's body and drive away in a 1950-51 gray coupe.

446. Did Mr. Wright inform the police when they arrived?
Yes. However they paid *no* attention to him.

447. Why?
They had their "patsy."

448. What did Mrs. Wright do?
She called the "strangest police department in the world."

449. Is there any proof or evidence to substantiate her phone call?
Yes. Her call is entered into the police records.

450. Is there any corroboration that the police responded?
Yes. The police records showed that Mrs. Wright's phone call was relayed by the police to the Dudley Hughes Funeral Home.

451. What happened?
The Hughes Home dispatched C. J. Butler, the driver, and E. Kinsley, his assistant, to the murder site. The time was 1:18 p.m.

452. Did the Commission examine these four witnesses?
No!

453. Why?
No one can read another person's mind. One can only look at all the facts which were available and the only answer to the "why" is that the Commission *knew* that if they had these four witnesses testify the Commission's "case" vs. Oswald killing Tippit would be destroyed.

All witnesses who testified that they heard the shots heard only three. The Commission failed to explain how all these witnesses heard only three shots and the Commission "heard" four or five!

Or did the Commission, by stating that five shots were fired, attempt to indirectly inform the American people that, although three shots were heard, five bullets were actually fired, two of which were from a silencer?

454. Where did Oswald go after being seen at the bus stop at 1:04 p.m.?

No one knows. There is, however, evidence that Oswald was connected with a mysterious "police car" that signaled Oswald at his Berkley Street address between 1 p.m. and 1:04 p.m. In every event which involved the "activity" of the police the evidence revealed that the Commission relied solely upon the police's explanation. 4H443; 26H195.

455. Was there a police car involved in this episode?

Neither the Commission nor the Dallas police say "no." The officer in charge of that police squad car simply testified that he gave that car to a police sergeant. The car then disappeared for three hours! The sergeant, in turn, was not asked by the Commission whether or not (1) he did use that car to drive to Oswald's rooming house; or (2) did he give that car to someone else to use. The Commission was *scared* to ask! 7H74-76; 12H341-46; 25H170-71, 914.

456. Where was Oswald seen after 1:04 p.m.?

He was seen "sneaking in" a theater by a shoe store manager.

457. Did this manager know Oswald was wanted for murder?

No. He testified that Oswald made him suspicious because (1) he was running; and (2) his "messed up" hair made him look frightened.

458. Was this true?

No. The official photograph released by the USIS showing Oswald immediately after his arrest does not show any "messed up" hair. He is not looking frightened and the police say he was not frightened.

459. What happened at the Texas Theatre where Oswald was arrested?

If the murder of the president of the United States was not a joke, then a "Mack Sennett" comedy occurred.

460. How many witnesses did the police use to verify the arrest?

Only two witnesses, yet there were more than twenty patrons.

461. Who selected those two witnesses out of twenty?

The police testified that they did not know who selected those two witnesses.

462. How valuable was the testimony of these two witnesses?

Worthless! They contradicted each other in every aspect.

463. Did the Commission then call the other witnesses?

Although the police said they had the complete list, the Commission did *not* call any other witness.

464. What happened in the theater?

Not even the policemen, of which there were fifteen, knew.

465. What does the evidence, published in the "Hearings," reveal?

An incredible state of affairs! Patrolman McDonald, the one credited with Oswald's arrest, had Oswald pointed out by the shoe store manager. Since the lights were on, Oswald could be seen easily.

466. What did Officer McDonald now proceed to do?

Believe it or not, this is what occurred. McDonald stepped off the stage and went down the aisle toward the "murderer" of the president of the United States and a fellow "cop." However, on his way to this "killer," Officer McDonald, with his back toward Oswald, engaged in a polite conversation with other patrons sitting in front of Oswald. Then McDonald stood up, turned around, and approached Oswald with a gun in his (McDonald's) hand.

467. Then what happened?
Oswald then drew back his fist and struck McDonald in the face. At this time, Oswald did not have a gun in his hand! 3H299.

468. Incredible?
Not to the Commission. This "killer," a "cop killer," calmly sitting back while fifteen policemen are searching for him in a theater with no escape route, permitted a police officer to turn his back and then strikes out with his fist.

469. What did the Commission publish regarding Oswald's capture?
"McDonald struck back with his right hand and grabbed Oswald's gun with his left hand." 3H300.

470. What is wrong with this statement?
The Commission failed to inform the American reader how McDonald struck back with his right hand and grabbed Oswald's gun with his left hand. In one hand McDonald had his own gun, in the other hand he grabbed Oswald's gun, and with his third hand he grabbed Oswald around the waist and struggled with the "killer."

471. Then what happened?
The Commission stated that McDonald "jerked" the gun away from Oswald and gave it to a Detective Carroll. This is incorrect R179; 3H300.

472. Why is the above in correct?
Detective Carroll testified that he went to McDonald's help and "saw a pistol pointing at me and grabbed the pistol and jerked the pistol away and stuck it in *my* belt and then I grabbed Oswald." 7H20.

473. What did Carroll do with this pistol?

He testified he gave it to a Sergeant Hill. 7H20-22.

474. Then what happened to this "pistol"?
It disappears in the Dallas police station.

475. How is the above statement proved?
By none other than Commissioner Senator Cooper! This cross-examination of McDonald by Senator Cooper destroyed the Tippet–Oswald case.

476. What answer did Carroll give to Senator Cooper when he asked Carroll: "Who had the pistol (during the struggle) at that time?"
Carroll replied: "I don't know, sir!" 7H20.

477. How did Senator Cooper's adroit cross-examination of McDonald uncover the possibility of some police personnel in the Tippet murder?
Patrolman McDonald, under oath, said he put "his mark on it"; that is, he marked the pistol.
However, he had already testified that he had *no* time to put his "mark" on the pistol since Detective Carroll "jerked" it and gave the pistol to Sergeant Hill
In addition, Senator Cooper brought out the fact or statement that McDonald had testified that he "found six live bullets in the revolver but he only put his 'mark' on one of them." 3H301-02.
Now, Senator Cooper, not [one of] the seventy-five-dollar-a-day "legal beagles," asked the key question: "When did you (McDonald) put your mark on it?"
The patrolmen's answer then blew the case wide open by saying: "He put his mark on it at the *police station*"! R304.
McDonald then admitted to the senator that he never saw the gun after it was "jerked" from his hand by Detective Carroll. Thus, as the senator pointed out, McDonald could not have (1) placed his "mark" upon the pistol; and (2) or upon any bullet!

478. What *legal* axiom did the senator give to the "legal beagles?

The senator, who is also an attorney, pointed out to McDonald and the legal beagles that McDonald could not identify the alleged Oswald revolver and that McDonald had put his mark upon *a* revolver at the police station. The senator added that what McDonald was saying, under oath, was that some police officer, at the police station, gave Oswald a revolver, said it was the revolver taken from Oswald at the Texas Theatre, and commanded him to "put his mark upon it."

Thus, said the senator, in law, McDonald was simply stating that he put his "mark" upon a revolver but that, at the Commission "hearing," McDonald could *not* legally identify the Commission's Exhibit of Oswald's revolver as *the* revolver taken from Oswald.

McDonald admitted that what the senator said was true and correct. With this admission, the Oswald–Tippit case blew up. R304.

479. Did Detective Carroll testify that he "jerked" the gun from Oswald?

No. Never! 7H20.

480. Did Sergeant Hill testify that he obtained the gun from Oswald?

No. Never!

481. Did either McDonald, Carroll, or Hill testify that the Commission Exhibit of Oswald's revolver was the *identical* one taken from Oswald?

No! Never!

482. What could have happened at the theater during the struggle?

One logical explanation could be that the pistol "jerked" from someone's hand by Detective Carroll was the pistol belonging to Patrolman McDonald. He testified that he had his own gun in his hand during the struggle and it is entirely possible that his gun was the one "jerked."

483. Is this a "far out" theory?

Not necessarily. Police Captain Fritz, on November 22nd, informed a press conference that Oswald's gun had "two empty shells" in it. There were, according to Detective Carroll, six *live* bullets in the "gun." Now, if Oswald's "gun" had *two empty shells* in it, plus four *live* bullets (the "gun" held six bullets) when it was examined at the police station, then it must follow that the revolver taken from *Oswald at the Texas Theatre was not Oswald's revolver.* 7 H22; press conference: November 26, 1963.

484. Were the bullets taken from Tippit's body from Oswald's gun?

The *FBI said "no"!* R171-72; 3H475; 26H263.

485. What federal agency said these bullets "were of *no* value"?

Mr. J. Edgar Hoover informed the Commission that the bullets sent to the FBI Laboratory *were of no value!* Three of the four bullets sent to the FBI were too mutilated to be tested and the fourth one "may have come from the revolver, from Oswald's pocket, or the U.S. Secret Service."

486. Where *did the Commission suppress Mr. Hoover's letter?*

In File Number 87, Commission Document Number 774. National Archives!

487. Did the Commission attempt to solve the conflict in testimony between Officer McDonald, Sergeant Hill, Detective Carroll, Captain Fritz and the FBI?

Of course not. They *knew* Oswald was guilty. The Commission did not ask Captain Fritz to explain how three police officers testified that the Oswald "gun" had six live bullets in it and Captain Fritz informed the press and the world that the same gun, *at the same time*, had only four live bullets and two empty shells.

Someone was lying. The FBI was simply reporting a ballistic fact concerning the bullets "sent" to them. The FBI did *not* state that the bullets sent to them came from any revolver and certainly *denied* the fact that the bullets came from Commission Exhibit Number 143–the Oswald "revolver."

488. In a court of law, was there any ballistic evidence, or revolver evidence to convict Lee Harvey Oswald of the murder of Officer Tippit?

No. There is *no* autopsy report on the body of Officer Tippit. Thus, in a court of law, there is *no* legal certification of how he died!

Was he killed by three bullets, four bullets, or five bullets? Was he even killed by a bullet? There is *no* legal report regarding the method of death!

The people of the United States pride themselves on the fact that their government is one of *law*. This rule must be applicable to all its citizens regardless of the alleged crime.

The *revolver taken from Oswald* has been "lost" and the fact that no *policeman* involved with the arrest of Oswald identified Commission Exhibit Number 143 *as the revolver taken from Oswald at the theater* is, in a court of law, a strong presumption in Oswald's behalf.

However, the final and conclusive factor in Oswald's innocence of the Tippit murder is the *FBI report*, suppressed by the Commission, that the bullets allegedly taken from Tippit's body did not ballistically match Commission Exhibit Number 143.

The fact that Oswald purchased a .38 revolver is, in law, of no value. The fact that one of the shells found at the Tippit murder site could be fired only from an *automatic* rifle is of great value, for Oswald's gun could not discharge any type of automatic shell.

489. Who testified that Oswald's revolver was Commission Exhibit Number 143?

A former member of the Soviet Communist Party, Mrs. Marina Oswald.

490. When she did this did she point out any *identifying features*?

No. R174; 1H120.

491. Who accepted her testimony as being "basic American justice"?

The chief justice of the United States Supreme Court.

492. Where was Mr. Craig, who was the "conscience of the Commission"?

Somewhere around. However, he was to act only for Mrs. Oswald.

493. What would have an impartial judge have said of Mr. Chief Justice?

That William Shakespeare would have been envious of the chief justice's interpretation of "basic principles of American justice"!

494. What did Mrs. Marina Oswald's testimony prove?
Nothing!

495. Why?

For the reason that she had informed the Secret Service and also testified for the Commission that she knew nothing about firearms and could not tell the difference between a revolver and a pistol and that she did not distinguish between various sizes of bullets.

A first-year law student would have been able to prevent any questioning of Mrs. Oswald, not on the basis of the husband-and-wife doctrine of not being able to testify for or against each other but on the basis of Mrs. Oswald had admitted she did not know anything about firearms.

This is not a legal "technicality" but a basic principle of American law that a witness, who was giving vital evidence concerning a specific fact, must know, not guess, evidence.

The Commission *used* her "testimony in an attempt to convince the American people that it was Oswald's revolver that "killed" Officer Tippit. Yet the evidence proved that Oswald may have "owned" a revolver but it did *not* prove *that* revolver was *used* to murder Tippit.

Again, the reader is referred to the FBI report volume one, which always printed the word "owned" and not the word "used."

496. Did the Commission prove that Oswald had purchased ammunition?

No. The Commission admitted that no police agency, federal or state or local, ever located any gun shop selling "ammo" to Oswald.

497. Did the Commission ever prove that the "holster" found by the police, [which] was "found" in Oswald's room, was actually "found" in that room?

No! Mrs. Roberts, under oath, testified that she never saw any holster, at any time, anywhere in the room. She was the person who cleaned the room, including putting on clean bedsheets. 6H440-42.

498. Was Mrs. Roberts present when the police "found" the holster?

No!

499. How did other police departments characterize the Dallas police?

To be the greatest "finding" police department in the world! Whenever evidence was needed to convict Oswald, the Dallas police was on the job. They "found" a thirty-four-inch bag which was seen by nobody but two police officers who arrived forty-five minutes after the murder of President Kennedy; they "found" a revolver but whose it was no one knew; they "found" a holster no one else had ever seen; and they also found three men who left no fingerprints on any of the items they touched.

Truly, the greatest "finding" police department in the world.

500. What happened, after Oswald's arrest, in the police station?

Nearly two hours elapsed and then the police decided to search Oswald. They found, they say, five live cartridges in his pocket.

501. Were these cartridges tested by the Dallas police?

No one knows! The Commission did *not* ask. The reason for not asking was the fact that if the cartridges did not match the bullet markings found on the bullets "taken" from Tippet's body, the Dallas police would be in the soup. The Dallas police, known only to themselves, willfully violated every known police rule and procedure.

Yet, the Commission never sought to find out "why" the Dallas police persistently violated these standard rules of police procedure.

502. What was the first police broadcast at the Tippit murder site?
A man with a "white jacket, a white shirt, and dark slacks." R175.

503. Was a further description broadcasted?
Yes. The first one, above, went out at 1:22 p.m. The second one at 1:33 p.m., by Patrolman Summers, who said: "I have an 'eyeball' witness ... who saw a white male, approximately five-foot eleven inches, about twenty-seven, 165 pounds, *black* wavy hair, fair complexion, wearing a *light gray* Eisenhower jacket." 17H416.

504. What other information went over the police radio?
At 1:44 p.m. Sergeant Stringer informed police headquarters that "the jacket the suspect was wearing over here on Jefferson bears a laundry mark with the letter 'B9738.' See if there is any way you can check. "

505. Did the clothing description match the clothes Oswald wore?
No.

506. Did the physical description match Oswald's?
No.

507. Did Oswald have "dark wavy hair"?
No.

508. Did Oswald have on a "white" shirt when captured?

No.

509a. What happened to the jacket with the laundry mark "B9738"?

Ask the Dallas police or the Warren Commission 17H411.

-7-

THE 100% ACCURATE WITNESS

509b. Who "fingered" Oswald as the murderer of President Kennedy?
Howard L. Brennan.

510. What did the Commission say regarding this witness?
"He made a positive identification of Oswald as being the person at the window." R250.

511. What did he actually prove?
As the evidence will show, nothing!

512. How is the above statement proved?
At the identification lineup held on November 22, Mr. Brennan identified another man, *not* Oswald. R145.

513. What did he inform the FBI at this lineup?
That he was unable to positively identify Oswald. 3H147.

514. What did he inform the FBI on December 17, 1963?
That Oswald was the man at the window. R145.

515. What did he say on January 7, 1964?
He changed his statement and said he could *not* identify Oswald.

516. When confronted by the Commission what did he say?
He said that his statement to the FBI was "intended as an accurate account of what he said on November 23, 1963." R145.

517. Again, what did he say on November 22, 1963?
"He was *unable* to make a positive identification." R148.

518. How did this Commission handle their "meandering witness"?

"It does not base its conclusion concerning the identity of the assassin on when Brennan first saw him, Oswald, in the line." R145.

519. Is this a true statement?
No.

520. Why?
The Commission proudly stated that "Mr. Brennan made a *positive* identification of Oswald as the person being at the window." R250.

521. Why was Brennan's identification of Oswald important?
His "evidence" was the *only* evidence to place Oswald at the window.

522. Who was Mr. Brennan?
He was a forty-five-year-old steamfitter. He admitted his eyesight was "not so good." He wore glasses regularly but not on that day. 3H141-43.

523. Where was Mr. Brennan when the shots were fired?
It was about 120 feet away from the southeast corner of the sixth floor and about 110 feet away from the base of the building. 22H847.

524. What did Mr. Brennan say he saw?
He saw a white man at the sixth-floor window several times between 12:22 p.m. and the time the final shot was fired. The man "appeared to be standing up and resting against the windowsill, with gun shouldered to his right shoulder, holding the gun with his left hand and taking positive aim and fired his last shot." 3H142-44.

525. How did he describe this man to the Dallas police?

"To my best description, a man in his early thirties, fair complexion, slender but neat, slender, possibly five-foot ten, weight from 160-170 [pounds]."

526. According to this one hundred percent accurate witness, what did he do next?

He ran to a policeman who, in turn, took him to a man Mr. Brennan identified as Inspector Sorrels, of the U.S. Secret Service. 3H158.

527. Was this man Inspector Sorrels of the U.S. Secret Service?

No! Inspector Sorrels was in the lead automobile that guided the president's car to Parkland Hospital. The inspector testified that it took at least twenty minutes to return to the Book Depository.

528. What does this prove?

That Mr. Brennan could "identify" a man six stories above the ground and while glancing *directly* into the sun, could tell a man's height, weight, complexion, but could *not* describe a man to whom he was talking who, in turn, was less than thirty-six inches away from his eyes! 7H341, 347-48.

529. What policeman gave the police radio a description of the man?

Police Inspector J. H. Sawyer. 6H321.

530. What was the broadcasted description?

"The wanted man is a slender white male about thirty, five-foot-ten inches, carrying *what looked like a 30-30* type of Winchester." 6H321.

531. What other important statement did the inspector state?

Headquarters radio: "Any clothing description?"

Inspector: "Current witness cannot remember that!" 6H[321]; 21H392.

532. Was this the description given to Officer Tippit?

Yes. This substantiates the author's statement that at no time was any clothing description ever flashed over the Dallas police radio.

Notice also the fact that a *Winchester rifle* is mentioned, and read questions twenty-eight to thirty-eight inclusive in chapter 1.

533. Who was this "current" witness?

Inspector Sawyer did *not* know! He did *not* know whether "he was young, old, short or tall." But he was a "white man." 6H322-23; 21H392.

534. Did Inspector Sawyer say it was Mr. Brennan?

He did not. He did not know "current witness's name or address."

535. But what did the Commission [do] regarding the inspector and Mr. Brennan?

They printed a statement that it was Mr. Brennan who spoke to the inspector. However, Mr. Brennan never testified to that effect.

536. What time did the broadcast by Inspector Sawyer go over the radio?

12:45 p.m. Inspector Sorrels was at the hospital. 23H843-44.

537. Did Mr. Brennan ever give a clothing description to the police?

Yes. After he went to the police station, Mr. Brennan then made an affidavit stating that the man was wearing a light jacket. 7H349.

538. Was Oswald wearing a light jacket or shirt at the Book Depository?

No!

539. What other "evidence" did Mr. Brennan give?

He testified that he "saw a man standing up and resting against the left windowsill, take positive aim, and fired his last shot." 3H144.

540. Is this a correct statement?
No. Highly incorrect. The Commission had photographs, taken during the murder, which showed the window opened only four inches! 19H563.

541. What is the implication?
The rifle bullets would have shattered the window glass and the Commission admitted *no* glass window was broken. 19H563-64.

542. What *two police officials proved Brennan one hundred percent inaccurate?*
None other than Police Captain Fritz and Inspector Sorrels.

543. What testimony did the captain give to the Commission?
The captain testified: "Some officer said we think the man who did the shooting out of the window is a tall, white man; that is all I had. That didn't mean much, you know, because you can't tell five or six floors up whether a man is tall or short!" 4H237.

544. What did Secret Service Inspector Sorrels testify?
The inspector testified that he was able to view, and *did* view, all the windows in the Depository Building. He said he saw the window at the southeast corner and: "I do not remember seeing any object or anything like that, such as a rifle or anything pointed out of the windows; there was *no* activity, *no* one moving around." 7H342.

545. Did the Commission believe its own "one hundred percent accurate witness"?
No! The Commission said: "The carton was so placed at the side of the window that a person sitting on a carton could look down Elm Street towards the overpass and *scarcely be seen.*" R6.

546. Did the Commission prove its own witness, Brennan, inaccurate?

The reader is referred to Commission Exhibits 723 and 1301. In Number 1301, the carton is so far away from the street that no person could be seen from the street where Brennan was positioned. Since the Commission stated that the killer fired from a crouched position, it was a physical impossibility for Brennan to see any rifleman. In Number 723, the head of the sitting person would be blocked. R80, 138.

547a. Was there anyone near the southeast window prior to the shots?

Yes. Two men.

547b. Who testified to that statement?

Mr. Rowland, who had 20/20 vision when tested by the Commission, was standing at the west entrance to the Dallas County Building which is about 150 feet across from the Book Depository. From this angle the rays of the sun did not affect the viewer's eyesight.

548. What was Mr. Rowland's testimony?

At approximately 12:15 p.m. or a little later, he noticed two men of whom one was at the window, with another man standing slightly behind. The man he saw was "holding a rifle–a .30-odd size six that had a telescopic sight. The man was rather slender in proportion to size, with dark hair, but light complexed and the man was wearing a *light* shirt, open at the collar, and he had a regular T-shirt under this, and wore dark slacks or blue jeans. The man weighed about 140 to 150 and [was] in his early thirties."

549. When was the last time Rowland saw these two men?

About 12:22 p.m. This was the time Mr. Brennan *first saw* his man. 2H167, 174; 17H896.

550. Did Mr. Rowland give this evidence to any government agent?

Yes, on November 23 and November 24, 1963. 2H183-84.

551. What else did the Rowlands give to the Commission?

That he had seen a Negro man hanging out of the window from the southeast corner about five minutes *before* the president's auto passed by. R174, 178.

552. Did the Commission ask Mr. Rowland why this evidence was not in his affidavit given to the FBI?

Mr. Rowland stated the FBI agent refused to put it in. 2H184.

553. Was there any photographic proof to uphold Mr. Rowland?

Yes, many Commission exhibits revealed this fact.

554. Did the Commission ask the FBI agent why he selected testimony?

No, for the Commission feared that the agent would confess he had left out the Rowland statement.

555. To whom was Rowland's initial statement made?

To a Deputy Sheriff R. Craig who testified that, within ten minutes after the shots rang out, the Rowlands reported to him that Mr. Rowland had seen two men, one with a rifle that had a telescopic sight, at the sixth-floor window. They thought nothing about these two men because they thought they were Secret Service agents protecting the president. R251.

556. How did the Commission decide to negate the Rowland evidence?

By printing in the "Report" an implication that Mr. Rowland was a liar. The Commission perverted his testimony by perverting Mrs. Rowland's testimony in such a way that the Commission had her calling her husband a liar. A despicable piece of work by the Commission. R250-52, 483, 495-98.

557. How else did the Commission attempt to discredit Mr. Rowland?

They "sicced" the FBI onto the Rowlands in an attempt to find evidence that could lead to a perjury indictment. None was found.

558. Was there evidence that corroborated Mr. Rowland?

Yes. Damaging evidence against the Commission, not Mr. Rowland. (1) The Commission had pictures of a Negro leaning out the window of the sixth floor just prior to the shots which proved Oswald was *not* at the window; (2) the uncontradicted statement of Miss C. Walther that she also saw two men in an upper window, one of whom had a rifle; (a) a Negro boy who informed Sergeant Harkness that he saw a Negro man at the same window. The sergeant radioed this information to police headquarters. The time was 12:36 p.m. R64; 2H201-10; 7H349; 24H552; Commission Exhibit Number 7.

559. Was Oswald telling truth when he said he had seen a rifle in the building prior to the murder of President Kennedy?

The truth! A Mr. Caster, a tenant of the building, admitted that he owned a .30 06 *Sporterized Mauser* with a *telescopic sight* and that he had shown this rifle to various persons in the Book Depository. Mr. Caster also admitted to being a member of various right-wing organizations. The FBI informed the Commission that Mr. Caster was not in Dallas on the day of the murder and he told them his rifle was at home. R610-12; 7H612, 386. There is no testimony that the FBI ever subjected this rifle to any ballistic tests, since the rifle matched the description of the police broadcast and to that of Rowland's evidence. What would the FBI have done with such a rifle if it had been owned by a member of the left-wing organizations?

560. How did the Commission attempt to deceive the American people?

The Commission, in spite of the evidence to the contrary in the "Hearings," printed a statement in the "Report" that said that five witnesses supported Brennan's "truthfulness." R144, 845.

561. Was the Commission's statement "truthful?

No! Every witness: Policeman Barnett, U.S. Secret Service Inspector Sorrels, Mr. Norman, Mr. Jarman and Mr. Rowland testified to facts which did *not* support Mr. Brennan in any manner, shape or form. 3H197, 6H322.

562. Did Police Captain Fritz?
No! 4H237.

563. Who performed the "coup de grace" upon the Commission?
None other than the chief of police, Police Chief Curry.

564. How?
(1) President Kennedy was murdered on November 22 at 12:25 or 12:30 p.m.
(2) Brennan informed the police he could identify the killer.
(3) Brennan is taken to the Oswald lineup and *cannot identify him*.
(4) After the lineup, Police Chief Curry went on national television and informed the world that the police did *not* have any identity of the killer. WFAA-TV.
(5) The next day, November 23, on KRLD-TV, despite the fact that Oswald was in custody and had been put through an "ID" lineup, Police Chief Curry again reiterated his "no identification."
(6) Both statements had been made after Brennan had made his trip to the lineup.
(7) *Thus*, the highest-ranking police officer in the Dallas Police Department *knew* [he] had no legal identification of the killer.

565. Where was Lee Harvey Oswald when the shots rang out?
He was standing *outside* the main entrance of the book building.

566. Is there any proof of this statement?
Yes, a photograph by J. Altgens of the AP photo news division.

567. Who did the Commission say this "man in the photo" was?
A Billy Lovelady. R149.

568. Was it Billy Lovelady?
No.

569. Who proved it was not Billy Lovelady?
Billy Lovelady!

570. How?
Billy Lovelady, testifying under oath, stated that when he was at the entrance of the Book Depository he had his "shirt buttoned up to the neck." 22H749; National Archives Exhibit Number 457.

571. Does the man in the photo have his shirt buttoned up to the neck?
No. In fact, the man in the photo is wearing the identical clothes worn by Oswald at the time of the murder and his jacket is open at halfway down the front!

572. Where can this picture be seen?
The *New York Herald Tribune*, May 24, 1964, or in the National Archives.

573. What FBI official impliedly said the "photographed man" was Oswald?
None other than *J. Edgar Hoover!*

574. How was this [statement] made?
In a letter from Mr. Hoover to Mr. Rankin, general counsel of the Commission, dated March 9, 1964, page 5. "He (Billy Lovelady) was standing in the doorway … He stated he was wearing a *red* and *white vertical striped shirt and blue jeans.*" FBI "Lovelady" photos.

The "man in the doorway" *is not wearing such a shirt* and, in addition, it is *not* buttoned up to the neck. Shaneyfelt Exhibit volumes 15, 21, 23.

Mr. Hoover, in his March 9, 1964 letter *never* stated that the man in the doorway was Billy Lovelady; he *never* affirmed the

Commission's own "self-serving" statement published in the Report.

Mr. Hoover's letter is *suppressed by the Warren Commission* and can only be found in the National Archives, File Number 157!

575. What high-ranking FBI official *proved* Brennan was "mistaken" when he said that he saw *no* rifle recoil or white flash?

Again, none other than Mr. Hoover, FBI chief! A letter by Mr. Hoover to the Commission stated that when the Italian Mannlicher-Carcano rifle was discharged, *white smoke* was clearly visible. Mr. Brennan, the man who saw the killer with sufficient "accuracy" to give the killer's height, weight, slenderness, saw *no* smoke. 26H811.

576. Who saw Oswald enter the Depository on the morning of November 22?

An employee, Mr. Dougherty. R131.

577. Did he testify that the "bag" was big enough for a rifle?

What rifle? Mr. Dougherty never saw any package! R131, 6H673-82.

578. Did not this testimony corroborate the Frazier–Randle?

Absolutely, yes! Any person carrying "curtain rods" knows that rods are thin enough to be "cupped" in the palm of one's hands and one end put under the armpit so as not to show.

But this cannot be done with a 34.8-inch rifle since (1) the rifle butt would extend beyond the dimensions of the palm; and (2) a rifle of that size would extend beyond the armpit.

In addition, the FBI testified that Oswald's palm print was a "cupped" print. Thus, Oswald could have easily carried the curtain rod package into the Book Depository and not have it seen by Mr. Dougherty.

However, from a *legal* standpoint, the Commission cannot have it both ways. Therefore, the Commission simply "printed" its own statement that Oswald carried a "rifle" into the Book

Depository; yet *no legal evidence* supported their own "self-serving" statement.

579. Who saw Oswald on the sixth floor?

A member of the sixth-floor maintenance crew, Mr. Givens. He saw Oswald, at about 11:55 a.m., with a clipboard under his arm, walking away from the southeast corner window. He saw *no* "shield of cartons."

580. Is the clipboard important in this Oswald "affair"?

Very important.

581. Why?

The Commission said the clipboard proved Oswald was at the sixth-floor window *when the president was shot.*

582. Does the clipboard prove the Commission's statement?

No! It proved that Oswald was *not.*

583. How is the clipboard used to prove a conspiracy?

(1) The Commission stated that on December 3, a fellow employee of Oswald's said he found the clipboard behind some cartons near the southeast corner. It was the clipboard he had loaned to Oswald.

(2) The Commission "forgot to print the facts that on (1) November 22, the sixth floor was (A) thoroughly searched by members of the Dallas police, members of the Sheriff's police, members of the FBI, members of the U.S. Secret Service, and newspaper reporters. (B) None of these persons saw a "clipboard."

(3) The Commission also forgot to print the fact that *every carton* within forty feet of the window was *lifted* and *photographed for fingerprints.*

(4) These cartons nearest the rifle window were all lifted and it was these cartons that the Commission said "formed a shield."

(5) As every carton that formed the "shield" was lifted it was impossible for a clipboard, 8 x 14 inches, with *white invoices on*

it, not to have been seen by all those more than twenty-five police agents.

584. Where was this "clipboard" found?

According to the Commission: "Hidden in the northwest corner of the sixth floor at the west wall *a few feet from where the rifle was found.*"

585. Who searched that area?

Deputy Sheriffs Weitzman, Boone, and Mooney, who found the rifle and the bullets, and twenty-five other police agents!

586. What did the Commission expect its readers to believe?

That all the searchers had been competent to find (1) chicken bones; (2) prints of Oswald on cartons that had to be moved to photograph them; (3) a rifle that was first a "Mauser" and then a "Carcano"; (4) a disappearing lunch bag; (5) take more than forty photographs; but despite all this activity, no one saw this *8 x 14 inch clipboard with white invoices.*

587. Would a jury of rational people believe the Commission?

Is the reader a rational person?

588. Did the Dallas police find Oswald's fingerprints on the clipboard?

There is *no* testimony that Oswald's prints were found!

589. What did the Commission [say] regarding this clipboard?

That the clipboard proved Oswald was at the sixth-floor window at the time of the murder.

590. Is this a true statement?

As true as the one saying "horses have feathers."

591. Who proved the fact that Oswald was *not* on the sixth floor at the time the shots were fired?

None other than Mr. Allen Dulles, former head of the CIA!

592. Where did the Commission "bury" this proof?
Three volumes away from the "Report." 3H169-173.

593. How did Mr. Dulles "blow" the Commission's case vs. Oswald?
By his adroit cross-examination of Mr. Bonnie Ray Williams.

594. What did Mr. Williams testify to before the Commission?
That he was a Book Depository employee who worked on the fifth floor. At 12:00 noon, the employee's lunch hour, he went *up* to the sixth floor to eat his lunch.

595. How long did he remain on the sixth floor?
From 12:00 noon to about 12:15 to 12:20, looking out the window at the crowd waiting for the president to arrive. 3H169-173.

596. What *vital* questions did Mr. Dulles ask Mr. Williams?
If Mr. Williams had (1) Heard anyone; (2) Seen anyone; (3) Heard anything; (4) Seen anything?

597. How did Mr. Williams answer under oath?
No. No. No. No.

598. Was Mr. Dulles satisfied with the answers and [with] his aides?
Yes! The record showed *no* aide disagreeing with the answers *nor* was there any evidence given to contradict Mr. Williams.

599. In other words, Oswald was not seen and not heard?
Yes, that is correct.

600. Where was Oswald from 12:00 noon until 12:31 and 1/2 p.m.?
Uncontradicted testimony by Junior Jarman, an employee, saw Oswald *eating his lunch!* 3H276.

601. Who saw the "chicken bones" first and who, in turn, proved it?

The "chicken bones," a vital piece of evidence willfully overlooked by the Commission, were first found by Officers Haygood and Brewer of the Dallas police when searching the sixth floor for evidence, then seen by Dallas Detectives Montgomery and Johnson, and finally seen by Deputy Sheriffs Mooney and Sergeant Hill of the Dallas police. Six officers.

602. Who said he saw "no chicken bones"?
Dallas Detective Lee.

603. What time did this detective arrive on the sixth floor?
Several hours *after* the "chicken bones" were found.

604. Why did the Commission use Detective Lee's statement?

It was necessary to destroy Mr. Williams' testimony even though Mr. Dulles' cross-examination proved him to be correct and honest. By destroying the Williams' testimony that he was eating lunch between noon and 12:15-12:20 p.m. and the "chicken bones" proved he was eating lunch, the disappearance of the "bones" would have "proved" that Mr. William's was lying since he said he had put them on the floor.

Now, this attempt to discredit Mr. Williams failed because *six white police officers upheld* Mr. Williams' statement, who was a Negro.

605. Did the Commission confront Detective Lee with the six officers?
No.

606. What did the Commission try to prove?
That "chicken bones can fly"!

607. What happened after the testimony was given by Mr. Williams?

The aides realized that a Commission member had proved Oswald innocent. Why this cross-examination was made of Mr.

Williams by Mr. Dulles will have to be answered by Mr. Dulles, who, perhaps, wanted the American people to read the testimony in the "Hearings," not the "Report."

608. What did the Commission say that Oswald must do, between 11:55 a.m. and 12:31 1/2 p.m., in order to murder President Kennedy?

(1) He must construct a "shield of cartons" to hide himself.

(2) Go to the place he "hid" his dismantled rifle.

(3) Assemble that rifle.

(4) Return to the "shield of cartons."

(5) Fire three rapid shots while adjusting his defective sight.

(6) Fire his first shot within .8 of a second when he sees Kennedy.

(7) Wipe off the rifle "in a well-oiled condition" with *no* cloth.

(8) Run *across* the sixth floor and *down* the stairway four floors.

(9) Take money out of his pocket, put it in the vending machine, wait for the "Coke" to drop, uncork it, and drink from it; without showing any anxiety, until a policeman sticks a gun in him!

609. Did the testimony [rely] upon the Commission's theory?
"Let's Look at the Record"–by Alfred E. Smith.[7]

610. Did the testimony prove that Oswald "built" a "shield of cartons"?

No. The record revealed that Mr. Truly, the company superintendent, stated that the "cartoons were lying around at random." He saw *no* shield.

[7] Alfred E. Smith (1873-1944) was elected governor of New York four times between 1919 and 1928. In 1928 he ran as the Democratic Party candidate for president and became the first Catholic to secure a major party presidential nomination. "Let's Look at the Record" was one of his campaign slogans in the 1928 race; it's also the title of a memorial book that contains some of his more well-known quotations.

611. Did Mr. Givens or his fellow maintenance crew see this "shield"?

The Commission aides never asked; the question is therefore "No."

612. How many cartons constituted this "shield of cartons?"

Commission Exhibit Number 732 revealed a minimum of twenty-eight cartons.

613. What was the total weight of the cartons?

The Commission said the average weight was fifty pounds or 1,400 lbs.

614. Was this "shield of cartons" constructed *prior* to the murder?

According to Mr. Truly, no.

615. Then who made it?

It was not Oswald, as the evidence showed.

616. How does the evidence prove the above statement?

Mr. Truly testified there was *no* shield when he was on the floor. Mr. Williams testified, uncontradicted, that from 12:00 until 12:15 to 12:20 p.m. he neither saw nor heard anyone at that sixth-floor window.

Thus, if Oswald was constructing a "shield of cartons" from cartons lying around the sixth floor "at random," weighing more than a ton and a half, Oswald would have either been seen or heard by Mr. Williams.

Therefore this "shield" had to be completed in less than fifteen minutes.

617. Did the alleged killer have fifteen minutes as the Commission stated?

No. The alleged killer had to go to the hiding place where he had secreted this weapon, assemble it, and return to the "shield."

618. Where was this hiding place?

There was no hiding place, only the Commission's imagination!

619. How long did the Commission say it took to assemble the rifle?

The Commission said it took their expert "six minutes with a ten-cent piece."

620. Is this time limit correct?

The Commission assumed that since their expert took only six minutes, everyone would take six minutes. Their assumption is as valid as the medieval assumption that the Earth was "flat." Or, because one man can run the hundred-yard dash in 9.1 everyone can do it.

621. Assuming that the alleged Oswald could assemble a rifle in six minutes, how much time is left for the construction of the shield?

Theoretically, nine minutes.

622. Is it actually nine minutes?

No. Some time must be consumed when "Oswald" went to his "hiding" place and then returned to the "shield." Since he was not heard he must have crawled silently so that he would not be heard or seen by Mr. Williams. So, in theory, subtract a minimum of two minutes.

623. In the remaining time period what did "Oswald" then do?

Two from nine leaves *seven* minutes to construct a "shield" of cartons. The killer had to pick up twenty-two cartons scattered all over the sixth floor, carry each one to the rifle window, and carefully construct a shield five-feet high. The weight was a minimum of 1,100 pounds. The "shield" had to be constructed so that it would not topple over.

624. What did the Commission constantly forget?

That the murderer *never knew the "exact" time the president of the United States would appear in his telescopic sight*.

625. What did the Commission want the public to forget?

That the "time" element was conceived entirely in the mind of the Commission and that the evidence was selected by the Commission to "prove" their own theory.

626. Was there any local radio broadcast of the president's car?

No.

627. Then the killer had *no* knowledge when he would see that car?

Yes.

628. Then he had to be ready to fire the moment the car was seen?

Yes. The time period it took the president's auto to make [the turn] from the corner of Main and Houston Streets, then a right turn to the corner of Elm and Houston Streets, was approximately two minutes.

During this time period the killer had to keep the president within his telescopic sight. Thus, the alleged "sixth-floor killer" never had six or nine minutes to construct the "shield of cartons."

629. What time can be [considered] reasonable?

For a total time of fifteen minutes, the Commission *must* subtract, to be honest with its readers of the "Report," a minimum of six minutes to assemble the rifle, two minutes to go from the rifle's hiding place, thus leaving a gross time of seven minutes at the maximum. From there, the maximum time to construct a shield composed of twenty-two fifty-pound cartons would be a mere seven minutes, but, as the Commission itself pointed out, Oswald, the alleged murderer, never knew the exact moment when the president would appear in the telescopic sight.

630. As the president's auto stopped at Elm and Houston Streets, why was he not shot then?

According to Mr. Hoover, FBI chief, "Oswald" could not shoot at President Kennedy because "there were some trees between his

window and the cars as they turned and went through the park."
5H105.

631. Is this statement by the FBI chief correct?

No! Mr. Hoover's aide did him a gross injustice. Commission Exhibit Number 875 proved there is not a single solitary tree or bush that would have hidden the president's auto from the sixth-floor window. It is incredible that the chief would make such a statement unless he was misinformed by his own aides. In addition, as the evidence revealed, the president's car came to a *complete stop* at this corner and made a perfect target, as Commission Exhibit Number 875 showed.

The reason why no shot was fired at President Kennedy at the corner of Elm and Houston is due to the fact (1) that there was *no* rifleman at the sixth-floor window; and (2) *the rifleman was on the second floor of the "Dal-Tex" Building* which prevented that killer from firing at President Kennedy.

632. At what time was Oswald seen by Officer Baker and Superintendent Truly?

The Commission said at exactly 12:31 and 1/2 p.m.

633. How was Oswald's appearance and condition at that time?

Officer Baker and Superintendent Truly testified that he was calm, cool, and collected. He was not agitated and was breathing normally.

634. Was there anything abnormal about the condition of his hands?

No. Thus, in view of the FBI report that they received the rifle in a "well-oiled condition" and the Commission's statement that Oswald had *no* wiping material [and] wore no glasses, then it stands to reason that Oswald's hands should have oil deposits on them.

However, Oswald had *no* oil stains on his hands or clothes. Furthermore, the Dallas police admitted that the paraffin test tests given to Oswald revealed *no* oil deposits.

Finally, the FBI and the Secret Service, in reporting on the condition of Oswald's clothes and paraffin tests, made *no* statement regarding oil or oil stains. The Dallas police, in its report on the paraffin tests, revealed that Oswald had no oil deposit.

This factor is final, conclusive proof that Oswald did not "use" the Italian Mannlicher-Carcano rifle.

635. In a law court, of what value was the evidence that the police found only one index fingerprint on only one carton, and one palm print on two?

No value whatsoever! This evidence tended to *substantiate* Oswald's innocence. How could any man, who moved and lifted twenty-eight cartons, leave only one index fingerprint and two palm prints?

636. Are not those prints "proof" in a court of law?

Proof of what? Oswald was an order-picking clerk whose duty it was to select books out of cartons to fill orders. His duty took him to the sixth floor every day at every hour. This fact is slid over by the Commission in its "Report" to leave an impression that, on November 22, Oswald was on the sixth floor in violation of his job requirements.

637. What did the Commission conceal from its "Report"?

That those three prints were between a day and a day-and-a-half old!

638. Who gave this information to the Commission?

The Federal Bureau of Investigation's fingerprint expert, Latona.

639. What did the Commission legally prove?

That Oswald was not only (1) the world's fastest runner; (2) the world's greatest marksman; but (3) the world's strongest man.

640. How did the Commission prove (3) above?

Commission Exhibit Numbers 1301, 1302 shows where the fingerprint and palm prints were located on the three cartons. Only a man of superhuman strength could lift a fifty-pound carton with either one finger or palm print!

641. What about fingerprints or palm prints on the remaining cartons?
Astonishing. The police found no prints of Oswald's!

642. How did he move and lift those remaining cartons?
By levitation.

643. Where did Oswald go after leaving the Depository at 12:31 and 1/2 p.m.?
He was seen by Deputy Sheriff Craig getting into a light-colored station wagon, a Rambler, driven by a Negro, at 12:45 p.m. 6H266; 23H817.

644. Why is this time element addressed?
At 5:30 p.m. on November 22, Deputy Craig was called into Captain Fritz's police office where Oswald was being questioned. 6H270; 23H817.

645. What did Deputy Craig do in the captain's office?
He identified Oswald as the man he had seen enter the station wagon at 12:45 p.m. No "if's," "and's," or "but's." Oswald was the man!

646. How did the Commission attempt to negate the deputy's evidence?
The Commission put Captain Fritz on the stand and he called the deputy a liar, in a polite way, of course.

647. Did the captain "prove" his statement?
Of course not. In fact, the captain opened up a can of worms!
The Commission wished he had never testified.

648. What did the captain testify that caused confusion?

The captain testified: "He (Deputy Craig) was telling me some things that I knew wouldn't help us." And "his (Deputy Craig) story *didn't* fit with what we knew to be true."

649. Did the Commission's legal beagles ask what he meant? What, and expose a conspiracy!

650a. What is the implication behind the captain's testimony?

(1) Captain Fritz testified that he was at Parkland Hospital at 12:45 p.m. and returned to the Depository at 12:58 p.m.

(2) The Italian rifle was *not* found until 1:22 p.m.

(3) Lieutenant Day did *not* find the "palm print" until 8:00 p.m.

(4) The FBI *never* found this "invisible" print.

(5) Dallas Police Chief Curry, on November 22 and 23, admitted on national TV that the police had no witnesses to identify the killer.

(6) Oswald had been in custody and in a police lineup.

(7) At 12:45 p.m. Deputy Craig saw Oswald get into a station wagon.

(8) At 5:30 p.m. Deputy Craig identifies Oswald as that man.

Now comes the intriguing question: Since *no* palm prints of Oswald had been identified by Lieutenant Day until 8:00 p.m. on November 22 which would "connect" Oswald with the Italian rifle; since the FBI, in Washington DC, had *not* received the rifle sent to them by the Dallas police; since the FBI, at 5:30 p.m. had not yet connected Oswald with "Hidell"; and since the Dallas police had *no* witness to identify Oswald as the "killer," then how did Police Captain Fritz, at 5:30 p.m. on November 22, know, *in advance*:

(1) that what Deputy Craig was saying "would not help us"; and

(2) "didn't fit in with what *we* knew to be true"?

650b. Today, in 1967, what is the implication made by the captain?

The reader should do his own thinking!

651. Did the Commission ever ask Mrs. Paine where her station wagon was?

If it is in the record, it is hard to find.

652. According to the Commission what did Oswald do after 12:31 1/2 p.m.?

(a) Oswald left the Depository by 12:33 p.m.

(b) Then he walked seven blocks *east* on Elm Street, which was directly *away* from his Berkley rooming house.

(c) He changed his mind and took a *bus* back to the same area from which he had left.

(d) Left the bus and took a six-block walk.

(e) Tired of walking, hired a cab which took him six blocks *beyond* his rooming house.

(f) Walked back the six blocks to his rooming house.

(g) Ran into the rooming house and took a secreted revolver.

(h) Put on a *dark zipper jacket*, not a light or white one. 7H439.

(i) Set a world record for the nine-tenths-mile run.

(j) Pumped three, four, or five bullets into Officer Tippit.

(k) Ran to the Texas Theatre, six blocks away; that took twenty-eight minutes!

(l) Called attention to himself by "sneaking" into the theater.

(m) Calmly watched fifteen policemen searching for a "cop" killer and, when approached by a policeman, struck the "cop" with his fist.

653. Is this what happened?

Yes, according to the Commission.

654. Who did the Commission say saw Oswald first?

A bus driver, Mr. C. McWatters.

655. Did the bus driver identify Oswald as his passenger?

No! He identified a man "who grinned" when McWatters told the "grinning man" that President Kennedy had been shot.

656. Was Oswald the grinning man?

No, Mr. Milton Jones was the "grinning man." 2H280-83.

657. How did the Commission convert McWatters' "no" to a "yes"?

By accepting a perjured exhibit from the Dallas police which stated: "Cecil J. McWatters, positive identification." Commission Exhibit Number 2003.

658. Did Mr. McWatters deny the validity of the Commission Exhibit Number 2003?

Yes, under oath, and at a public hearing. The Commission refused to have anyone from the Dallas police confront McWatters. 2H270, 279; 14H347! Hence, under American law, the police committed perjury.

659. Who was the next witness to identify Oswald on the bus?

Oswald's former landlady who owed him money, Mrs. Bledsoe.

She testified that Oswald "looked like a maniac, his sleeve was out there, his shirt was undone, his face was distorted." 6H409.

660. Was her testimony corroborated by the bus driver or passenger?

No! She was the only one to see this "maniac." 2H264-65; 15H900.

661. [Who] assisted Mrs. Bledsoe to "identify" Oswald?

Mr. Sorrels of the U.S. Secret Service, who brought to her a white shirt and he told her it was the one Oswald was wearing. Did she now recognize it? Of course she did! She said she "tended to forget." 4H112.

662. Was her testimony of any value in a court of law?

Very little since she was not substantiated in any manner by the other two witnesses whose testimony was accepted by the Commission, Mr. McWatters and Mr. Jones. Those two witnesses saw "no maniac."

663. Who was the next witness that identified Oswald for the Commission?

A cab driver who drove Oswald to his rooming house.

664. What testimony did he give before the Commission?

He picked up Oswald at 12:30 p.m. and drove Oswald to his rooming home on Berkley Street. The trip took fifteen minutes. The cab driver substantiated his testimony by showing his "trip ticket" to the Commission which showed he had picked up Oswald at the Greyhound bus station and left him off at the 500 North Berkley block. *Seven blocks away.* 2H254; 16H996.

665. At the police lineup whom did this cab driver identify?

None other than an eighteen-year-old boy. R161.

666. What did the police "request" this bus driver do?

Prior to the lineup, the police *compelled* the bus driver to sign an affidavit that he had selected Oswald, before being seen! 6H430-31.

667. Did the cabbie identify Oswald's clothes at the Hearings?

No.

668. Where was Oswald "sitting" while in the cab?

In the front seat, next to the driver! 2H256.

669. Did the cab driver ever identify Oswald?

No. Never. Thus, the Commission perpetuated the height of unmitigated gall. Although the cab driver had this passenger sit right next to him, in the front seat, and *refused* to identify his passenger as Oswald, the *Commission* perverted his testimony and they said it was Lee.

670. How were the identification lineups conducted?

In *violation* of every state and federal court decision. The cab driver, the bus driver, Mrs. Markham, and five other witnesses viewed a lineup that was one hundred percent illegal in view of all recent decisions rendered by the United States Supreme Court,

Earl A. Warren, chief justice. The method can be read in: 2H267, 280, 294, 270; 24H215; 25H901.

671. Did the police compel the cab driver to change his testimony?

Since a cab driver's livelihood depends upon a police department, the driver attempted to change his testimony but did not succeed since he admitted he was now confused by the police. 2H253-62; 6H428-35.

672. After all the testimony is read, where was Oswald?

The *one* and *only witness* who identified Oswald between 12:33 p.m. and 1:00 p.m. was Deputy Sheriff Craig. The bus driver, his passenger, Mr. Jones, and the cab driver *never* identified Oswald and, in fact, denied they even saw Oswald. Mrs. Bledsoe saw a man no one else saw on the same bus she was riding as a passenger. In addition, her memory and eyesight were refreshed by a Secret Service inspector. The Commission *never* found a single witness who corroborated Mrs. Bledsoe's "evidence." Thus, in a court of law, the only witness would be Deputy Sheriff Craig.

-8-

THE COMMISSION VERSUS MEDICAL SCIENCE

673. When did President Kennedy arrive at Parkland Hospital?
The Secret Service says: 12:38 p.m.; the medics say 12:43 p.m.

674. What alarming fact is revealed by the Parkland Hospital report?
That the report was tampered with in such a manner that it would not be admissible in a law court! It is addressed to no one; *no one signed it.*

675. What is the official cause of death of the president?
"A massive head and brain injury from a gunshot wound of the *left temple*"! Dr. R. N. McClelland, R526-27; reaffirmed in 6H30.

676. Is the autopsy signed by Commander Humes of any legal value?
In law, *no* value, worthless. He admitted he destroyed his original notes to the Naval Medical School autopsy report A-63-272. 2H371.

677. Why did the commander destroy his original notes?
The Commission was frightened to ask this pertinent question since the commander stated that he did so at "command of higher authority"!

678. What would the commander have to do to prove his original notes?
In a law court, the commander would have his secondary report carefully scrutinized and those notes would have to be corroborated.

679. Were the commander's "rough notes" corroborated?

No. *New York Times*, November 23, 1963; *New Republic* November 27, 1963; 6H42, 45; 17H4; 20H333.

680. How accurate were the "rough notes"?

In Navy parlance: not an "e"! The commander not only admitted his "rough notes" were, in turn, altered, but [that his report was] also based on a newspaper report of the *Washington Post* of November 23, 1963!

681. Are autopsy reports based on newspaper stories?

Not in accordance with AMA rules of practice.

682. How long did it take the commander to prepare his "official report"?

It took him two days to prepare a report from "rough notes." 2H350, 372.

683. What was the conflict between the commander and the FBI?

The commander said the following FBI report was not true: "that the president had been struck by a bullet which entered his *back* just below his shoulder to the right of the spinal column at an angle of forty-five to sixty degrees downward, there was *no* point of exit, and the bullet not in the body."

684. The Commission said *no* FBI was present at the autopsy. Is this true?

No. False. (1) An FBI agent was in the autopsy room all the time during the autopsy. (2) With the agent were two Secret Service men. (3) *All* agents confirmed the FBI "report" that the physicians announced the fact that the bullet in president's *back* did *not* go through his body. The agent's names were O'Neill and Sibert. 2H93; 18H740-45.

685. What other statement did the FBI issue to the Commission?

"Medical examination of the president's body had revealed that the bullet which entered his *back* had penetrated *less* than a finger length.

686. Did the FBI statement issued in January 1967 retract the above?
No, their report of January 13, 1964 remained unsullied!

687. What is the common sense reply to the Commission?
That a person does *not* have to be a physician to *hear* what a physician has said and then report what the physician has said.

688. Who was the physician who said there was *no* exit wound?
The Army's number one authority on ballistic wounds, Lieutenant Colonel Finck, Chief of Wounds, Ballistic Branch, Armed Forces Institute of Pathology.

689. Was lack of a path consistent with a *low* velocity bullet?
Yes. 6H58.

690. Where did one bullet strike the president?
In the front of his neck, "a penetrating wound." R519.

691. Where did another bullet strike the president?
One shattered the right side of his head. 6H48.

692. Where did a third bullet strike the president?
Near or over the left temple! R527; 6H30; 17H11-12; 29-46.

693. The evidence thus disclosed how many bullets involved?
Four bullets: the (1) back; (2) the front of the throat; (3) the right side of the head; and (4) over *left* temple.

694. Did another *independent bullet strike Governor Connally?*
Yes. *All* evidence supports the answer of "yes"!

695. Were *more* than five bullets fired at the presidential car?

Yes! The evidence revealed two more fired, with two more probable. In addition, the governor may have been struck three times.

696. Why did the Commission willfully conceal the number of bullets?

The Commission had *no* faith in the American people that they had the strength to withstand the shock of a conspiracy. Seven men believed they knew their countrymen better than the countryman [knew] themselves. These willful seven men decided that it was better that the conspirators go free than convict the guilty. Of course, the wealthy, powerful right-wingers, who contribute to both political parties, had no part in the Commission's decisions. These Commissioners are "all honorable men."

697. Where was the president's *back* wound?

[An] FBI agent testified: "I found on the *back* of the president's shirt, a hole, 5.75 inches below the top of the collar, and as you look at the back of the shirt, 1 1/8 inch to the *right* of the mid seam." R91-92.[8]

698. Did the Commission aide *admit* there was a *back* wound?

Yes, but this admission is buried in volume 2 where the aide asked of the Parkland Hospital physician: "Start with the head wound, or the *back* wound, *either* one." 2H380.

699. Then the Commission lied when it said there was *no* back wound?

Yes. A back wound is *not* a neck wound. 2H380.

700. What other famous Commission authority agreed with the aide?

None other than Commander Humes! 2H365-66; 18H240-45.

---

[8] Testimony of FBI Agent Robert Frazier.

701. Who substantiated Frazier, Humes, and the Commission aide?
Agents Kellerman and Hill. R111; 2H365-66; 18H240-45.

702. What did these bullet holes prove?
A conspiracy existed.

703. What is the medical evidence regarding the throat wound?
The bullet wound in the front of the president's throat was caused by a *neat, round hole* which, in ballistic science, can only be caused by an entry wound. 3H9, 361; 5H78; 6H42, 54; 17H848.

704. How large was the wound at the entrance of the throat?
Only five millimeters in diameter. 3H372.

705. How could a 6.5-millimeter bullet leave only a five-millimeter hole?
Ask the Warren Commission. They repealed scientific laws.

706. What did Dr. Shaw state in reference to the throat wound?
Dr. Shaw, [chief] of thoracic surgery, Parkland Hospital, said: "The first bullet entered the president's trachea, *in front of his neck*, coursing downward into his right lung." *New York Times*, November 23, 1963.

707. What did Dr. Clark say regarding this same wound?
The president was "hit by a bullet in the throat just *below* the Adam's apple." *New York Times*, November 23, 1963.

708. What did Dr. Perry state regarding this wound?
The president was hit by a bullet *at the necktie knot* and that the bullet ranged downward in the throat and did not exit. *New York Times*.

709. What did Dr. Carrico and Dr. Jones also testify to what fact?
That the wound was an *entrance wound*. R519; 17H4.

710. Did *any* physician of Parkland Hospital, in the operating room, testify, under oath, that the wound was not an entry wound?

No! Unanimously, every physician said it was an *entry* wound.

711. Who had both the X-rays and papers of the autopsy?
The U.S. Secret Service.

712. Who has them now, in 1967?
The National Archives, Washington, DC. However, there is now evidence that the archives does *not* have the complete set of papers or X-rays, for the archives received and signed only for those items given to them but *no* one knows if what the archives received is the complete set of papers and X-rays. This is one reason why the public does *not* believe in the Warren Report.

713. Why did the Commission conduct such a "sloppy" examination?
The greater the "slop," the greater the confusion; the greater the confusion, the greater difficulty in proving a conspiracy!

714. What would Mrs. Jacqueline Kennedy testify to at the "Hearing"?
The Commission's excuse to withhold her testimony was absurd. The Commission's "sensibilities" did not extend to prevent a man to abuse the president for 132 pages! Mrs. Kennedy testified that her husband was hit in the throat first; that she saw him clutch his throat, at the front, with *both* hands; then she tried to catch him as he fell toward her and she saw the back of his head covered with blood; and as the third bullet hit his head and drove his body away from her, she leaped to grasp him. She testified that she saw the president clutch his throat and remembered the head wounds.

715. Why has Mrs. Kennedy kept silent?
Mrs. Kennedy has two lovely children. If the combined forces of the Secret Service and the FBI could not protect her husband,

the president of the United States, how can they protect her and the children as long as the conspirators remain free?

716. How did the Commission attempt to negate the physician's words?

Several methods were used. The Commission *refused* to permit any physician to use his *original* report; refused to permit them to examine the X-rays *which were in the possession of the U.S. Secret Service* and the FBI; refused to permit them to see the photographs in possession of the same agencies; refused to permit the physicians to see and hear the TV tapes which were offered to the Commission and the Secret Service for a small sum of $450 per tape (President Kennedy's conspirators are going free because the United States of America could not afford $450), and then the Commission had the gall to ask the physicians to answer a hypothetical question based on assumptions, not facts.

717. Is this legal?

No, for a hypothetical question must be based on facts in the trial record.

718. Did any of the physicians unqualifiedly accept this question?

No! Every physician asked the hypothetical question by the Commission qualified his answer: "Assuming the facts are true ..."

719. What legal document was suppressed in the "Report"?

The official *autopsy report* which is known as Commission Exhibit Number 397. This official report on the autopsy of the president's body clearly shows the back wound of the president, the *front neck wound*, and the *two wounds in the head of the president*.

720. What other autopsy report was suppressed?

The report relating to Officer Tippit. In *both* autopsies, the Commission had the legal right to demand their appearance.

721. Did the Commission ever solve the "bullet in the back"?

No, for in the Commission's mind, it never existed! It is the only bullet that made a "self-sealing" path for itself.

722. How many bullets did the conspirators fire at the president?

One bullet hit the president in the front of his throat; one bullet hit him in the back; one bullet hit him on the right side of the head; one bullet on the left side of the head; one bullet hit Governor Connally; one bullet hit the curb; one bullet fragmented and its portions were found on the inside *front* seat of the automobile.

Thus, a *minimum* of seven bullets were fired at President Kennedy.

723. Was there a possibility of more than seven bullets?

Yes! Three additional bullets may have been fired. (1) A bullet may have shattered the Dealey Plaza street sign. This sign has mysteriously disappeared and has been replaced. (2) FBI Agent Frazier testified that the *cross strip*, which is across the top of the windshield, was struck by bullet fragments, however, these fragments may have been part of the fragments found on the front seat. (3) A bullet hole was seen in the grass and photographed. UPI code number DAP 112226: November 22, 1963.

724. Is there proof that the front seat fragment was an independent one?

Yes. The FBI examined the fragments and found no blood or matter on them. The direction of the bullets striking the president's head was against the Commission's theory that those fragments were part of the head bullets. Furthermore, the front seat fragments were *too* large.

725. What startling evidence did the "Report" suppress?

That the president was struck in the head by *two* bullets.

[Editor's note: The enumeration skips ahead here, from 725 to 728.]

728. Is there any evidence in the "Hearings" to support this charge?

Yes! A close analysis of the Zapruder film, frame numbers 311-322. In frame number 311 the president's head is driven *backward* and toward his left. This means, in the law of physical and ballistic science, that the bullet came from the front, *not* from the Book Depository.

At the time Zapruder took this film, by frame 311, the president is already seen clutching his throat.

From frame 311 to 322 there is *no* forward motion of the president.

Mr. Hoover has admitted that, by error, frames 314 and 315 were transposed in volume 18 of the "Hearings." This statement cleared the air, for the unintentional transposition showed the president as if he was struck from a bullet in the head driving him in a different position. Thus, the bullet *did come from the front and right* and this proved a conspiracy.

729. Was the president hit on the left side of the head?

Yes! As previously stated, Dr. Shaw unqualifiedly stated that President Kennedy was also struck on the left side of the head. The physician stated "that the cause of death was due to a massive head and brain injury from a gunshot wound of the *left* temple. "6H30-33.

730. Was his testimony corroborated by other physicians?

Yes. Doctors Giesecke and Jenkins. Thus, three examining physicians upheld a wound over the left side. 6H48, 17H12.

731. Were there any civilian eyewitnesses to the above wound?

Yes, two witnesses: (1) Mr. J. Altgens, who took the famous Altgens photo of Oswald in the doorway; and (2) Mr. N. Similas, a Canadian visitor. Mr. Altgens, standing on Elm Street to the left of the president's auto, stated that "flesh particles flew out of the side of his head in my direction." Thus, the president had to be hit on the left side of his head. 7H518.

(2) The second civilian witness was Mr. N. Similas who stated that he was a mere ten feet from the president's car and that he "could see a hole in the president's left temple, and his head and hair were bathed in blood." *New York Times*, November 23, 1964.

732. Was there another civilian witness to this wound?

Yes. Father O. L. Huber, a Catholic priest who administered the last rites to the president. Father Huber stated that he "noticed a 'terrible wound' over his left eye." Philadelphia *Sunday Bulletin*, November 24, 1963.

733. Does the official autopsy report, *Exhibit Number 397, uphold* a bullet wound over the upper left-hand side of the head?

Yes. A black dot, with a figure in centimeters appears. This is the official method of locating wounds in the body!

734. Where can all this evidence be found?

In: 4H30-33; 6H48; 7H518; 17H11-12, 17H45.

The evidence is *conclusive* that President Kennedy was struck twice in the head. One bullet hit him on the right side of the head, and this conclusion is supported by every eyewitness, and *supported by the physicians* and the official autopsy report.

The Zapruder film supports the uncontradicted fact that the wound at the *rear* of the president's skull was an *exit* wound since his head is driven *backwards*.

Agents of the various federal and state police *testified* that President Kennedy was struck on the *right* side of his head. These witnesses include: Secret Service Agents Kinney[9] and Hickey; [J.

---

[9] Sam Kinney drove the car directly behind JFK's limousine in the cavalcade. His daughter Susan Rosser later reported that Kinney "found a piece of the skull. It was about the size of a small ashtray. He put it in his pocket until he saw White House doctor Admiral Burkley. Burkley put it into his pocket. Nobody ever asked him about it again. That bothered him." See Lona O'Connor, "Momentous seconds in Dallas 50 years ago haunted secret service agent who retired to Palm Beach County," *Palm Beach Post* (online), November 21, 2013.

Hurchel,] a Texas Highway Patrolman; Agent Kellerman, USSA [Secret Service, Assistant Special Agent]; and an additional two civilian witnesses, W. E. Newman, and S. Kantor of the accredited Washington press corps. Their *uncontradicted evidence can be read in:* 18H731, 765, 801; 19H490; 20H353, 2H81.

The Warren Commission willfully and deliberately buried this testimony to deceive the American people that a conspiracy existed which conspiracy was directed and executed by persons who were either citizens of the United States or under the command and control of an agency of the federal government.

735. What was Commission Exhibit Number 399?

A *planted* bullet that was used by the Commission as an excuse by the Commission to support *their* contention, in spite of all evidence to the contrary, that this number 399 struck *both* the president and Governor Connally.

736. What were the opposing viewpoints?

The FBI, the Secret Service, and the medical profession, *plus* the immutable *laws of physical and ballistic sciences* proved bullet number 399 could not and *did not* strike both men; the Commission, who had only its own prestige to support its theory, stated that bullet number 399 did go through and in the body of two men.

737. Who does the public believe?

The public, after listening and reading the activities of this "prestige" Commission, has, by a vote of nearly seventy percent, supported the view of the FBI, the Secret Service, the medical profession, and the immutable law of science.

738. Who introduced this bullet theory that violated science?

A Commission aide who admitted to Allen Dulles that he knew he would find evidence to support his "theory."[10] 2H368.

---

[10] The origin of the theory is generally attributed to Arlen Specter, who served as assistant counsel for the Warren Commission.

739. Did this "knowledgeable" "legal beagle" have documentary proof that his "theory" was supportable?

Yes, in the possession of the Commission were two *official* documents from (1) the FBI and (2) the Secret Service which positively stated that this bullet number 399 was found on the stretcher used to carry President Kennedy to the operating room in Parkland Hospital.

As usual, these documents were hidden from the American public; they can be found in the National Archives (or they were there, but, in view of the fact that many papers are *now missing*, they may not be), entitled Commission Document Numbers 3, 5, and 7.

740. Where did bullet number 399 come from?

[According to] the uncontradicted testimony of the finder, Mr. Tomlinson, from the *president's* stretcher! 2H368.

741. What was the condition of bullet number 399 when found?

(1) It was in a clean condition; (2) it had lost *only* 1/180th of an ounce in weight! 3H430; 4H113; 17H49.

742. Where was the location of the president's *back* wound?

As previously pointed out in questions 697 to 702, the *back* wound was *not* a neck wound. "A shot (that) hit the president about four inches *down* from the right shoulder" is *not* a neck wound. R111; 18H470.

743. What did the Commission expect the public to swallow?

That a bullet that lost less than 1/100 of an ounce caused the following damage: went through the neck of President Kennedy, *changed* direction, shattered four inches of Governor Connally's rib, blasted his right wrist to pieces, changed direction, and pierced three inches *into* his left thigh, and lo and behold, emerged as a *perfect* normal bullet!

744. Could any bullet do all this damage and be perfect?

Medical and ballistic science says "No"! 3H340, 399; 4H113.

745. Did the Commission's *own* physicians uphold the Commission?

Commanders Humes and Boswell said *"No."* 2H374-77; 17H418.

746. Did Lieutenant Colonel Finck, the Army's number one ballistic surgeon, uphold it?

No! 2H375-82.

747. Did Dr. Shaw, the Connally operating physician, uphold it?

No! 4H113-14.

748. Is it honest to state that *no* physician upheld the Commission?

Yes! There is not a single piece of testimony by the medical profession that upheld the Commission's theory.

749. The Commission said the "bullet tumbled" and this "tumbling" created all the damage. (R95). Can a bullet "tumble"?

No, and there is *no* forensic evidence to prove it.

750. Who upheld the above answer? When?

Three and one half years after the release of the "Report" a Commission aide admitted (1) You can't fire a bullet that "tumbles"; and (2) the Commission's own test bullets did *not* match bullet number 399 in any shape, manner or form! This admission appeared in the August 1966 issue of *Greater Philadelphia Magazine*, by Gaeton Fonzi.[11]

Again is seen the deceit practiced by the Commission.

751. Can this aide's statement be corroborated?

Yes. *Buried deep*, deep, deep in the "Hearings" are the *actual* photographs of the various tests conducted by the Commission.

---

[11] A reference to Fonzi's interviews with Arlen Specter. The audio tapes of these interviews are available online.

Compare bullet number 399 with Commission Exhibit Numbers 572, 858; 17H851!

752. What do these "test" bullets reveal?

Every one of them was deformed and were *not* ballistically capable of being examined! R80.

753. What other method was used to "support" the Commission theory?

(1) The aide who examined the Commission's own two experts was none other than the aide who "created" the theory. This would be like a trial judge being asked to conduct an examination of his conduct on an appeal by the accused protesting the judge's conduct! (2) The experts were asked, and answered, questions pertaining to material not involved in the tests. The Commission then used these immaterial answers as a proper solution to bullet number 399! 5H90-92.

754. What *federal agency* upheld the FBI reports of December 9, 1963 and January 13, 1964 which stated, and then reaffirmed, that the president had a *distinct* back wound, *not* a wound in the back of the neck?

The Warren Commission *suppressed* the official document of the *United States Secret Service* which specifically stated that (1) the president was shot first; (2) then Governor Connally received a bullet; and (3) then the president was hit with *another* bullet.

This *Secret Service document* is *buried* in the National Archives and is dated November 28, 1963, with code number 2-34, 030. It is titled: "Preliminary Special Dallas Report #1." Signed by Inspector Kelley.

Notice that the date of the Secret Service report is November 28, 1963. The "official" autopsy report was released on November 24, 1963. The FBI first report was dated December 9, 1963; and the FBI *reiterated* its first report on January 13, 1964.

As of this date, Mr. Hoover has never denied the statements made by the FBI agents to the Commission that it was a wound and that Governor Connally was struck by an independent bullet.

Is the Commission contending that *both* agencies are incompetent?

755. How can a citizen, not an attorney, physician, FBI agent, or Secret Service agent, reading the evidence given to the Commission under oath, decide for himself (or herself) the question: "Was the president struck in the back by an independent bullet?

Based strictly on its theory, the bullet in the president's back would have, after it had entered the president's back, traveled *upward through his body*, come out of his body, made a right turn and entered his neck; then as the bullet passed through his neck, take another partial right turn, *downward*, and strike the governor. The Commission admitted that there is no tissue or bone in any person's neck to deflect a bullet and the Commission also stated that the bullet left the neck below the breastbone since the Commission said that the bullet's path was fifteen degrees.

If the average citizen believes that a bullet can change its path, in midair, and hitting nothing that can cause deflection, if the citizen believes that, then he believes the Commission is correct.

However, the citizen would have to refuse to believe *all* the evidence and tests conducted by the Commission itself.

756. What did the evidence reveal as to the *angle* of the bullets?

(1) Commander Humes stated that the bullet came in at a forty-five degree angle; (2) the FBI report said forty-five to sixty degrees; (3) Governor Connally's bullet hit him at a twenty-seven-degree angle; and (4) the official surveyor for the Commission said the bullet hit the president at a seventeen-plus-degree angle.

Every one of the angles *proved* that two bullets were fired at the president; and one independent bullet hit the governor! This fact, alone, proved the existence of a conspiracy.

Evidence, not theory, proved that there were a minimum of three riflemen firing at President Kennedy. As has been seen, and will be seen, one rifleman was hidden on the second floor of the *Dal-Tex Building*. Two riflemen were in front of the president.

The evidence, as has been shown, proved that Lee Harvey Oswald could not, and did not, fire any bullets at the president of the United States or the governor of the State of Texas.

He was a "patsy," part of the conspiracy, but not the "sole and exclusive killer" of President John F. Kennedy.

-9-

PICTURES CAN BE MADE TO LIE

757. How did the Commission compel the "camera's eye" to lie?

The Commission again *suppressed* an FBI report which stated that the camera used by Mr. Zapruder was set for twenty-four frames per second (fps), but the Commission had it set for only eighteen-plus frames per second.

This report can be found in the National Archives, File Number 7. Dated December 4, 1963, code number DL89-43, signed by Robert M. Barrett, Dallas, Texas. Typed by /gmf.

758. What does this mean?

That the Commission's reconstruction and the testimony of FBI Agent Shaneyfelt was a deliberate fraud upon the public. The agent is not condemned for he was simply instructed, by the Commission, to use 18.3 seconds (fps). He may *not* have known of File Number 7.

759. Would a law court accept the reconstruction or testimony?

Absolutely not! The reconstruction and testimony must be based on *facts* which must be proved to be accurate.

760. What was the purpose behind this fraudulent reconstruction?

To conceal the truth.

761. What was the effect of changing the speed of the camera?

It increased the action of the film by 33.3 percent!

762. How did the change of speed affect the testimony?

It changed the time between the shots! Agent Shaneyfelt said: "The camera operates at an average speed of 18.3 fps.... *The maximum* time for firing the rifle in succession is approximately two-and-a-quarter seconds.... This gives us this figure of forty-one to forty-two frames ... and establishes two points in the film where two successive shots *could have been fired.* R153-54.

763. How did Agent Shaneyfelt obtain his "reconstruction"? Believe it or not, from a *copy* of a *copy!* 5H177.

764. Did the Commission have the *original* Zapruder film? Yes.

765. Then why did the Commission refuse to give it to him? And have the agent prove Oswald did not fire those shots?

766. On what facts did the agent [base] his "reconstruction"? "On information furnished by the Commission, and photographs taken by the Dallas Police Department." 5H145.

767. What new formula did the Commission thus create? A lie plus a lie equals the truth.

768. Was Agent Shaneyfelt a key witness for the Commission? He was the key photographic witness. His testimony revealed that he was only the producer, but the script was written by the Commission. 4H279; 5H138, 176; 7H410; and 15H686.

769. Why would a law court refuse to admit the "reconstruction"? The agent's reconstruction would be inadmissible because: (1) The agent worked with a copy of a copy of the Zapruder film. (2) The original film was developed on sixteen-millimeter film and the copy was made on an eight millimeter film. Thus, clarity was completely lost. (3) The original speed of twenty-four frames per second was reduced to 18.3 fps. (4) Much of the reconstruction was made at 6:00 a.m., not at 12:30 p.m. Thus, the light conditions were false.

(5) The Commission suppressed the fact that the Dallas Police Department had falsely reconstructed the street conditions. 17H875.

(6) The Commission also suppressed the fact that frame numbers 208-221 are *not* available and were not printed in volume 18.

(7) Frame number 212 is mutilated beyond repair.

(8) Frame numbers 314 and 315 were transposed thus creating the impression that the president had been struck in the head from a bullet behind the president. Mr. Hoover has stated that the frames in volume 18 are incorrectly transposed.

(9) The Zapruder film revealed that the bullet that struck the president in front of the throat was fired prior to frame 210.

(10) The Zapruder film also revealed Governor Connally was hit at frame 225. This makes another distinct bullet.

770. What type of film and photographs have been suppressed?
The film and still photographs taken immediately prior, during and after the murder.

771. Why?
The only reason given by the Commission was that "it was against the national interest." However, another reason could be that the Commission did not want persons who could have been seen, seen.

772. What vital picture was suppressed?
The Mary Moorman Polaroid picture. She was given a receipt but the picture has never been published. This is a picture of the sixth floor *at the instant the shots were fired*. 2H44; 18H59-69; 19H635-36; 19H467-87.

773. What is the famous *Altgens* photograph?
A photograph taken by Mr. Altgens, a twenty-five-year veteran with the AP, who took the photograph of the "man in the door entrance."

774. Who was the "man in the door entrance"?

The evidence clearly supports the fact that it was Oswald.

775. Why did the Commission have to dis-approve this fact?
Oswald in the doorway could not be Oswald on the sixth floor.

776. Is there any proof that the man was Oswald?
Yes. In the Commission files (again, we find suppression of facts) is a picture of the man the Commission says was the man in the doorway, a Billy Lovelady. The picture shows Lovelady in the *clothes he wore* at the time the murder was committed. The picture revealed the fact that Lovelady wore a "red and white vertical striped shirt." R113; Shaneyfelt Exhibit Number 24.

777. What did the "man in the door entrance" wear?
The same color shirt, in the same manner, as Oswald's!

778. Did Mr. J. Edgar Hoover write a letter concerning this?
Yes. A suppressed letter to the Commission, dated March 9, 1964 to Mr. J. Lee Rankin, general counsel. Mr. Hoover stated that Mr. Lovelady informed his agents that when he wore his shirt it was buttoned up *all the way to the neck* and had red stripes!

779. For what other reason did the Commission distort this photo?
The photograph was taken when the president's car was about twenty-five to thirty feet away from Altgens' location. The president and the governor had already been hit. Thus, the Commission had the exact location of the car, and it should have should been used by Agent Shaneyfelt. 7H520-22.

780. Did any evidence substantiate the Altgens location?
Yes, Agent Shaneyfelt testified that the picture was taken exactly at frame 225 of the Zapruder film. 5H158.

781. How did the Commission attempt to negate the exact location?

It published a false exhibit. The Commission had Mr. Altgens place a spot on a map locating his standing place. Then, this actual spot is placed in the area which negated his location. 16H949, Exhibit 354.

782. How else did the Commission deceive the American public?

Published Exhibit Number 893 as a true reproduction of frame number 210. The Commission admitted that frames 210 to 211 were destroyed in *Life's* photo laboratory. Then how could [Exhibit] Number 893 be frame 210?

783. Why did the Commission publish this fraud?

The Commission labeled this Exhibit: "Photograph through Rifle Scope." The "picture" shows the president's "head" through tree branches *as it was to be seen by a rifleman on the sixth floor*. The Commission created a "theory" and *manufactured evidence to support their theory*.

784. What did the Commission do to the Altgens photograph?

The Commission deceived the public by "cropping" the entire *right side* of the picture. In law, this is fraud.

785. Why did the Commission publish a "cropped" photograph?

The picture, in its entirety, proved that one of the bullets which struck President Kennedy was fired from the second floor of the *Dal-Tex Building*.

The Dallas police, it should be remembered, arrested a man in this building immediately after the shots were fired, and held him on a charge of "suspicion of murder." *This arrest is recorded in the published police log.* Yet, *the federal agencies did nothing. Why?*

The reader should also recall the fact that the angle of the bullet corresponded to a bullet fired from the *Dal-Tex Building!*

786. Why did the Commission lie about the photographic evidence?

To *conceal* the vastness of the *conspiracy.*

787. How did the Commission create its own "red herring"?

By the use of fraudulent evidence, they attempted to prove that Mr. Zapruder's film showed the president hit *after* frame number 210. R98.

788. How and "who" proved that the president was hit prior to number 225?

The "who" is the "eye" of the Zapruder camera. Mr. Zapruder, after waiting seven months, testified that the president was first struck in the *front of his throat* in frame number 185. 7H571-73.

789. How did the Commission attempt to confuse Mr. Zapruder?

By showing him pictures of a film in black-and-white thirty-five-millimeter *slides.* His original film was in eight-millimeter size and in color.

790. Did the Commission have the legal right to show the film?

Yes. Although the Commission said that the film was the property of *Life*, the Commission had the *legal right*, under Executive Order Number 11130, and by joint resolution of Congress, to subpoena those films. After seeing the films, *Life* would then receive them from the Commission.

The Commission had no qualms in seizing the Mormon pictures or the Altgens picture and *keeping them.*

Did the Commission, under Chief Justice Warren, create a new American principle *that the size of a person's pocketbook determines the kinds of law to be used to determine principles?*

791. What does *film number 205* reveal?

Another Commission deception! The Commission stated that the president's head was not visible to any rifleman until frame number 210. However, frame number 205 revealed his head very clearly.

792. How did the Commission *prove* that *they* had lied?

It is an old proverb that give a liar enough rope and his lies will hang him. The Commission, ironically, used its own rope!

The Commission adopted its own formula which proved they lied:

(1) The killer needed 2.3 seconds between shots.

(2) The camera's speed, the Commission said, was 18.3 fps.

(3) Therefore, the minimum number of frames proceeding through the camera was 18.3 fps x 2.3 seconds or a total of 42.09 frames per shot.

(4) The Commission admitted the president had been struck by frame number 225, and in this frame the president is seen clutching his throat. Thus, subtract 42.05 frames from where the Commission stated the president had *first* been hit, and this is frame number 183 *which showed the president's hands clutching his throat*. This supports Mr. Zapruder.

793. Is there another way to prove that Mr. Zapruder was correct?

Yes, by using the same Commission formula:

(A) Governor Connally was struck in frame number 230.

(B) By even using the Commission's theory that the same bullet struck both the president and the governor, and allowing the smallest time for the governor's reaction, then by simply subtracting 42.09 frames from number 230, the final figure is frame number 185.91 *where the film revealed* that President Kennedy is already clutching his throat!

794. Is there still another method to prove the Commission was wrong?

Yes. The Commission stated that the president's head wound can be seen originally on frame number 311.

Thus, by using this frame, the Commission, in spite of themselves, *proved* that President Kennedy was struck *prior* to frame number 225.

The Commission stated that all three shots, including the one that missed, were fired in a total time period of 5.6 seconds.

The evidence revealed that the president was clutching his throat when he and the governor were hit. Thus, the only fact to be solved: "Did the president become struck in the throat prior to frame number 225?" If the president's hands were at his throat prior to frame 211 then he must have been struck in the neck first.

Now, since frames 210 to 211 inclusive have been destroyed, does frame 209 show the president's hands at his throat?

The answer is "yes"! By moving the film backward, it can be seen that the hands remain on the throat until [frame] number 185 and, continuing backward, the hands can be seen dropping away.

795. What did the condition actually prove?
The existence of a conspiracy.

796. What *federal agency had its official survey suppressed?*
The Commission *suppressed* the reconstruction of the murder site, the location of the president's automobile when the shots hit the president, and the number of shots fired. This suppressed report *proved Oswald innocent* of the Commission's charge. File 87.

-10-

THE COMMISSION VERSUS BASIC PRINCIPLES OF AMERICAN JUSTICE

797. What was the *legal* duty of the Warren Commission?
To evaluate facts and ascertain the truth.

798. Was the Commission to act as prosecutor, judge, and jury?
No.

799. What [was] the Warren Commission?
Originally, it was to be a fact-finding Commission; however, it acted as a star-chamber committee and obscured the truth.[12]

800. Was the president of the American Bar Association necessary?
No. Mr. Craig was appointed to make sure the Commission followed "basic principles of American justice." He followed.[13]

801. Did the Commission adhere to those principles?"

---

[12] According to *West's Encyclopedia of American Law*, the Star Chamber, "named for a room with stars painted on the ceiling in the royal palace of Westminster where the court sat," was "an ancient high court of England, controlled by the monarch, which was abolished in 1641 by Parliament for abuses of power." "The term *star chamber* has come to mean any lawless and oppressive tribunal, especially one that meets in secret. The constitutional concept of Due Process of Law is in part a reaction to the arbitrary use of judicial power displayed by the Star Chamber." *West's Encyclopedia of American Law, Second Edition* (Farmington Hills, MI: The Gale Group, 2008), online.

[13] By saying "He followed," I believe Marks is implying here that Craig "followed orders" rather than following the basic principles of American justice.

No. The Commission permitted outright hearsay; it permitted perjury; it permitted its aides to use threats to obtain "evidence" to convict Oswald; it accepted fraudulent photographs; it *suppressed* evidence that would have proved the Commission's theory wrong; and the Commission permitted their aides to act above and beyond the established legal rules of procedure.

802. Was Oswald legally indicted by legal methods?

This question is now subject to great doubt. The unquestioned facts are as follows:

(1) At 11:26 p.m. on November 22, Oswald was hauled before a press conference. At this conference Oswald was asked if he had been charged with the murder of President Kennedy.

(2) Oswald answered "No"; only with the Tippit murder.

(3) Both the district attorney and his assistant then admitted that Oswald had only been charged with the Tippit murder.

(4) At the conference the assistant held up an "affidavit" and the press took pictures of It.

(5) Oswald, according to the Commission, was then brought before a justice, on November 23, and charged with the murder of President Kennedy at 1:35 a.m. He had no attorney present.

803. Then what happens?

In the United States, nothing. However, in Europe, when this picture was published, something that escaped every attorney in the United States was seen by Mr. Joesten, an author of anti-Nazi books. He said nothing until his book was published, titled *Oswald: Assassin or Fall Guy?* The book was released prior to the Commission's "Report."

804. What did this book say?

That the "affidavit" held up by the assistant district attorney had (1) *no* judge's signature; and (2) no person signed the "affidavit" as an "affiant"! The "affidavit" was worthless as a legal document.

805. Then what happened?

Warned, the Commission set about to "cure" the mistake.

806. What was the sequence of events?

Captain Fritz, who gave conflicting testimony, under oath, said he made no "rough" notes but then made a report based on "rough notes." In the captain's report is the statement that Oswald had been charged with the Kennedy murder before Justice Johnston.

However, on page four of this "report," the captain said that Tippit had been arraigned for the murder of Tippit! Yet, the Commission accepted the captain's report as true. According to the captain, Oswald was charged with the Kennedy murder at 1:35 a.m.

807. Is there another affidavit published by the Commission?

Yes, in the Warren "Report" is an affidavit printed on the regular report stock paper, and the assistant D.A.'s picture on glossy enamel stock. A person can count the number of lines *below* the DA's fingers and there is *no* writing and *no* printed material.

808. What is the new affidavit photograph?

This "new" photograph is published as the Johnston Exhibit Number 4. What is glossed over by the Commission is the fact that on the side of this reprint is some very strange writing. This writing is *not* on the affidavit but on the side, outside of the four corners of the affidavit.

Someone has handwritten in some words and dates: either January 26, 1964 or June 26, 1964. Justice Johnston did not testify before the Commission on either date; nor is it in D.A. Wade's or Captain Fritz's handwriting.

809. What else is strange about Johnston Exhibit Number 4?

The fact that the published photograph is torn completely across about two-thirds of the way down. *The two parts do not match!*

810. What is another mystery?

That the Alexander "affidavit"[14] and the torn Johnston Exhibit Number 4 are *inadmissible* in a court of law. Both are worthless.

811. Did the police file a report on the Oswald arrest?
Yes, a very strange one.

812. Why so strange?
That the Dallas police *knew* that Oswald was the murderer of President Kennedy despite the fact that:
(1) at 2:30 p.m. on the day of the murder, less than three hours had elapsed [yet] the Dallas police knew Oswald was the "killer"!
(2) although Police Chief Curry was to go on national TV after the police lineup and say no identity was made, they *knew!*
(3) although *no* fingerprints were found to connect Oswald with the rifle or cartons, the police *knew!*
(4) although the FBI had not yet traced "Hidell" to Oswald as the purchaser of a rifle, *the police knew Oswald was the killer.*

813. How is this knowledge proved?
By the statement made by the arresting officers which appears on the *charge sheet*:
"This man shot and killed President *John F. Kennedy* and Police Officer Tippit. He also shot and wounded Governor John Connally."

814. Where can this "charge" sheet be seen?
In the illustration section of the "Report." Note (1) the time when arrested; (2) *no* policeman signed the charge sheet; (3) the vacant spaces below the policemen's names; (4) charge space.
The Commission has admitted that *none* of the officers participating in the Oswald arrest knew that he was wanted in the murder of President Kennedy. Then how did the arresting officers *know* that Oswald was the "killer"? Note that the policemen used the word: "killed."

[14] District Attorney William ("Bill") Alexander was photographed holding what he claimed to be an affidavit charging Oswald with the assassination of JFK.

[The author skips ahead here, from Q&A 814 to 819.–Ed.'s note.]

819. Who was the Commission's key witness against Oswald?
Mrs. Marina Oswald, his wife.

820. Was she in protective custody?
Yes! This is discovered by delving into the National Archives and reading Commission Exhibit Number 344. Mrs. Oswald gave a long statement when interrogated by FBI and Secret Service agents. The statement was made on December 1, 1963, "where Mrs. Oswald is being held at 'Inn of Seven Flags.'"

821. What evidence did she give concerning the rifle?
That the rifle she had seen in her New Orleans home had *no* telescopic sight. Commission Exhibit Number 344, National Archives.

822. Did Mrs. Oswald identify *that* rifle to the Dallas police?
No! It was shown to her on November 22, 1963. 1H164; 4H24; 24H219.

823. Did she ever state that Oswald owned, possessed or used a revolver?
No! She only said a rifle with *no* telescopic sight. Commission Exhibit 344.

824. Did she identify the bullets allegedly from *that* rifle?
No! She said the bullets she saw were much smaller. 1H119.

825. When did Justice Warren *know* she would identify the rifle?
The day *before* she testified! *New York Post*, February 5, 1964.

826. Was Mrs. Oswald threatened with deportation?
Yes, by all three federal agencies. 22H194; 740-64; 23H363-400.

827. In a law court is her testimony of any value?

No value at all. This is not based on the principle of husband cannot testify, or the wife, against each other but based simply on her statement to the federal agents on December 1, 1963.

Since the Commission accepted her statement and testimony the Commission, under basic principles of American law, cannot accept pieces or sections to prove their case. They cannot impeach their own witness.

828. How did the Commission handle evidence they did not want?

The Commission (1) placed evidence against its theory in the section entitled "Rumors and Speculations." The average reader would conclude that the "rumor" had been investigated and discredited. Were not the Commissioners "all honorable men"? (2) Failed to call witnesses who would give evidence upsetting the "theory." (3) *Suppressed written* evidence, charts, surveys, and photographs. (4) Selected only those facts that agreed with their "theory."

829. What were "off the cuff" interviews?

When the witness was not giving testimony to support the "theory," the aides used this method to "convert" the witness!

830. What was said by the aides during these "interviews"?

According to the witnesses who did talk after the examination, threats were used to change the testimony. This is called, in law, "suborning a witness" and is a criminal offense. A perjury indictment was threatened against a policeman who refused to change his testimony. 5H213; 254-58.

831. Were "smear" tactics used by the Commission?

Yes, in the form of "leaks" to the press, radio and TV. The policeman's case, cited above, was a "smear" tactic. In the Joesten *Oswald: Assassin or Fall Guy?* case, the Commission had the CIA go to the *Gestapo files* to try and prove that he [Joesten] was a "communist"![15]

832. Was Mr. Zapruder also "smeared."
The Commission charged him with "profiteering" for selling his film to *Life* for $25,000.

833. Was this true?
A half-truth is more vicious than an outright lie. Mr. Zapruder *gave* the entire amount to Officer Tippit's family![16]
The above are just a few samples of the Commission's interpretation of "basic principles of American justice."

834. How did the police forbid legal advice for Oswald?
They informed the Dallas Civil Liberties Union that Oswald had said he had an attorney. 7H322.

835. What did the Civil Liberties Union do?
What could they do? Force their way into Oswald's cell? Call the state police? Ask for a Texas judge? 7H322-23; 20H685.

[15] "The Warren Commission obtained certain detailed background information on Joesten. Mark Lane made this public in 1967, when he told an audience that federal authorities had gathered data on most of the critics. 'One of the files in the National Archives,' he said, 'is a document submitted to the Warren Commission by the CIA, listed as a "basic source material" relied upon by the Warren Commission. What is it? A Gestapo file. The Gestapo prepared a file on Mr. Joesten back in 1937. Can you imagine the chief justice poring over the Gestapo file [concerning] the political reliability of one of the Commission's critics?'" John Kelin quotes from a tape recording, in the Ray Marcus archive, of Mark Lane in a debate with Wesley Liebeler on January 21, 1967, held at the University of California, Los Angeles. Since LA was Stanley Marks' locale, it's quite likely that Marks learned of this firsthand, by attending the debate. John Kelin, *Praise from a Future Generation* (San Antonio, TX: Wings Press, 2007), p. 171.
[16] The film was sold for $150,000, plus royalties. Mr. Zapruder donated the first $25,000 to Tippit's widow.

836. How did the Commission handle this violation?

Like all lawyers: with a smattering of truth caking over the facts with a gloss of words. The evidence revealed that the police refused to permit the union to see Oswald because Oswald had not requested their service. How could he request their service if he did not see them? R200, R598-636.

837. Did Oswald, at first, request an attorney?

Yes. He requested the services of a Mr. Abt, a New York lawyer. The police said they had placed a phone call to him and he rejected Oswald's request.

838. Was this true?

No. The Dallas police committed outright perjury. Mr. Abt denied any such phone call. The Commission refused to subpoena the telephone company's records to verify the police statement. R627; 10H16; 20H685.

839. Were Oswald's other rights violated?

Yes. Illegal searches were made of his home in Irving and Dallas, Texas. R177-80; 7H177, 188-91; 21H603-699.

840. Did the Commission investigate the arrest of the two other suspects seized by the police on the murder day?

Of course not. Oswald, the "patsy," was dead. Nor did the Commission investigate the man on the fire escape seen in the famous "Altgens photograph." Nor did the Commission investigate the conditions surrounding the man captured in the *Dal-Tex Building with a rifle in his hands.* Nor did the Commission ask any questions regarding the man captured on the "grassy knoll" with a rifle in his hands. *Both rifles* were of the caliber used to fire the bullets which struck the president. Nor did the Commission ask Mr. Couch, of WFAA-TV, to show his film taken of the Dal-Tex Building during and after the shooting.

These films revealed a rifle-like object from the second floor. 6H160.

Nor did the Commission ever ask the Dallas police who owned the jacket found near the Tippet murder.

841. Was the jacket Tippit's jacket?

No! Mrs. Oswald testified that she never sent any of his shirts or jackets to the cleaner since her husband objected to the cost. This jacket was used by the Commission as a key piece of evidence to connect Oswald with the Tippit murder. *No* witnesses ever testified that they saw this jacket. The FBI, who could trace the Russian spy, Abel, by a hollowed five-cent piece, could not locate the owner of the jacket that had a clothing serial number on it! Believe it or not![17]

842. Did the Commission believe the police were efficient?

Efficient? The Commission could not find enough words in the English language to praise the Dallas Police Department.

To achieve this praise, this paragon of police departments did the following:

They: (1) found evidence; (2) lost evidence; (3) had *no* stenographer at Oswald's interrogation; (4) had *no* tape recorder either; (5) conducted illegal searches; (6) seized private property which was never returned; (7) threatened witnesses; (8) committed perjury; (9) switched evidence; (10) did not know the difference between a German "Mauser" and an Italian "Carcano" rifle; (11) found chicken bones; (12) lost chicken bones; (13) took pictures of a "bag" that was not there; (14) found fingerprints; (15) had three members of the force who left no fingerprints; (16) found a holster; (17) lost vital radio logs; (18) reconstructed a murder site but first changed the street scene; (19) lost a revolver; (20) found a revolver; (21) arrested and then released men charged with "suspicion of murder"; and so on and on and on!

For the above, the Commission *profusely praised the police.*

---

[17] Abel: a reference to Soviet intel agent Vilyam Genrikhovich Fisher, a.k.a. Rudolf Ivanovich Abel (1903-1971), and the FBI's Hollow Nickel Case. (The hollow coin contained a hidden microphotograph.) In 1957 Fisher was convicted for conspiracy as a Soviet spy.

843. How can the interpretation of the phrase: "basic principles of American justice" be made in reference to the Commission?

On both moral and legal plateaus the Commission was a disgrace to "basic principles of American justice."

-11-

INVESTIGATORS OR "FALL GUYS"? THE FBI

844. What was the role of the FBI under Executive Order Number 11130?

To cooperate with the Commission.

845. Was the function of the FBI to interpret or evaluate the facts?

No.

846. Was it their function to suppress or distort facts?

No.

847. Was the murder of President Kennedy a federal crime?

No. The State of Texas had sole jurisdiction. Only those acts specified in the U.S. Code were and are federal crimes.

848. Where does the Jim Garrison "Affair" come into the picture?

Mr. Garrison, the district attorney of New Orleans, Louisiana, secured an indictment of a man allegedly connected with a *conspiracy* that involved the murder of President Kennedy.

849. How could he secure an indictment if the murder was in Texas?

The State of Louisiana has a *state* law which prohibits persons to *conspire* to commit a crime. The *crime* is the *conspiracy*, not the conclusion, successful or not, of the conspiracy. Thus, although the culmination of the conspiracy takes place outside of the state's boundary, the crime is the *conspiracy* itself.

850. Is this why Mr. Garrison refused to give his information to the FBI, the Secret Service, and the CIA?

Yes. *None* of the *federal agencies* have any jurisdiction to prosecute any act that is not a crime as defined by the U.S. Code. There is *no* federal law regarding the murder of the president of the United States nor any act regarding a conspiracy to murder him.

851. Could Mr. Garrison have gone to the Dallas police?

How could they know the difference between a crime and a conspiracy? Seriously, the State of Texas has *no* right to interfere in the acts of Louisiana. States' rights, you know.

852. Has Mr. Garrison requested the services of the Dallas police, the FBI, the Secret Service, and the CIA?

Yes, and all of them are going out of their way to interfere with Mr. Garrison's investigation. None of those agencies can afford to have a conspiracy proved since the proof of the conspiracy would automatically involve each agency with the charge of, at the minimum, gross negligence. As to the Dallas Police Department, many of its members were involved in (1) the Kennedy murder; (2) the Tippet murder; (3) the Oswald murder; and (4) the Ruby murder. Mr. Garrison has attempted to secure the testimony of a witness who fled to Texas but the Dallas authorities have blocked this attempt. If this witness is involved, he does not have long to live and his confidence is misplaced!

853. How did the FBI become the "fall guys" for the Dallas police?

Only Mr. J Edgar Hoover can answer this question! Present and future historians will seek the answer and it will never be solved as long as Mr. Hoover remains silent.

On the day of the murder, although the FBI had no authority to investigate, various FBI members were involved in the activities commenced after the murder. There is evidence of this as this book will soon show.

The FBI, on the afternoon of the murder, knew from the reports issued by the various official physicians conducting the operations to save the life of President Kennedy that the president's neck wound had come from the front. The FBI also knew from the same reports that the cause of death was a wound over the left temple and also the fact that the president had been hit on the right side of the head. This was a classic crossfire setup. It could only mean that a conspiracy existed. By the night of the next day, the FBI also knew that the president had a back wound. Again, confirmation of a conspiracy.

The FBI also had the public statements of Police Chief Curry that the police had *no* witness to the murder. By the end of four days the FBI had the autopsy report, the rifle, the bullets, the revolver, and in spite of this evidence, the FBI conducted itself on the theory that Oswald was the killer.

That is why only Mr. Hoover can answer this question.

854. When were the FBI "reports" issued?

The "reports," consisting of five volumes, were issued, volumes 1-4, on December 9, 1963; the fifth volume on January 13, 1964.

855. What are the main features of the "report"?

The many "red flag" signals that the average person would immediately [recognize as evidence] that the Dallas police were involved.

856. What was the first "red flag"?

The use of the English language and the construction of words and phrases. Thus the constant use of the word "owned" in reference to the rifle. The strange statement that the rifle barrel of the rifle may have been changed. The refusal of the FBI to verify the police statement that Tippet stopped Oswald based on radio broadcasts. The fact that the FBI named every witness who said they saw Oswald *except* Mr. Brennan–yet Mr. Brennan's name was in every newspaper and spoken over the air.

857. What is the major difference between the Warren and FBI reports?

The total disagreement between the FBI and the Commission.

Thus, when the FBI agents testified, under oath, their testimony either totally disagreed or was qualified in regards to the "facts" written in the Warren "Report."

On every major issue regarding the facts used by the Commission to "convict" Oswald, the FBI disagreed [with], and this disagreement generally applied to, all ballistic tests and fingerprint evidence.

858. What key witness supported the FBI's bullet "in the back"?

None other than the Commission's own witness, Commander Humes.

He confirmed the FBI statement that the bullet hole in the president's back was "5 3/4 inches below the top of the collar and two inches to the right of the seam." R91-92; 2H365. This admission is buried in volume 2.

859. Then a conspiracy did exist?

Yes!

860. Was the FBI statement that only two bullets hit the president correct?

No. The minimum had to be three. The neck, the throat, and the head. The reason why the FBI did not say two bullets were in the head is due to the fact that this evidence was not brought out until the physicians testified before the Commission. However, in view of the fact that Dr. McClelland had notified the press that the president's death was the result of a bullet over the left temple, the FBI should have been more cautious. There was *no* excuse by the FBI not to bring the facts up to date in their January 13, 1964 report.

Despite this failure, the FBI had put the Commission on notice that a minimum of two bullets hit the president, and one hit the governor.

861. What other the facts were disputed by the FBI?

(1) The bullets sent to them by the police did not match the Italian rifle sent to the FBI by the Dallas police.

(2) The bullets sent to the FBI by the Dallas police from the "Oswald" revolver did not match that revolver.

(3) The slug sent to them by the police did not match the rifle sent to them by the Dallas police.

(4) No fingerprints were found on the rifle sent to the FBI.

(5) The prints taken from the carton were between one day and a day-and-a-half old.

(6) The rifle had to be repaired to be used.

(7) The telescopic sight was fitted for a left-handed man.

(8) Oswald was right-handed.

(9) The rifle sent to them by the police was worthless.

(10) Oswald was not a member of any communist party.

862. Did the FBI have any evidence of a possible conspiracy?

Yes. A Miami, Florida newspaper, in February 1967, published a story that the Miami, Florida, Police Department had obtained a statement from a man, a member of several right-wing fascist organizations, that President Kennedy would be assassinated.

This man admitted that his organization had committed several murders against civil rights organizers, bombed schools, and injured many Negroes and whites who were civil rights members. In addition, the man told the police *how* President Kennedy would be assassinated.

The Miami police checked his statement and found that many of the facts related in it were true.[18]

863. What happened to this tape recording?

The Miami, Florida police sent it to both the FBI and Secret Service.

864. Did the agency deny receiving the tape recordings?

No.

---

[18] A reference to right-wing extremist Joseph Milteer, who was secretly tape-recorded thirteen days before the assassination by a Miami police informant. Milteer was a leader of the National States' Rights Party and a member of the Congress of Freedom and the White Citizen's Council of Atlanta.

865. Did the tape recording reveal the future date of the murder?

No.

866. How did both agencies attempt to negate the tapes?

The bureaus informed the public that the person who gave the information did not know what he was talking about since the president's Dallas trip was a last-minute affair.

867. Was this a true statement?

No! It is a matter of record that the Dallas trip was planned [with] a minimum of a ninety days' notice to the Dallas Police Department. The only element in question was whether the president would be there on the twenty-second or twenty-third of November. However, this is *not* the point at issue. The conspire-ators *knew* he was to visit Dallas on one of two days. A conspiracy does not need to know a year or two in advance; they only need to know the approximate date; the rest is all mechanics.

Neither bureau, to this day, has denied the facts on the tape.

868. What is the importance of the tape recording?

The tape recording has on it the names of the executives of the organization which has, and still is, committing crimes in violation of the Civil Rights Act. Several Miami, Florida police members have stated that the names involved are high in the political, economic, and social structure of the nation. Since these names had prior knowledge of the conspiracy they are "accomplices before the fact," which is a criminal offence.

869. Are the tapes still in existence?

Ask the FBI and the Secret Service.

870. How did the Commission handle its first crisis with the FBI?

By aiding the FBI and attacking its accuser!

871. What were the facts?

The Commission had been informed, on January 24, 1964, by the Texas attorney general and District Attorney Wade, that a newspaper reporter, Mr. Hudkins, had informed the Houston U.S. Secret Service bureau that Oswald was an FBI informant, code number "S172."[19]

872. Did the Bureau actually have this information?
Yes, under File Number 00-234, 030. 5H242.

873. What did Mr. Wade say to the Commission?
That his experience as a former FBI agent led him to believe Mr. Hudkins. He said that FBI informants generally used a PO Box and also the agent's automobile license number.

874. Who was Oswald's FBI contact?
The district attorney stated that the agent was FBI Agent Hosty, and Oswald had Hosty's phone and auto license number in his notebook.

875. Were the other names in the book revealed?
No. In addition, page seventy-four has been suppressed.

876. Was Hosty's name ever submitted by the FBI to the Commission?

---

[19] Although Oswald may have been an FBI informant, it later emerged that "S172" was a fictitious badge number and part of a hoax played upon the Bureau. Dallas County Assistant DA William Alexander suspected that the FBI was tapping his phones, so he decided to play a trick. He arranged a conference call with his friends Lonnie Hudkins and Hugh Aynesworth, reporters who also suspected that their lines were bugged. (They were said to be investigating the possible connection between Oswald and the FBI.) The trio had prearranged to discuss Oswald's "payroll number": was it S172 or S179? "Within half an hour" of the call, "FBI agents, flashing their badges, showed up at the offices of all three of these marplots asking what they knew about Oswald's government payroll number." Gerald D. McKnight, *Breach of Trust* (Lawrence, KS: University Press of Kansas, 2005), p. 139.

No, his name had been removed. 5H112; R242-43.

877. Did Oswald and Hosty know each other?
Oswald knew Hosty well enough to demand that Hosty be removed from the interrogation room after his arrest.

878. Could the Commission prove or disprove the Hudkins story?
The Hudkins story was based on a report given to him by Mr. Allen Sweatt, the chief of the Criminal Division, Sheriff's Office, Dallas, Texas. U.S. Secret Service file: 00-2, 34-030, Houston, Texas.

879. Did the Commission have the legal power to summon both men?
Yes. Under Executive Order Number 11130.

880. What excuse did the Commission use to "weasel" out of their responsibility?
By giving the excuse of "privileged communication."[20]

881. Was this legally correct?
No. When Mr. Huggins gave his story to the Secret Service, Mr. Hudkins waived that right. Thus, the Commission only had

---

[20] "If pursuing the 'Agent Oswald' matter 'to final conclusion' was what the commission was all about, then Sweatt should have given testimony under oath. There were numerous compelling reasons why Sweatt should have been called before the Commission. He was in charge of the sheriff's investigation into the Kennedy assassination. The crime had been committed almost directly outside his office. Minutes after the assassination police and sheriff's deputies had crowded witnesses into his office, where statements were taken and sworn to under oath. Sweat identified and spoke to witnesses who were unknown to the Commission and promptly collected all available pictures of the assassination and the crime scene. There is no question that Sweatt could have been a source of additional useful information." McKnight, *Breach of Trust*, p. 135.

to ask Mr. Huggins who gave him the story and receive the answer.

882. Did the Commission do this?
Of course not. The Commission had lawyers who had passed the bar. However, by refraining from having both men testify, the Commission could brand both men "liars"–in a polite way, of course.

883. How did the Commission handle this story?
The Commission had seven frightened men. The man who had given the story to Mr. Huggins was not a "man on the street" but the *chief of the Criminal Division* of the Dallas Sheriff's Office.
Therefore, to discredit both men the Commission had a "special" counsel from Texas investigate the story and he dutifully reported to the Commission that the story was a "rumor," i.e., a lie.

884. Who, in turn, said the Commission's "rumor" was the truth?
None other than the FBI! The FBI never admitted that the Hudkin's story was incorrect but evaded the charge by admitting that Hosty's name was in the Oswald book for reasons "fully known to the FBI." 5H112.

885. Did the Commission have the courage to ask "why?
No.

886. What did the Commission uncover regarding Agent Hosty?
Mr. Hosty was a steady bridge-playing partner to a Mr. Surrey who, in turn, was a personal aide to ex-Major General Walker, who ...

887. Did the Commission ask the FBI to investigate itself?
Yes. They asked the FBI to inform the Commission whether or not Oswald was, or had been, an FBI informer on their payroll.

888. What was the result of the FBI investigating itself?

A clean bill of health. The Bureau submitted a statement by the agent in charge of the Dallas office stating that they "never used Oswald's services or paid for his time" and that the *Dallas* files revealed no payment for any type of service to Oswald. R22, 327, 840; 17H.

889. What value, in a law court, would this statement have?

Nothing of value. The statement limited itself to the Dallas office but many citizens know that the FBI has many offices. A careful reading of the affidavit or statement revealed the fact that the FBI did not state Oswald was not an informer, only that the Dallas office never paid him for his information.

Furthermore, as in many police operations, the informer is paid out of a special fund and Mr. Dulles cited his experience as a former CIA chief.

Since the FBI did not answer the question, the answer must be that Oswald was an FBI informant.

890. Did the FBI offer the Oswald file to the Commission?

There is no question that the FBI, through Mr. Hoover, did give the Oswald dossier to Commission Chairman Earl Warren. He refused to read it. The "Report" now states that "an independent survey was made of the dossier" *but no report was made to the Commission!* Epstein's *Inquest* categorically states that an aide told him *no* investigation was made of the file. R327 of 5H13.

891. Were many false statements made by FBI agents to the Commission?

Yes, very many. In fact, a three-judge panel in New Orleans has already ruled that the Warren "Report" and "Hearings" is nothing more than "hearsay piled upon hearsay."

892. What method did the FBI use to confuse the issues involved?

Witnesses, before the Commission, complained time and time again that the FBI agent had (1) failed to write down the remarks made to the agent by the witness; (2) quoted the witness incorrectly; (3) put words in their mouths; (4) deleted words or sentences that changed the context of the statement; and (5) took no statement by warning the witness to keep his mouth shut. The latter occurred when Secret Service agents attempted to interview the Klein officials concerning the purchase of the alleged Italian rifle.

893. Did the Commission place any agent on the stand to deny those charges?
No, the Commission never confronted the agent with this fact.

894. Did the U.S. Secret Service complain about the FBI's conduct?
Yes. Many times. R326, 433-39, 364; 15H783; 16H638; 2H93, 191. Etc.

895. Did the FBI have any right to suppress evidence?
The FBI had not a single law to stand upon to suppress evidence. Evidence, in law, can also be suppressed by not investigating facts that have been brought to their attention. Suppression can only lead to an assumption that the FBI had something to hide … like the names that were on page seventy-four of the Oswald notebook ... like the names of persons affiliated with the Batista wing of the anti-Castro forces in the United States ... or Jack Ruby's telephone number ... or the Texas people behind the Kennedy advertisement that appeared in the Dallas newspapers on the morning of his foul murder.
One fact is certain, no "Red" name was in Oswald's book.

896. How did the investigating bodies conduct the Oswald interrogation?
By violating his constitutional rights. He had no attorney and there was no stenographer or tape recorder to record his statements.

897. In a law court would Oswald's statements be of any value?

No. Absolutely worthless. The police, Secret Service and FBI notes all contradicted each other or made no mention of various facts. A reading reveals the contradictions. R600-40; 7H309-19.

898. Was Oswald a "blatant" liar as the Commission alleged?

Since the Commission had to rely upon the notes made at the interrogation, and since the notes were legally worthless, what was Oswald lying about?

899. What evidence supported Oswald against this charge?

Oswald told the truth when he said he saw a Negro eating lunch in the lunchroom near his eating table. Mr. Jarman confirmed this. Oswald said he saw a Mauser rifle prior to the murder. Mr. Caster confirmed this. R622; 7H386.

The evidence confirmed Oswald when he said he did not have or carry a rifle into the Depository on the morning of the murder.

Oswald admitted he owned a .38 revolver. He made this statement voluntarily to Captain Fritz.

The evidence confirmed the fact that Oswald did not attempt to murder Mr. Walker; therefore Oswald's denial was the truth.

The evidence confirmed the fact that Oswald did not murder Officer Tippit; therefore Oswald's denial was the truth.

The evidence confirmed Oswald's denial that the "A. Hidell" rifle was used by him for the murder of President Kennedy.

The FBI never stated that Oswald "used" that rifle.

The only method used by Commission to "convict" Oswald was to brand him a "liar," and this would not hold in a law court!

900. How many attempts were made upon President Kennedy's life?

Buried *deep* in the "Hearings" is the strange account of another attempt upon his life in the Parkland Hospital.

901. What were the circumstances surrounding this attempt?

While the president was in the operating room, a man approached the door and was stopped by Secret Service Agents Berger and Johnsen. The man showed them credentials purporting to be those of the CIA. The agents had never seen this man and after an argument refused his entrance. The man's name was never taken by the agents or his CIA code number. If he was a CIA agent why was the CIA involved in the internal affairs of the nation? Or was he an agent of the CIA acting for his own group within the CIA that was running wild with the Batista anti-Castro forces contrary to President Kennedy's instructions? Was he a conspirator that had to make sure that the president was dead? Why did the Secret Service agents fail to take this man's name or hold him in custody? Did not the man have a pistol in his possession?

Why did the Commission fail to question the CIA on this matter?

At 1:30 p.m., a white male attempted to enter the operating room and both Secret Service agents actually used their fists to subdue this man. This man then admitted, or said, he was an FBI agent but neither Secret Service agent had ever seen him before in the FBI Dallas office. The man was carrying a pistol. The Secret Service agents had his height, weight, and age. They forgot to record his name!

Prior to the appearance of these two men, an FBI agent by the name of Drain approached the door with another man in tow. The Secret Service agents knew Mr. Drain. The FBI agent informed the Secret Service agents that he had received instructions from Mr. Hoover, who was in his Washington, DC office, that Agent Drain was take this unknown man into the operating room since this unknown man was a "doctor" and Mr. Hoover wanted this "doctor" to "watch" the Parkland Hospital physicians operate.[21]

---

[21] Marks is essentially correct on all these points. Secret Service Agent Andrew E. Berger (stationed with Agent Richard E. Johnsen right outside Trauma Room One), reported that he encountered the following four figures at Parkland Memorial Hospital, who each attempted to gain entry to the room: FBI Agent Drain, accompanied by a "doctor friend." An "unidentified CIA agent," who possessed credentials. And an "unidentified FBI agent," who did not possess credentials. See Vincent Palamara, *Survivor's Guilt: The Secret Service and the Failure to Protect President Kennedy* (Walterville, OR: Trine Day, 2013), pp. 271-272. Palamara concludes: "Berger's report was totally ignored by just about everyone." Author Gerald McKnight adds that the

The FBI trusted Oswald but not the physicians.

The Commission *never* investigated the FBI regarding both incidents. Why did the FBI want a doctor in the operating room? To spy upon them? What reason was there for any FBI agent in the operating room? Were there communists there or was the real reason the fact that the FBI had knowledge that there was a Cuban exile employed in the hospital who was a member of the Batista Cuban group?

Now, by 1:30 p.m., in the halls of Parkland Hospital, there were three men, with pistols, running around doing what? No one knows. The Commission had no desire to know. 18H795-99.

902. Who was responsible for the safety of the president?

The U.S. Secret Service. It is incredible that the Secret Service was "awed" by a cardboard saying the bearer was an "FBI" or "CIA" agent; but they were.

903. Did the FBI attempt to censor Manchester's *Death of a President*?

Let the facts speak!

In April 1967, Mr. Manchester, in his *Look* article, casually wrote that he was "interrogated" by four FBI agents in his Dallas motel room. He mentioned this at the conclusion of a sentence on page sixty-six.

If nothing occurred, why mention the visit at all? Why use the word "interrogated," which is generally used by authors when writing about police matters? Was this Mr. Manchester's method of warning the reader that his book had been censored by the FBI?

Was he influenced by the fact that these four uninvited FBI agents, each with a revolver in his possession, was conveying a warning not to write about certain aspects concerning Dallas

---

unidentified FBI agent who attempted to push his way past the Secret Service "was instantly slammed to the wall and fell to the floor after receiving a haymaker from one of the Secret Service agents. The FBI agent was later identified as J. Doyle Williams." See McKnight, *Breach of Trust*, pp. 272-273.

"higher-ups" involved in the conspiracy? Mr. Manchester was alone in his motel room. The agents were not invited by him to visit with him in Dallas. But, out of the blue, four agents decide to visit with him. For "casual" purposes?

904. What is frightening about this episode?
The new assumption of the power of censorship by the FBI in a democratic society. Mr. Hoover has remained silent concerning this episode and has not rebuked those four agents.
Are all future books relating not only to the Kennedy murder but other national issues to be impliedly censored by the FBI?

905. What is the other frightening matter involved?
The abdication of the press and the absolute silence by every publisher, editor, and commentator to discuss this episode.
Can a free press remain "free" if their readers are slaves?

906. Did the FBI warn the Commission that Oswald was innocent?
Yes. Many times. This fact has been overlooked by many of the critics of the FBI in the Kennedy murder. The fact that the Commission refused to heed those "red flag" warnings was not the responsibility of Mr. Hoover and his Bureau.
The fact is that the FBI did warn the Commission.

907. What "red herring" was "set up" by the Commission?
The critics have run all over the place in attempting to prove that Oswald was or was not an FBI agent or informant; whether he was or not a CIA agent; whether or not he was or was not a member of the anti-Castro conspiracy; whether or not he knew Jack Ruby or Officer Tippit. These are "red herrings."
The critics must convince the American people that Oswald did not murder President Kennedy; if they prove that point then it will follow, as night follows day, that the intelligence of the American people will accept the next step: that President Kennedy was murdered as a result of a conspiracy–even if Oswald was part of that conspiracy. If the Commission's eight conclusions are false, then a conspiracy must follow.

It is dangerous and foolish to place the responsibility upon the FBI. When one honestly analyzes the total testimony of the Bureau, the only conclusion anyone can obtain is the FBI's proof that Oswald "was not the sole and exclusive killer of President Kennedy."

What more do the critics desire? The abolishment of the FBI? Mr. Hoover's head?

The Federal Bureau of Investigation gave to the Warren Commission a minimum of eleven pieces of vital evidence that proved that the Commission's conclusions were totally incorrect. They have been discussed in the previous chapters of this book. Even if Oswald was proven to be either an FBI or CIA agent, does this prove he did not murder the president? Of course not! Or vice versa?

The president, Mr. Johnson, ordered the FBI to cooperate with the Commission and to uncover the evidence. The evidence the FBI uncovered was more than sufficient to prove the Commission wrong.

908. Did the FBI write the "Warren Report?
No!

909. Then how can the FBI be held responsible?
An unanswerable question.

There is no question that the agents exceeded their authority many times. However, the Bureau was still answerable to the Commission. However, if the Commission lacked the "guts" to bring the FBI to heel, that is not the responsibility of the FBI. A government agency will always seek power where a vacuum exists.

It was not the duty or responsibility of the Bureau to tell the Commission how to conduct its investigation. The Commission had full authority to seek and use other investigators. Certainly, the "Hosty" affair was a warning to the Commission that the Bureau had something to conceal. But the Commission took the easy way out. The fact that the FBI was lukewarm in proving a conspiracy is proved by various pieces of evidence scattered in the "Hearings."

But, in a real sense, what could the FBI do *after* it had submitted all its evidence, its tests, its various letters to the Commission? Denounce the "Report" as a fraud? There is no evidence that the FBI knew what would be included or excluded from the Report or the "Hearings."

To criticize the Bureau for submission of unintelligible charts or photographs, or for taking too much time in answering questions submitted to them by the Commission is begging the question. The Commission had only to request, and then demand; if the Bureau refused, the Commission could go to the president. The Commission could have compelled the FBI to resubmit those charts and photographs.

Nor should the Bureau be censored because the "legal beagles" on the staff did not know how to act as lawyers. The damage was not done by the FBI; it was done by the aides.

The events that have occurred since the issuance of the "Report" in regards to the conclusions stated by the Commission bear out the FBI.

What is strange is the fact that the FBI has accepted the defense of the "Report" when the Bureau need only point to the evidence and show the American public that the Bureau *had* uncovered this evidence but that the Commission *refused* to publish it.

Thus, by making themselves a party to the defense of the Commission, the FBI is now in the position that everything the Commission printed is being upheld by the Bureau in spite of the evidence that the Bureau, itself, uncovered!

The voluntary involvement of the FBI in the New Orleans investigation conducted by Mr. Garrison will, in the long run, harm the Bureau. The Bureau can no longer stand with its finger in the dike, called the "Warren Report," and prevent the truth from flowing.

Two years ago, the Commission accepted the "glory"; the FBI should not prevent the Commission from accepting the disgrace.

-12-

THE OTHER SERVICES:
THE DALLAS POLICE, THE SECRET SERVICE, AND THE CIA

910. Were the Dallas police involved in (1) the murder of President Kennedy; (2) Oswald's; (3) Tippit's; and (4) Ruby's?

Under the principles of American law there is now no question that certain police personnel were involved in all four murders either as (1) accessories before the fact; or (2) after the fact.

911. What proved the involvement of Dallas police personnel?

The tapes from the Dallas Police Department.

912. Where can some of the tapes be found?

The transcript of some of the tapes can be found in 17H361-494; 6H325-27; 21H388-400. Also known as Commission Exhibit Numbers 705 and 1974.

913. Did the FBI assist in analyzing the tapes?

The FBI assistance created more confusion. As pointed out in the previous chapter, 11, the Commission accepted the FBI report in regards to the tapes when the Commission should have *commanded* the FBI resubmit their examination to *uncover* the facts. The Commission, instead, meekly accepted a batch of unintelligible words.

914. What do the tapes from the Dallas radio reveal?

Since the radio tapes from the Dallas Police Department were accepted by the Commission as true and representative of the facts, then various members of the police were perjurers and involved in the murders as "accessories after the fact."

915. Is Officer Tippit, according to the Commission, legally dead?

He may be dead, but he was not murdered since the Commission has never published his autopsy, which was not given to them by the police.

916. Why?
To prevent the knowledge that Tippit was not shot by Oswald. The autopsy report would have involved the Dallas police as accessories after the fact.

917. Is there any evidence to support this accusation?
Yes, the number of bullets recovered "from the body" does not match the number of bullet holes in the body; the number of shells found beside the body does not match the bullet holes in the body; that is, an automatic shell was found. R171-72.

918. What Secret Service document was *suppressed* by the Commission?
A document signed by Secret Service Agent E. W. Moore, dated December 11, 1963. Commission File Number 87, National Archives.

919. What is in this suppressed Secret Service document?
It proved that someone in the Dallas Police Department committed gross perjury to conceal the real murderer of Officer Tippit!
Agent Moore stated that a Dr. E. Rose, the medical examiner, informed him that three bullets penetrated Officer Tippit, and the *fourth* one did not penetrate Tippit's body because it "hit a bullet on the officer's coat."
Agent Moore's report went on to state that the autopsy report said "*three* bullets hit Tippet in the chest and the *other* one hit him in the head."
Agent Moore then stated that another police officer, R. Davenport, informed him that "a .38 caliber bullet was taken from the stomach of Officer Tippit."

920. Where can this "fabulous" report be found?

Commission File Number 87, Document 563, Autopsy Report Number M63-352; date: November 22, 1963, 3:15 p.m., Parkland Hospital.

921. What did Inspector Kelley of the U.S. Secret Service state?

"Tippit was shot once in the head, and *twice* in the chest."

922. What did Mr. Hoover warn the Warren Commission about the bullets?

The FBI chief stated that the bullets sent to him for laboratory ballistic inspection were too mutilated to be tested, three of them; the fourth bullet, Mr. Hoover stated, "may have come from Oswald's pockets, from the revolver, or the U.S. Secret Service."

Mr. Hoover *never* stated that the bullets sent to him by the Dallas police were *the actual ones taken from the alleged revolver.*

In fact, in rereading his letter, Mr. Hoover is telling the Commission that the *fourth bullet is a fraud! A plant!*

How? Oswald *did not have any bullets in his pocket that had been fired.* The police testified that they were cartridges, *not bullets.* The bullet, the fourth one, was *unmarked*; then how could it have been fired through a revolver? Commission Document Number 774, File 87.

923. Is Officer Tippit legally dead?

In view of the testimony, who knows? From a legal standpoint, the Warren Commission has yet to prove he is dead; someone in the Dallas Police Department had some explaining to do.

Three bodies are involved: (1) One body has three bullets in the chest, and one in the head. (2) One body had a .38 caliber bullet hole in its stomach. (3) One body has two holes in his chest and one in the head.

924. Is there a fourth "Tippit" body?

There is! Way, way, down deep in the "Hearings" is a statement by Detective J. Leavelle that Tippit "was shot three times: one time each in the hand, chest, and stomach." Now, a hand wound appears. 24H253, Exhibit Number 2003. This is the fourth "body."

925. Who is perjuring himself?
Who knows? The Commission made sure it did not find out.

926. Was the FBI directed to solve this mystery?
No. Officer Tippit was a case for his department to solve.

927. Who informed the world that Oswald was murdered with the connivance of the Dallas Police Department?
The sworn testimony of the Parkland Hospital staff.

928a. How is the above answer substantiated?
At least one hour before the murder of Oswald by someone in the Dallas Police Department and assisted by one of the conspirators (Ruby only shot Oswald, not fatally wounded him, as will be shown), the staff at the Parkland Hospital was notified to prepare an operating room for Oswald. 21H170-71, 182-91; 215, 227.

928b. What Dallas official refused to cooperate with the FBI and its investigation of the Oswald murder?
Sheriff Decker. 19H452.

928c. Did the Dallas police have any knowledge of an attempt to murder him?
Yes. It is the sworn testimony from the FBI and Secret Service that the Dallas police were notified that an attempt would be made. 4H223; 19H770.

928d. What and where are the citations bearing on the Oswald murder?
As usual, the Commission made this task as difficult as possible. Here they are: R208-16; 4H223; 4H150-51; 5H254-58; 12H250, 431-33; 15H124-33, 641; 19H406-09, 452-53, 464-65 and 19H410-13.

928e. What is the overall evidence in the above citations?

(1) Chief Curry, prior to the day of Oswald's murder, announced, contrary to all police regulations, the *time* when Oswald was to be moved.

(2) That the FBI and Secret Service had informed the Dallas police that an attempt would be made upon Oswald's life.

(3) That fifteen minutes before moving Oswald from the upstairs interrogation room, Oswald agreed to talk to Inspector Kelley of the U.S. Secret Service if he had a lawyer present. R630.

(4) The Parkland Hospital staff prepared an operation room for him an hour before the murder. Price Exhibits, 21H.[22]

---

[22] Marks is referring to an affidavit featured in Price Exhibit Number 7 (*Warren Commission Hearings and Exhibits*, volume 21), dated November 24, 1963. Composed by Steve Landregan, the assistant administrator at Parkland Memorial Hospital, it reads in part:

"Shortly before 11:30 [a.m.], Geilich received a telephone call from Mr. Struwe advising him that large crowds had gathered at both the City Hall and the County Courthouse in anticipation of the transfer of Lee Oswald from the City Jail to the County Jail. Mr. Struwe noted that there was a possibility of an incident and suggested we might want to alert the Emergency Room. Mr. Geilich, following the telephone call, advised me of the call, which at that time I understood him to say was from Mr. Price and asked if I felt it was indicated, which I did. Mr. Geilich then proceeded to the Emergency Room to alert the Emergency Room and asked them to delay any lunch hours until after the transfer had been effected.

At approximately 11:30, I was standing in the corridor talking with one of the members of the Highway Patrol concerning the transfer of Oswald, discussing the great amount of attendant publicity. At approximately 11:30, an Associated Press reporter dashed up to us in the hall and stated that Oswald had been shot and they are bringing him here."

Peter N. Geilich was an administrator at the hospital; Robert Struwe was comptroller; and Charles Jack Price was administrator, Dallas County hospital district, which included Parkland Memorial Hospital and Woodlawn Hospital.

(5) Jack Ruby, a known police character, entered the station with assistance from someone in the department.

(6) The truck that was to be used to transfer and protect Oswald was known to be inoperable in the basement.

(7) That Jack Ruby *shot* Oswald but did not murder him. An unknown detective straddled Oswald's body and gave him artificial respiration in spite of the fact that this treatment *pumped the blood out of Oswald's body.*

(8) A belly wound, by today's medical standards, is not a fatal wound. Nearly seventy percent of the cases show recovery if assistance is rendered quickly. Someone in the police department could not afford to have those odds working in Oswald's favor.

(9) An unidentified man, who looked like a doctor, was also seen over Oswald's body. This man, of twenty-three, was permitted to leave by a policeman who "thought he was a doctor." 19H410-13.

(10) The Dallas police know both their names.

The CIA

928f. What did George Washington warn about the CIA?
"Let there be no change by usurpation; for though this, in one instance, may be an instrument of good, it is the customary method by which free governments are destroyed."

928g. What did Thomas Jefferson say about CIA?
"Whatever power in any government is independent, is absolute also."

929. What did Harry S. Truman say about the CIA?
"It has become an operational and, at times, a policy-making arm of the government."

930. What is now the fourth branch of government?

The CIA, who is responsible to no one; an independent government by itself who talks of the angels but walks with the devils. A "lip serving" democratic organization.

931. Is the CIA subject to any control?
According to the law which created it, to the Senate. But one knows that many watch dogs watch the burglars burgle the house.

932. To whom does the CIA report?
To the president, to the National Security Council, the Senate.

933. How did the CIA "cooperate" with the Commission?
With utter contempt.

934. Is there any evidence to link Oswald with the CIA?
A thin link whose chain never seems to end.

935. What is one of the links that fits this chain?
A letter to the CIA by J. Lee Rankin of the Commission. Mr. Rankin asked the CIA to clear up certain questions that had come to the attention of the Commission. The information desired by the Commission was needed as soon as possible.

Mr. Rankin requested information from the CIA regarding press reports that Jack Ruby was connected with the anti-Castro groups. (2) He also requested information regarding the report that a Chicago-based U.S. anti-Castro informer had stated that the "anti-Castro forces were behind the Kennedy assassination." (3) Mr. Rankin desired information that reports were being circulated that various arms cache built in the United States were directed by a retired U.S. Army colonel. (4) Mr. Rankin also wanted to know if the John Birch members were involved; and (5) if the Las Vegas gambling interests were involved.

936. When was this request made?
On February 24, 1964. A second request on April 2, 1964. Nine months later, on September 15, 1964, the CIA decided to answer this "upstart" Commission and did file a letter that answered *none* of the questions.

937. What did the CIA write to Mr. Rankin?

That the CIA had no knowledge of any anti-Castro activity concerning Lee Harvey Oswald! Thus, for some unknown reason, the CIA inserted Oswald's name in a letter that never sought any information of Oswald, the CIA, or Jack Ruby. 26H466-70.

938. Were any of Mr. Rankin's questions answered?

In an eight-month investigation, the CIA found nothing to implicate anybody.

939. What did the Rankin–Helms letters lead to?

To the opening gun by District Attorney Garrison of New Orleans in his investigation of a conspiracy that first saw light in New Orleans. It was the implications in this letter relating to the anti-Castro groups and to the arms caches in the U.S. that opened the door. The "brush off" of the Rankin letter by Mr. Helms and his failure to deny was an implication of the affirmative.

Furthermore, Mr. Garrison, as the district attorney of New Orleans, had access to the New Orleans Police Department division which kept a watch on all Cuban organizations. In its files is evidence of the CIA involvement in various anti-Castro groups and the supply of weapons and ammunition by the CIA to those groups.

940. Was Oswald a CIA agent?

The answer must depend on the interpretation of "agent."

Is a person an agent if he supplies the CIA with information on a voluntary basis? No. Is a person an agent if he supplies the CIA with information at their request but receives no pay? Yes. Is a person an agent [if he] accepts the direction and command of the CIA even though he receives no payment? Yes.

However, Mr. Allen Dulles, former head of the CIA, in his discussion with his fellow Commissioners over the Oswald–Hosty affair, seems to imply it was strictly a matter of a legal contract. He cited the Powers–U-2 situation where Powers was under a contract through a company controlled by the CIA. It will never be known whether or not Oswald was paid by the CIA through a dummy company. However, payment is not the criteria but the understanding is.[23]

941. What does the evidence reveal regarding Oswald's activity?

Lee Oswald enlisted in the U.S. Marine Corps in October 1959. After his basic training, he was of sufficient intelligence to be trained as an electronics specialist with specific training in radar and highly classified coding and decoding equipment.

He was sent to Japan where some newspapers have reported that he received special CIA training at a secret CIA Japanese air base. While in Japan, he received a Class A security clearance by the Marine Corps. After his return from this special training, he commenced to "sound off" with praise for the Soviet Union.

If he was serious, then why did the U.S. Marine Corps give him a Class A clearance; and why did they not cancel that clearance if the Counterintelligence Division knew about his "conversion"?

The only answer can be that Oswald was setting up his "front" as a "communist," and Marine Corps Intelligence knew all about his CIA front.

Oswald still retained his Class A security clearance when he returned to the U.S. with his company. His commanding officer had testified to the Commission that when Oswald did go to the Soviet Union, the Corps did change their codes. Volume 8H.

942. What was Oswald's background for his trip to the USSR?

On September 4, 1959, while still in the U.S. Marine Corps, Oswald applied for a passport for travel to the Soviet Union. He

[23] "Powers–U-2" refers to American pilot Gary Powers, who survived a crash over the Soviet Union while flying the secret U-2 spy plane. Marks is again being prescient here when he suggests that Oswald may have been paid through a CIA front company. For more on the CIA's use of proprietaries during this period, see "Rand Development and U.S. Intelligence" by Gary Hill and "Creating the Oswald Legend" by Vasilios Vazakas, each featured at Kennedys and King.com, September 2020.

did not hide this move from any of his fellow marines. He bragged about it. On September 10 he received this passport.

One day later, the known "pro-communist" marine, who was leaving for the Soviet Union, was transferred to the U.S. Marine Corps from "active" duty to the "U.S. Marine Corps Reserve"! He still retained his *Class A security clearance*. Volumes 19 and 20: Hearings.

On the day of his transfer, September 11, 1959, Oswald received a "hardship" discharge and ten days later he was on his way to the USSR. R265, 393, 439.

Was the Counterintelligence Division of the U.S. Marine Corps stupid or was the Division taking orders from the CIA?

943. What did Oswald sign upon his release from the Marine Corps?

He agreed and signed a statement which held him liable for criminal prosecution if he revealed any classified information to foreign nations or unclassified persons.

944. What did he do in the Soviet Union?

He attempted to obtain Soviet citizenship and announced to the press in the USSR that he had given to the Soviet officials his knowledge of the codes he had in his possession.

945. Why did Oswald return to the United States?

Oswald soon discovered that the Soviets did not trust him (in fact, they knew all about him and his CIA training, as Yuri Nosenko stated), and he desired to return to the United States. He applied for a visa for himself, his wife, and his child, but it was not until May 1962 that the CIA was able to twist the arm of the State Department to obtain his visa for him.

946. Was Oswald arrested upon his return to the United States?

According to the law he should have been arrested. His name was on the passenger list, and he had received wide publicity in the United States when he "defected." The State Department made no effort to conceal his return.

Thus, the moment he stepped on U.S. earth he was liable to arrest by the U.S. Marine Corps for divulging code information. But was he? Of course not.

Did the FBI, who could trace down Mr. Abel when he lost a five-cent coin and received a twenty-year sentence for its loss, arrest Lee H. Oswald? Of course not.

Did the FBI arrest Oswald when they had him in the New Orleans jail and he requested assistance from the Bureau? Of course not.

Does anyone believe that the U.S. Marine Corps should "lay off" this "defector" unless the Corps received instruction to "lay off"? Does anyone believe that the FBI would refuse to arrest this defector who "betrayed" code secrets to the archenemy unless they had received instructions to leave Oswald alone?

947. Then what happened?

Six months after his return, Oswald calmly walked into the passport bureau and requested and received another passport to the Soviet Union and other places, including Mexico. What a farce!

The State Department gave him a passport in twenty-four hours. What power did this young man of twenty-three have over the U.S. Marine Corps, the FBI, and the State Department? R744; 11H360; 18H324.

What power? No power except that he was working with the CIA.

948. Is there proof that Oswald held a clearance from the FBI because the Bureau knew Oswald was a CIA agent?

Yes. There is a document in the archives belonging to the Dallas Police Department which carries a sentence including the phrase "Subject checked with the FBI and they told him that Oswald was all right." The "subject" was a Mr. and Mrs. Meller who befriended the Oswalds when they lived in Fort Worth, and this couple was afraid that Oswald was a communist. The Commission never investigated the Mellers and the FBI's "all right" of Oswald. Dallas Police Department Criminal Intelligence. Dated February 17, 1964. Detective Hollinghauser.

The Secret Service

949. Who has the duty of protecting the president's life?
The Treasury Department, through the Secret Service.

950. How did the service conduct itself on the Dallas trip?
Negligibly.

951. Did the service have knowledge of the Miami police tapes?
Yes. They admitted the receipt.

952. Did the service know of the "double detour"?
The evidence is conflicting in the "Hearings." Yes and no.

953. Did the service have knowledge that Oswald was "dangerous"?
No report was given to them by any federal agency.

954. How many agents were assigned to protect President Kennedy?
Only nine agents. This, despite the fact that the service knew how deeply the president was hated by the Dallas power structure. Nine men where a police officer was head of the local KKK!

955. How many Secret Service agents protect a sleeping president?
Two agents!

956. Where were the other seven agents during the night of November 21?

"Boozing it up"! Gossiping over a friendly drink until *3:00 a.m.*[24]

957. When the shots rang out, how did the agents react?
Very slowly, according to a World War II marine: Senator Yarborough.

958. Were any of the agents reprimanded or punished?
No.

959. Why?
The answer given to the Commission was that to punish any agent would cast a stigma of blame upon the agent or agents.

960. How does this affect the future protection of a president?
By logic, it follows that it would be better if the president dies. The service regulations provide instant dismissal for any agent for tippling while on presidential duty. However, if he is murdered, the agent faces no punishment.

961. Did the service inform the Commission that Oswald was innocent?
Yes. Secret Service Report Number 2 and 34-030, November 28, 1963!

962. What did this *suppressed report* inform the Commission?

---

[24] "Nine of the agents from Kennedy's White House Detail drank alcohol the night before the assassination in Fort Worth, at the Fort Worth Press Club and, presumably, The Cellar 'Coffee House,' including four who had critical duties in the follow-up car directly behind" the president's "limousine.... The owner of The Cellar, Pat Kirkwood, said, 'About 3:30 in the morning, these Secret Service men were sitting around giggling about how the firemen were guarding the president over at the Hotel Texas ... those guys were bombed. They were drinking pure Everclear.'" Agent Paul E. Landis, assigned to the follow-up car, remained in the Cellar until 5:00 a.m. Vincent Palamara, *Survivor's Guilt*, pp. 150, 258. Everclear vodka is 190 proof (95% alcohol) and is banned on over a dozen states.

"At the foot of Elm Street, at a point approximately 200 feet east of the Houston Street triple underpass, on the approach to Stemmons Freeway, President Kennedy, who was seated on the right rear seat, was shot. Immediately thereafter Governor Connally, seated on the right rear jump seat, was shot once. The president was then shot a second time."

963. Was this report consistent with the FBI report?
Yes. The Secret Service report was *after* they had received the official autopsy report. Thus, three shots were *definitely hits*.

964. What about the second head wound?
This was not brought out until the "Hearings."

965. *Why did the Commission suppress the Secret Service report?*
(1) It proved Oswald was *not* the killer. Note the spot where the Secret Service stated the president was *first hit*–250 feet east of Houston Street, which meant that the angle of fire prevented Oswald from hitting the president from the sixth-floor window. (2) The report confirmed the FBI report!

966. What about the "missed" bullet?
A "red herring" created out of thin air by the Commission. There is not a single piece of factual evidence that there was a missed shot. Who said there was? The Commission.

967. Why?
The "missed" shot was created in the same manner that the Commission created the fabulous bullet number 399. The creation of this missed-shot myth was done to "protect" the nation from a conspiracy!

968a. How can one prove that there was *no* "missed" shot?
By simply using the Commission's own "self-serving" statements!
The "missed" bullet, according to the Commission, *missed the president's automobile* completely. But, how could the bullet

"miss" the automobile when one takes into consideration the *angle of fire* which led to two bullets completely striking the target? According to the Commission, Oswald was a tremendous, cool, cold, calculating marksman, one of the best in the world.

Yet this young man was so "cool, cold, and calculating" that either his first or last bullet completely missed not only the target but a sixteen-foot automobile that was six-feet wide! When did Oswald lose his poise? Not only did he miss the president's automobile but this "missed" bullet failed to hit anywhere in Dealey Plaza, the street, the triple overpass and the spectators in the crowd lining the street. Every one of them, or the inanimate objects, were completely missed. What did Oswald shoot at, the sky?

The "missed" bullet is a figment of the Commission's imagination!

968b. What other Secret Service report was *suppressed* by the Commission?

The official survey made for the U.S. Secret Service by R. W. West!

969. What did this survey show and prove?

The *position* of the president's car at the time the president was hit first, then Governor Connally, and then the president again.

This survey *proved* that Oswald *did not fire any of those shots*.

The Warren Commission deliberately and willfully *suppressed* both the Secret Service report and survey from the "Report" and the "Hearings" to prevent the world from knowing a *conspiracy* existed.

970. Where can this "survey" be found?

In the National Archives, Washington DC. Files Number 87, 88.

971. What did the Secret Service report and survey prove?

They proved that the president was hit by at least one bullet which could have been fired from the second floor of the Dal-Tex

Building where the Dallas police arrested a man in that building and held him on a charge of "investigation of a murder"!

The Commission refused to conduct any investigation of not only this man, but the other two men arrested by the Dallas police. The Commission had an independent witness who saw a rifle-like object pointed out of this second-floor window and had obtained pictures, yet the Commission refused to investigate. Why?

The answer is simple; the Commission did not desire to ascertain the truth if the truth was a conspiracy.

The *angle* of fire from that second-floor window of the Dal-Tex Building was in direct line with the angle of the bullet striking President Kennedy in the back!

The FBI proved it; the Secret Service proved it.

-13-

THE RAPE OF THE AMERICAN CONSCIENCE

972. What *did* the Warren Commission prove?
That a conspiracy murdered John F. Kennedy.

973. What did the Commission believe?
They believed that those who could read would not read; that those who could see would not see; that those who could [talk] would not [talk]; and those who would investigate would not investigate.

974. Who was responsible for the "Report"?
In law, the seven Commissioners; in fact, the aides.

975. Did the Commission fulfill Executive Order Number 11130?
No. The Commission did not ascertain the truth and evaluate the facts.

The future historian of the affairs of the Warren Commission will have no easy duty to find the answer to the question: "Why and how did the Commission fail in its task?"

The Warren Commission cannot and should not be attacked or discredited because of the composition of the members. Whether each member should have undertaken the task can only be answered by each individual. Due to their duties it was an impossibility for five of the members to give the Commission one hundred percent cooperation. Congressmen, senators, and justices cannot be engaged in an investigation seeking the causes of the death of a president and also give their attention to their elective or appointed duties.

The most perplexing question to obtain any answer to is the fact that the Commission, at the very first moment of its investigation, had in its hands the FBI reports and the Secret Service reports.

Just on the basis of those reports the Commission could not find Oswald guilty of being the "sole and exclusive killer."

The members of the Commission did not achieve their status in the American social, economic, and political scale by being stupid; therefore one can only conclude that these seven had some understanding, whether spoken or implied, that this nation of 195,000,000 souls would be torn asunder if the Commission reported to them that a Conspiracy had murdered President John F. Kennedy. Yet, these seven men place their honor upon a report that would wilt in the noonday sun.

Was this implication, by osmosis, impressed upon the aides? The facts are clear that no control was ever exerted over these aides, who, time and time again, violated the rights of witnesses. The facts are also clear that these aides did not seek to bring forth the truth but sought only to confuse, to mislead, and to deceive the Americans.

A wise president, a man by the name of Harry S. Truman, once said "The buck stops here."

In a democracy no leader must be immune from criticism. Nor should the Warren Commission be immune from criticism when that criticism is based on truth.

Criticism is derived from critics and they should not be immune in turn. When, however, the critics are attacked on the basis of personality instead of the measure of their facts, then it is a sign that the criticism has been correctly established.

If the critics cannot criticize the Warren "Report" when the facts reveal that the "Report" is worthless, who can they criticize? An IBM computer did not write the "Report"

The Warren Report was the "sole and exclusive responsibility" of the members of that Commission. Therefore, criticism must be directed against the Commission as an entity. That the Commission was negligent and slothful in its responsibility has been proven beyond a reasonable doubt.

The Commission, neither as an entity nor individually, now has the right to say that they lost control of their aides and, thus, they have no responsibility for the manner in which the facts were either suppressed or expressed. Nor the right to say that the "Report" was hurried because the political scene demanded the

Report before the 1964 election. The American people wanted the truth, not a whitewash.

Thus, to whom does the American public go to seek the truth?

It can now be said that the American people do not believe anything stated in the "Report." Due to this lack of belief, a cynicism has now gathered among the Citizenry that bodes ill for the Nation. A Nation whose moral fiber has been torn and shattered cannot long live; for when the Nation's spirit is destroyed, no Nation will live.

The American Creed, which is expressed in the Preamble to the Constitution of the United States, has been violated and this violation has been condoned by the Warren Commission.

People, in all nations, must stand for an ideal. The United States of America was not born on the idea that its President could be shot like a dog in the street and his murderers be "shielded from this day on" because it would be "against the national interests."

The Spirit has in this year of 1967 been replaced by cynicism of everything "American." There was a Spirit when John F. Kennedy was president of the United States. There was a feeling that the United States of America was moving toward a goal enunciated in the Preamble of the Constitution. The Youth, upon which a Nation must have to exist, had a feeling within them that the Nation did not care for the future. There is no Spirit today.

How can there be? A Congress that laughs at black children, brown children, white children being bitten by the rats of the slums? This is the Spirit of America? A Congress that passes a law which drafts only the poor, white or black? A governor that destroys an educational system? A governor who believes that only the youth who has parents with money should enter the universities and colleges of his state? A governor that believes mental health can be cured with pills? This is the United States of America?

The Commission, deceased though it be, has its reputation being torn to shreds, not by the critics, but by the former aides to the Commission. It was their aides that stated that the Commission was a "joke," a "farce," "a nothing."

Thus, a full circle has been made and there is no answer to the question: "To whom do the American people redress this wrong?"

In criminal law, any person, who by untruthful statements or activity, prevents the law from securing the person liable for the prosecution of a crime, is called "an accessory after the fact."

Was the Warren Commission, morally, that type of person when the Commission concealed the truth from the American people?

Was the Commission, morally, an accessory after the fact, when it refused to question witnesses whose evidence was contrary to the theory created by the Commission?

Was the Commission, morally, an accessory after the fact, by suppressing evidence from both the "Report" and the "Hearings"?

Was the Commission, morally, accessories after the fact when they stated that the "Report" was substantiated by evidence published in the "Hearings"?

Was the Commission being cynical when it stated that if the American citizen and did not believe the "Report" they should buy the twenty-six volumes comprising the "Hearings"? Or contemptuous?

The use of words to obscure the truth, the suppression of photographs, charts, film, X-Rays, the FBI report (yes, the five-volume FBI report *is not in the "Report" or the "Hearings"*), the Secret Service report, the destruction of material evidence, the theft of evidence, is the reason why the "Report" is considered untruthful.

Was it planned this way?

Many years ago, Walter Lippmann wrote:

> The decay of decency in the modern age, the treatment of human beings as things, as mere instruments of power and ambition, is without doubt the consequence of the decay of the belief in man as something more than an animal animated by highly conditioned reflexes and chemical reactions.

For, unless man is something more than that, he has no rights that anyone is bound to respect, and there are no limitations upon his conduct which he is bound to obey. This is the forgotten foundation of democracy in the only sense in which democracy is truly valid and of liberty in the only sense in which it can hope to endure. The liberties we talk about were established by men who took their conception of man from the great religious tradition of Western civilization, and the liberties we inherit almost certainly cannot survive the abandonment of that tradition.[25]

The Commission agreed and accepted the first paragraph only.

The final verdict of history was summed up by Dean Sayre of Washington National Cathedral in his sermon the Sunday after the murder:

"By our silence, by our inaction, by our willingness that heavy burdens be borne by one man alone; by our readiness to allow evil to be called good and good evil; by our continued toleration of ancient injustices ... we have all had a part in the assassination...."

How long, o how long, Americans, will we permit our silence to perpetuate the evil in the Warren Report?

---

[25] Walter Lippmann, "The Forgotten Foundation," *New York Herald Tribune*, December 17, 1938.

-14-

THE CONSPIRACY THAT MURDERED PRESIDENT KENNEDY

"If they found another assassin, let them name names and produce their evidence." Allen Dulles to Mr. Knebel in *Look*.

This contemptuous statement directed at the American citizenry revealed the attitude of the Commission.

The Commission did not praise the president; they gave him a funeral and used his shroud to conceal his murderers.

The question is not the discovery of other assassins; the question is whether or not the Commission fulfilled its obligation to the American people

In that obligation the Commission was a total failure. Have you, Mr. Dulles, read an interview of one of your aides in the October 10, 1966 issue of *U.S. News & World Report*? What a revelation! The single bullet theory "is not indispensable" and the "back" wound is not a "neck" wound. Is he lying or [is] the "Report," which carries your signature, Mr. Dulles? You should read the August 1966 issue of the *Greater Philadelphia Magazine* where this same aide admitted that bullet number 399 *did not perform* in the manner stated in the "Report." Did he lie or did the "Report"?

Mr. Dulles, did the Commission accept an unauthenticated picture of the president's back wound? Why, Mr. Dulles, did the Commission suppress the Secret Service report concerning the location of the President's automobile and the number of bullets hitting the president? Was it because the report confirmed the FBI reports? Was it because *both* reports proved Oswald innocent?

Mr. Dulles, did the Commission actually see the X-rays and photographs or did the Commission rely upon "hearsay" evidence? Is the medical staff of both the Parkland and Bethesda Hospital so incompetent that physicians do not know the difference between a "neck" wound and a "back" wound? Since when, Mr. Dulles, does a bullet leave no path through the body? Since when, in medical history, is an autopsy based on a newspaper report? Why, Mr. Dulles, was the Commission too frightened to ask the autopsy physician the name of his "higher authority" on the burning of his notes? Why did he burn his notes?

Mr. Dulles, why did the Commission fail to investigate the three men arrested by the Dallas police on the charge of murder? Why did the Commission say it had inspected the FBI–Oswald dossier when it did not? Why did the Commission fail to examine Mr. Hudkins and Mr. Sweatt?

Why, Mr. Dulles, did the Commission refuse to subpoena the Zapruder film from *Life* but did not hesitate to confiscate the vital Moorman photograph? Why was the Altgens photograph "cropped"? To prevent the public from seeing a rifle poking out of the *Dal-Tex building?* Why, Mr. Dulles, did the Commission refuse to purchase any film from the various TV stations who had tapes of the complete assassination and the murder of Lee Oswald? Did you know about the tapes or did the aides conceal that matter from the Commission? The tapes were in existence as late as May 18, 1964. Mr. Dulles, you should read your own exhibits. The offer and letter can be seen in Commission Exhibit Number 962. Of course, the United States did not have $2,000 in the Treasury to purchase those tapes. But was not the real reason the tapes were not purchased due to the fact that positive, conclusive evidence would show where the president's car was, the faces of various persons entering, standing, and exiting from the Book Depository, and the man in the window of the second floor of the Dal-Tex building? Or where the people ran when they heard the shots? Or the detective who gave Oswald artificial respiration, or the "doctor" who also straddled his body, or how the detectives acted when they and Oswald saw Ruby point the gun at Oswald? In which direction did the detectives turn when they saw Ruby?

Why, Mr. Dulles, did the Commission say that Commission Exhibit Number 839 is frame number 210 of the Zapruder film when *no* such frame exists?

Mr. Dulles, how can other assassins be named if material is *not* in the National Archives? Was there a conspiracy, Mr. Dulles?

Of course, there was!

The inception of the conspiracy that murdered President Kennedy can be, and will be eventually, traced back to the disastrous "Bay of Pigs." The president relied upon the CIA, headed by Allen Dulles, whose information was one hundred percent wrong in the CIA's assessment of Castro's Cuba. Heads rolled but the CIA had many heads and the heads that remained never forgave President Kennedy.

One of the reasons why the invasion failed was discovered by the president after the collapse. To his dismay and anger the president was informed that the CIA, an organization that was organized and supported by a democracy, did not believe in democracy. His postwar investigation revealed that every anti-Batista leader and member of the anti-Castro movement had been either imprisoned on the day of the invasion or given menial tasks in the invasion army. One of the plans of this invasion force was to imprison every anti-Batista leader and, in some cases, the death sentence had already been imposed. This was kept from the president. This is and was the CIA belief in democracy.

Thus, in the wreckage of the "Bay of Pigs" were parts and persons of the CIA apparatus who had directed that operation. The hatred of this apparatus for President Kennedy was to cease only when these forces fired four bullets into his body.

It would be repeating the news stories, published nearly weekly since the "Bay of Pigs," of the various caches of weaponry and ammunition confiscated by federal agents or local police forces. In various police department records are listed the names of the persons creating those arms caches. In the files of the New Orleans Police Department are the names of the Cuban CIA fronts.

With the relaxation of tensions between the U.S. and the USSR after President Kennedy's confrontation with the Soviets in the Cuban Missile Crisis, the Batista–Cuban exile organization, with many members on the CIA payroll, decided that Kennedy must go. However, the murder of President Kennedy was the "spark," a means to an end.

The Kennedy conspiracy had a major and minor objective: (1) An invasion of Cuba; (2) an attempt to involve the Soviet Union with the invasion so that a war would ensue between the U.S. and USSR.

By early 1963, members of the conspiracy, who were both U.S. citizens and exiled Cubans of the Batista faction, had been selected.

It was during this period that Oswald entered the conspiracy. He thought he had a perfect "front." To the world (and FBI?) he was a defector, and he was branded as a "communist." A perfect "patsy"! Oswald, to himself, was a patriot, misguided, but still a patriot. Was not Hale a spy and a patriot? Did not many American newspapers and commentators call President Kennedy a traitor? Oswald was happy to assist in the removal of a "traitor."

Oswald's role was strictly that of being a decoy. He had no idea that he was also selected to be a victim. To assist him in this decoy was another man who resembled Oswald. That this is true can be found in the "Hearings" of reliable witnesses seeing "Oswald" in two or three places at the same time.

As history has shown, a conspiracy spreads rumors. The various assassination attempts upon President De Gaulle were always preceded by rumors and the French agencies took care to track them down. Yet, in spite of this, De Gaulle narrowly escaped death when the attempted killers received word one hour before the attempt.

Both the FBI and the Secret Service knew plans were afoot to kill President Kennedy as early as September 1963. Yet, nothing was done. When President Kennedy visited Miami, Florida in 1963, the police department refused to permit him to travel from the airport to the city, and he used a helicopter. Yet, the FBI and Secret Service did nothing.

Their excuse? The tapes from the Miami, Florida, Police Department, which has been discussed, meant nothing since both bureaus claimed that the president had not decided on the visit to Dallas. Was is this true? No! Both Dallas newspapers reported on

September 26, 1963, that President Kennedy would visit Dallas on either the 22nd or 23rd day of November. The bureaus did nothing.

With this announcement, the conspiracy went into operation. Oswald obtained a job at the Book Depository and of this factor the FBI was notified by Mrs. Paine. The rifle, that was also to be a decoy, had already been purchased under the name of "Hidell."

However, two elements were lacking: (1) the conspirators must know the route; and (2) how to implicate Castro and the USSR.

The evidence is that only two elements knew the *actual* route the president was to use: (1) the conspirators; and (2) some person or persons in Dallas who was either connected with the Dallas police or had connections with that department.

Oswald was such a minor figure in the conspiracy that if he dropped dead that morning or had departed from Dallas the conspiracy would have gone ahead. Since the president was not shot at from the Book Depository but from the Dal-Tex Building and the grassy knoll, Oswald was simply a "patsy."

There was only one map ever published in Dallas and that was not the *actual* route. There was no "double detour" ever printed so the mystery of why the police directed the crowd into the actual route used was never investigated by the Commission. Nor was the chief's statement concerning "they" ever investigated.

The Commission admitted that Oswald never knew the actual route of the cavalcade. Oswald never knew where the president's car was to be at: 12:20, 12:25 or 12:30; nor did he find out from the radio since that information was never broadcasted.

But someone in the police department did, for the police radio broadcasted the fact that President Kennedy was shot at 12:25 p.m. At 8:00 a.m. Oswald went to work and around 11 a.m. the rifleman entered the Dal-Tex Building, while two more went to the grassy knoll.

What was the plan after the murder of the President?

There is now evidence that three persons, one who looked like Lee Oswald, attempted to rent a plane from the "Red Bird

Airfield" for a long-distance flight. The operator of the flight was contacted on November 20 for a flight to take place in the afternoon of November 22, 1963. One of the persons asked the field owner if the plane could fly direct to Cuba. (See *Second Oswald*, R. Popkin.)

One of the conspirators was Mr. Ferrie, involved in the Garrison investigation, who was also a former civilian pilot for a major airline. He was to fly to Cuba, surrender to Cuban authorities, and ask for asylum. Then, he was to announce he had participated in the assassination! And then what would have happened to Castro and Cuba?

The press would have been in its glory. The president of the United States murdered by a "defector" to the godless communists. War now! The Birch Society with its vast propaganda machine, the professional anti-communists, now they had their proof.

Oswald was a communist, the FBI said so. A "defector" had fled to Cuba, that "Red" godless country, and had admitted it. Why did he fly down to Cuba if Cuba was not involved? That was the plot. The president's murder was only the spark. "Remember the Maine!" Remember Kennedy!

Far-fetched? Incredible? Fiction? Is it?

Then why did Assistant District Attorney Alexander, Mr. Wade's assistant, attempt to have an indictment issued which stated that Oswald and the Soviet Communists killed President Kennedy? Why did high officials in Washington, DC, when hearing of this canard, nearly have a heart attack? Why did the Secret Service rush an inspector to Alexander to compel this one hundred percent American not to do this act of madness? Why did the newspapers and columnists sit on this story for nearly four years until broken by Mr. Manchester in his book *Death of a President*?

Mr. Wade is an attorney, a district attorney, and he should know the law. He chose his assistant, Mr. Alexander, who is also an attorney. What was the purpose of the district attorney's office to secure such an indictment? Did the power structure of Texas and the oil interests of Texas want a war to follow President Kennedy's death? Why did Mr. J. Lee Rankin ask the CIA to investigate the involvement of Texas oil interests in the Kennedy murder? Why did the CIA refuse to answer his questions? Why is the Commission silent on the number of police in Dallas involved in the KKK? Why is the Commission silent on the fact that an official of the Dallas Police Department, who was on the police "team" to investigate the death of President Kennedy, also the head of the Dallas KKK? The same KKK group that engaged in attacks on the then Senator Johnson and later Ambassador E. Stevenson.

How was the president murdered? Today, after all the facts and evidence are in, just a careful reading of the "Report" and the testimony in the "Hearings" reveals the method.

Three killers were involved and the gunfire was synchronized at 12:25 p.m. when the Dallas police flashed their first radio alarm. The president was hit in the classic "crossfire," from the back and the side. His car came to a complete stop at Elm and Houston Streets. Now, if Oswald was the assassin, he had a perfect target from the sixth floor. Mr. Hoover said Oswald did not shoot because trees blocked the view. It can only be said that Mr. Hoover should have his glasses repaired. There is not a tree on Houston Street! But no shots ring out. The car proceeds.

As the car continues on Elm Street, the rifleman on the second floor of the Dal-Tex Building is waiting until his target approaches. He cannot fire at the President while the car is stopped at the corner of Houston and Elm Streets for the simple reason that the fire escape outside the window acts as a shield. Furthermore, he has a better shot when the car will proceed down Elm Street. About 175 to 200 feet down Elm Street the trigger is pulled and the president is hit in the back. At the same instant, the two riflemen behind the fence on the grassy knoll pull their triggers, and the deed is done.

A fusillade of shots is released, all directed at the president in his automobile. Two types of rifles were used. It was all over in fifteen seconds. Within fifteen minutes the Dallas police had three suspects, two of them with rifles, but since none of them was Oswald, the police let them go.

The evidence is clear and uncontradicted that many witnesses heard five or more shots. It was in the newspapers and in the testimony given to the Commission. A bullet struck the curb and fragments of that curb hit a man.[26] The bullet striking the curb did not come from bullet number 399; even the Commission admitted that fact. Parts of a bullet, some say the nose and base portion, were found on the front seat of the President's auto. No one has claimed, not even the "legal beagles," that those portions came from either bullet number 399 or the president's head. But what about the bullet that hit the windshield? So, Mr. Dulles, there was a conspiracy.

Now, back to the depository. At 12:22 Mr. Rowland sees two men, one with a gun. His eyesight is also verified by another witness, not Mr. Brennan, but by Miss C. Walther. They disappear. Where do they go? Nowhere, just away from the window so as not to be seen by anyone on the street. The shots ring out and they go to work. Two men now have, not fifteen minutes, but thirty-five minutes to construct and lift twenty-eight fifty-pound cartons that form the "shield of cartons." They then carefully placed the decoy rifle into a semi-hiding place and depart. Depart where?

They depart upstairs to the seventh floor, which was never searched by any police agent! When the mob of reporters invaded the building upon hearing of the found rifle, the two calmly descended, joined the mob as newspaper reporters, and left with the rest. A reporter's newspaper card is the easiest thing to forge. The police admitted that the building was never sealed off. In fact, the testimony revealed that the police first searched the third, fourth and fifth floors, although witnesses told them that the shots came from the sixth floor.

The entire Kennedy murder reeks with conspiracy. That some of the Dallas police were involved in it is not questioned today. Their activities, and non-activities, prove the involvement of some of the police, both in high and low places. The letters of Mr. Hoover, from the one [in which] he stated that Lovelady wore a "red and white striped shirt," thus could not be "the man in the doorway," it had to be Oswald, to his letter rejecting the

---

[26] Later identified as James Tague.

bullets for both the rifle and the revolver, is clear proof that a conspiracy existed.

Mr. Hoover and his FBI is not responsible for the negligence of the Commission, nor is the Secret Service.

No, Mr. Dulles, it was not the responsibility of the American citizen to find and name the assassins; that was your task. Your lack of responsibility to the task is the cause for your failure. You issued the "Report" under your name; you had at your disposal the entire operating machinery of the government of the United States. We citizens have only what you and your fellow Commissioners wrote. We read, we looked, we analyzed, we thought; and we, nearly seventy percent of us, now deliver our verdict on your work:

The Warren Commission was a failure.

POSTSCRIPT:

JIM GARRISON, "ST. GEORGE" VERSUS THE "DRAGON"!

By the time this book appears in print, the Kennedy conspiracy may claim another victim: none other than Jim Garrison, the district attorney of New Orleans, whose "lance of truth" has pierced vital organs of the conspiracy that murdered President F. Kennedy.

There is no question that Mr. Garrison's investigation has created a firm base in the theory that President Kennedy was the victim of the Batista backed anti-Castro groups in the United States. These groups, in turn, have the full support of the CIA.

The mass communication media, many of its organs either being paid by the CIA or having its agents in executive positions, have entered the battle against Mr. Garrison's efforts to reveal the existence of the conspiracy.

Never in the history of American journalism has the *entire* mass communication media entered into a plan to destroy, not only a case, but the person conducting the prosecution of a criminal case. In addition, this is being done on a national scale.

The original indictment in the "Shaw–Bertrand" case was upheld by a three-judge panel which, in American jurisprudence, means that the district attorney had sufficient facts revealed in open court to give the case to a jury. Upon the ruling of this three-judge panel the mass communication media went into an operation of deceit that is unparalleled in the history of American journalism.

Various members of the mass communication media bribed witnesses, hid witnesses, issued fraudulent interviews, had "witnesses" file suit against Mr. Garrison, produced nationwide television programs which upheld the findings of the Warren Commission. How incredible! Why?

The answer to "why" can be found in the fact that many of the inactive and active participants of the conspiracy will be found in the ranks of the government and the economic strata of our nation.

On August 13, 1967, a jury in New Orleans found Dean A. Andrews guilty of three charges of perjury in denying he knew who Clay Bertrand was, and if he knew that Clay Bertrand was actually Clay Shaw. Mr. Andrews' original testimony appears in volume 11H325-339 wherein Mr. Andrews stated he had seen a "Mr. Bertrand" as late as forty-five days before Mr. Andrews' appearance before the Warren Commission. At the grand jury investigation, he now testified that he could not identify either Mr. "Bertrand" or Mr. Shaw.

The new attorney general of the United States, Mr. Clark, had also gotten into the act and, acting upon the advice of the FBI, first stated that the FBI had investigated Mr. Shaw on the behalf of the Warren Commission, and the Bureau had found nothing incriminating about Mr. Shaw regarding the Kennedy murder. The attorney general was then flooded with letters from the critics of the Warren Commission who informed him that the FBI had testified to the Commission that "no such person as Clay Bertrand existed!" Therefore, the attorney general informed the public that he had "misunderstood" the Bureau and the testimony of the FBI was correct!

The National Broadcasting Company, known as "NBC," with the "peacock," and the Columbia Broadcasting Company, known as "CBS," with the "big eye,"[27] entered the fray with programs designed only to destroy Mr. Garrison and his prosecution of Mr. Shaw. Then the *Saturday Evening Post* got into the act. Of course, the reliability of the *Post* can and should be taken with a dose of salt in view of the fact that its "articles of exposing" seem to attract libel suits whose judgments have been upheld by various state and federal courts. Finally, the Associated Press, known by its byline "AP," circulated its "white paper" and lo and behold, the Warren Commission was found to be a document in the highest tradition of American state documents.

---

[27] The "peacock" and "big eye" were the trademark emblems of each of these respective corporations.

To whom does the mass communication system owe its loyalty? To the people who have fought, are fighting, and will continue to fight for the ideas of the "freedom of the press," or to its advertisers?

The NBC and CBS programs dealing with the Warren Commission in 1967 [are] nothing more than a distortion of the evidence and a deliberate misrepresentation of the truth. If this sentence is libelous then NBC and CBS have the right to sue this author for libel. Unfortunately, this will not occur, for it would be a means of obtaining a trial before a court of law where the "basic principles of American justice" would be invoked.

That the Warren "Report" is worthless as a legal document is proved by the fact that a three-judge panel in New Orleans has ruled the "Report": "Hearsay piled upon on hearsay"!

NBC has become so vicious in its attack upon Mr. Garrison that it is a known fact that this company, this "upholder and seeker of the truth," has paid a witness to flee the jurisdiction of the State of Louisiana. A Walter Sheridan, an independent investigator for NBC, and a Richard Townley, of NBC's New Orleans outlet, have already been indicted for attempting to suborn a witness, Mr. Russo. The mass communication media obtained the services of a Mr. Gurvich, who appeared on the CBS program, to go before the New Orleans grand jury and accuse Mr. Garrison of "illegal and unethical" methods. The grand jury threw his accusations out of their room.

CBS, however, did not inform the American public that the grand jury had thrown out the Gurvich statements. That would have been a blow to the CBS program extolling the Warren Commission!

The mass communication media is constantly proving Hitler's dicta: "The greater the lie, the greater the belief" and "Constant repetition of a lie converts the lie into the 'truth'"![28]

The media may succeed; for as the day for the [Clay Shaw] trial approaches, the greater the use of the media for the

---

[28] "If you tell a lie big enough and keep repeating it, people will eventually come to believe it"; "Repeat a lie often enough and it becomes the truth": both attributed to the Nazi Joseph Goebbels.

perpetration of the lie increases. If the forces behind the conspiracy cannot destroy Mr. Garrison's case, they may decide to destroy the man, either physically or by reputation.

It is speculation to attempt to find out the reasons why the mass communication system has entered into a program of hiding the facts and the persons either accessories before the fact or after the fact in the murder of President Kennedy.

That the CIA controls many of the news columns in both the press and magazines is now known. What is not known, and what will never be known, is how many agents of the CIA now work for various organs in the mass communication media.

The facts speak for themselves, but if the public is never given the facts those facts are worthless.

Thomas Jefferson once said that the most important factor in a democracy is a free press; he did not say a "privileged" press.

The hideous activity of NBC, CBS, ABC, and other organs of the mass communication media can lead to a conclusion that certain members of that media know that President Kennedy was murdered by conspirators and the conspiracy must never be allowed to face the light of day.

Books Cited in *MMF*

Epstein, Edward Jay. *Inquest: the Warren Commission and the Establishment of Truth*. New York: The Viking Press, 1966.

Joesten, Joachim. *Oswald: Assassin or Fall Guy?* New York: Marzani & Munsell, 1964.

Jones, Penn. *Forgive My Grief*. Midlothian, TX: The Midlothian Mirror, 1966.

Manchester, William. *The Death of a President*. New York: Harper & Row, 1967.

Lane, Mark. *Rush to Judgment*. New York: Holt, Rinehart & Winston, 1966.

Popkin, Richard. *The Second Oswald*. New York: Avon, 1966.

Sauvage, Léo. *The Oswald Affair*. Cleveland: World Publishing, 1966.

Thomson, George C. *The Quest for Truth: How President Kennedy Really was Killed*. (Glendale, CA: 1964.)

Weisberg, Harold. *Whitewash: The Report on the Warren Report*. Hyattstown, MD: Harold Weisberg, 1965.
– *Whitewash II: The FBI–Secret Service Cover-up*. Hyattstown, MD: Harold Weisberg, 1966.

ABOUT ROBERTA MARKS

Roberta (Bobbie) Marks was born and raised in Chicago. Upon graduating college with a degree in art, she moved to Los Angeles to work in the California fashion industry as a clothing designer. During this period she started a clothing-manufacturing company and owned two retail women's clothing stores.

In the 1980's she switched from clothing to interior design and opened the Los Angeles franchise of Designer Previews, the highly successful New York company run by Karen Fisher, which matched clients with interior designers. The LA office represented over sixty design professionals whose works were often showcased in top-shelf publications.

Now retired, Roberta continues to create, utilizing paper as her main medium. She makes figures that are clothed in all forms of paper, from heavy butcher paper to fine tissue, then paints and embellishes the paper and forms it into clothing. Papier-mâché and clay are also used to make heads that are adorned with elaborate headpieces. Roberta says that she's now come full circle: using her pattern-making training to make paper clothing.

About Rob Couteau

Rob Couteau's work as a literary critic, interviewer, and social commentator has been featured in books such as *Gabriel Garcia Marquez's 'Love in the Time of Cholera'* by Thomas Fahy, *Conversations with Ray Bradbury* edited by Steven Aggelis, *Ghetto Images in Twentieth-Century American Literature* by Tyrone Simpson, and David Cohen's *Forgotten Millions*, a book about the homeless mentally ill.

His published interviews include conversations with Ray Bradbury, Pulitzer Prize-winning author Justin Kaplan, *Last Exit to Brooklyn* novelist Hubert Selby, Simon & Schuster editor Michael Korda, LSD discoverer Dr. Albert Hofmann, Picasso's model and muse Sylvette David, Nabokov biographer Robert Roper, music producer Danny Goldberg, poet and publisher Ed Foster, and historian Philip Willan, author *Puppetmasters: The Political Use of Terrorism in Italy*.

In his early years as a writer, Couteau won the North American Essay Award, a competition sponsored by the American Humanist Association. His books, including the novel *Doctor Pluss*, the anthology *More Collected Couteau*, and the poetry collection *The Sleeping Mermaid*, have been praised in the *Midwest Book Review*, *Publishers Weekly*, and *Evergreen Review*.

His essays and interviews on the Sixties assassinations have been featured at the Kennedys and King website, and he has appeared several times as a guest on Len Osanic's Black Op Radio.

Visit his website at robcouteau.com

INDEX

A

B

C

D

J

K

N

O

Lightning Source UK Ltd.
Milton Keynes UK
UKHW040708221222
414324UK00002B/319